Selected Readings in
Rhetoric and Public Speaking

Selected Readings in Rhetoric and Public Speaking

With Introductory Comments
By
LESTER THONSSEN
College of the City of New York

NEW YORK
THE H. W. WILSON COMPANY
1942

Copyright 1942
By Lester Thonssen
Second Printing 1952

PRINTED IN THE UNITED STATES OF AMERICA

Library of Congress Card No. 42-13301

Speak of the moderns without contempt, and of the ancients without idolatry; judge them all by their merits, but not by their age....
——Earl of Chesterfield

PREFACE

This book contains selected passages from the more important contributions to the literature of rhetoric and public speaking. It embraces the work of twenty-three acknowledged scholars from Plato to Genung, taking from each such excerpts as, in the judgment of the compiler, tend to bring out the distinguishing characteristics of the individual's conception of rhetorical theory.

Although designed essentially as a reference book, this anthology should be serviceable in a collateral capacity for courses in Public Speaking, Rhetorical Criticism, Rhetorical Theory, and the Teaching of Speech. It assembles in compact form a body of material which throws some light upon the historical antecedents of contemporary speech instruction. The contents should bring into sharper relief many of the principles and techniques of speaking discussed in modern textbooks on the subject. Furthermore, the passages are, in the main, taken from old books which are generally inaccessible, except through the large research libraries.

The compiler is fully mindful of the fact that extracts from a book are not altogether satisfactory substitutes for the complete work. However, this collection is not intended to take the place of the originals in their entirety; it is not designed to discourage the careful examination of full editions of the books that make up the rhetorical tradition. On the contrary, it is hoped that this survey of enduring ideas on rhetoric will promote more extensive studies into the background of the subject.

With few exceptions, the selections from a particular book are presented in the order in which they appeared in the original. No attempt has been made, except in the general index, to assemble all of the material on a given subject in one specific section. To do so would, in all probability, make for a certain amount of artificiality; and it would unquestionably make more difficult the task of transmitting the spirit of the contributor through the medium of discrete, and in most cases, reasonably short excerpts. However, each passage, or set of passages, has a sufficiently descriptive title to indicate the nature of the contents. The basic pattern for the system of labeling derives from the traditional division of rhetoric into five parts: invention, or the gathering and analysis of materials; disposition, or arrangement; elocution, or style; memory; and delivery. Unless otherwise indicated in the appropriate footnote, the bracketed numeral at the end of each selection indicates the page on which the original material appears in the specified text.

If certain contributors to the literature of rhetoric and public speaking seem to have inadequate representation in this volume, the compiler hopes that the critics will benevolently attribute the shortcoming to severity of space limitation.

Grateful acknowledgment is made of the permission granted by the following publishers to use certain copyrighted materials in this volume: The Macmillan Company, for selections from J. E. C. Welldon's translation of Aristotle's *Rhetoric*; The University of Chicago Press, for excerpts from Frederic Ives Carpenter's edition of *The Arte or Crafte of Rhethoryke* by Leonard Cox; Ginn and Company, for excerpts from *The Practical Elements of Rhetoric* by John F. Genung; and D. Appleton-Century Company, for the passage from *The Senses and the Intellect* by Alexander Bain.

Colleagues and friends have offered helpful suggestions regarding the choice and arrangement of materials in this book. Special thanks should go to Mary Margaret Robb.

For unselfish devotion to this venture in compilation and for substantial assistance in all stages of its preparation, the compiler enters this word of appreciation to Dorothea Thonssen.

L. T.

New York City
October 10, 1941

CONTENTS

Preface 7

Plato
   Gorgias 11
   Phaedrus 26

Aristotle
   Rhetoric 35

Cicero
   De Oratore 65
   Orator 91
   A Dialogue Concerning Oratorical Partitions 96

Quintilian
   Institutes of Oratory 99

Longinus
   On the Sublime 159

Leonard Cox
   The Arte or Crafte of Rhethoryke 163

Thomas Wilson
   The Arte of Rhetorike 173

John Bulwer
   Chirologia 189
   Chironomia 199

François de Fénelon
   Dialogues Concerning Eloquence 207

John Lawson
   Lectures Concerning Oratory 209

John Ward
   A System of Oratory 213

Thomas Sheridan
   Lectures on Elocution 215

Thomas Gibbons
   Rhetoric 219

GEORGE CAMPBELL
   The Philosophy of Rhetoric 231
HUGH BLAIR
   Lectures on Rhetoric and Belles Lettres 251
GILBERT AUSTIN
   Chironomia 263
JAMES RUSH
   The Philosophy of the Human Voice 281
RICHARD WHATELY
   Elements of Rhetoric 287
THOMAS DE QUINCEY
   Rhetoric 301
HERBERT SPENCER
   The Philosophy of Style 303
ALEXANDER BAIN
   The Senses and the Intellect 307
EDWARD T. CHANNING
   Lectures on Rhetoric and Oratory 309
JOHN F. GENUNG
   The Practical Elements of Rhetoric 311
SUPPLEMENTARY BIBLIOGRAPHY 315
INDEX 319

PLATO

(c.428 B. C.-c.348 B. C.)

Although the *Gorgias* and the *Phaedrus* do not provide a complete system of rhetoric, they are of interest to the student of public address in at least four particulars: (1) They throw some light upon a period in Athenian life when rhetoric held a position of unusual prominence. (2) They reveal some of the most cogent objections hurled against rhetoric by those who disliked both the practice and its practitioners. (3) They suggest certain principles of speaking as brought out by the participants in the discussions. (4) They remind the present day teachers of the importance of holding up to students an ethic of discourse, an ethic which derives from the doctrine of *words with knowledge*.

In these *Dialogues* Plato condemns rhetoric because of what he considers its separation from truth, its questionable techniques, and its unwholesome influence on public life.

The participants in the *Gorgias* are Callicles, Socrates, Chaerephon, Gorgias, and Polus. Socrates shows that rhetoric is of little significance; this he does by refuting the arguments of Gorgias, Polus, and Callicles. Chief among Socrates' conclusions are the claims that rhetoric is not an art, and that it is of little use to a person.

Socrates and Phaedrus are the participants in the dialogue *Phaedrus*. The treatment of rhetoric results from a comparison of speeches, one of which is represented as the product of Lysias' rhetorical skill and the other two, the work of Socrates.

The *Dialogues* are probably of less value for what they explicitly state, than for what they suggest. Beneath the satiric condemnation of the art of rhetoric may be found certain principles of speaking which are in use today. There are also reminders of irregularities and evils to which undisciplined speech will always be an easy prey.

GORGIAS [1]

[*Nature of the Art of Rhetoric*]

SOCR. Well then, since you say that you are skilled in the art of rhetoric, and that you can teach another this art, tell me about what is rhetoric employed? just as the art of weaving is employed in the making of garments, is it not so?

GORG. It is.

SOCR. And is not music also employed in the composing of melodies?

GORG. Yes.

[1] From the translation by Henry Cary (1854). *The Works of Plato*, vol. I, London, Henry G. Bohn, 1854.

Socr. By Juno, Gorgias, I admire your answers, for you answer as briefly as possible.

Gorg. I think, Socrates, that I do this well enough.

Socr. You say well. Come then, answer me thus respecting rhetoric, of what is it the science?

Gorg. Of words.

Socr. What kind of words, Gorgias? Are they such as inform the sick by what kind of diet they may become well?

Gorg. No.

Socr. Rhetoric, then, is not concerned with all kinds of words?

Gorg. Certainly not.

Socr. Yet it makes men able to speak?

Gorg. Yes.

Socr. And does it not enable men to think on the same things on which it enables them to speak?

Gorg. Without doubt.

Socr. Does not, then, the medicinal art, of which we just now spoke, make men able to think and speak about the sick?

Gorg. Necessarily so.

Socr. The medicinal art, then, as it appears, is conversant with words?

Gorg. Yes.

Socr. And those that concern diseases?

Gorg. Just so.

Socr. And is not the gymnastic art also conversant with words that relate to the good and bad habit of bodies?

Gorg. Certainly.

Socr. And it is the same with other arts, Gorgias: each of them is conversant with those words that are employed about that particular thing of which each is the art.

Gorg. It appears so.

Socr. Why, then, do you not call other arts rhetorical, as being conversant with words, since you call that rhetoric which is employed about words?

Gorg. Because, Socrates, almost the whole science of other arts is conversant with manual operations and such-like actions; in rhetoric, however, there is no such manual operation, but all its activity and efficiency is by means of words. For this reason, I consider that the art of rhetoric is conversant with words, herein speaking correctly, as I affirm.

RHETORIC AND PUBLIC SPEAKING

SOCR. Do I understand what kind of art you wish to call it? but I shall soon comprehend it more clearly. However, answer me. We have arts, have we not?

GORG. Yes.

SOCR. Of all the arts, some, I think, consist principally in workmanship, and stand in need of but few words, and others of none at all, but their work may be accomplished in silence, as painting, statuary, and many others. With such arts, you appear to me to say rhetoric has nothing to do? is it not so?

GORG. You apprehend my meaning perfectly, Socrates.

SOCR. On the other hand, there are other arts which accomplish all by means of words, and require no work at all, or very little, such as theoretical and practical arithmetic, geometry, the game of dice, and many other arts; some of which require almost as many words as actions, and most of them more, so that altogether their whole activity and efficiency is by means of words. You appear to me to say that rhetoric is among arts of this kind.

GORG. You say truly.

SOCR. However, I do not think you mean to call any one of these rhetoric, although in the expression you used you so said, that rhetoric has its efficiency by means of words; and any who wished to catch at your words might reply, Do you say then, Gorgias, that arithmetic is rhetoric? But I do not think that you call either arithmetic or geometry rhetoric.

GORG. You think rightly, Socrates, and apprehend my meaning correctly.

SOCR. Come then, complete the answer to my question. Since rhetoric is one of those arts which make great use of words, and there are others of the same kind, endeavour to tell me in reference to what rhetoric has its efficiency in words. Just as if any one should ask me respecting any of the arts which I but now mentioned: Socrates, what is the arithmetical art? I should say to him, as you did just now, That it is one of the arts that have their efficiency in words. And if he should further ask me, In reference to what? I should answer, In reference to the knowledge of even and odd, how many there may be of each. But if again he should ask me, What do you mean by the art of computation? I should answer, that this also is one of those arts whose whole efficiency consists in words. And if he should further ask me, In reference to what? I should answer, as they do who draw up motions in the assemblies of the people, That in other respects computation is the same as arithmetic, for it has reference to the same object, that is to say, the even and the odd; but it differs in this respect, that computation considers what relation even and odd have to themselves and to each other in regard to quantity. And if any one should ask me about astronomy, and after I had said that its whole efficiency consists in words, should say, But Socrates, to what do words employed about astronomy refer? I should answer, That they are employed about the course of the stars, and of the sun and the moon, how they are related to each other with respect to velocity.

Gorg. And you would answer rightly, Socrates.

Socr. Now then do you answer, Gorgias. For rhetoric is one of those arts which accomplish and effect every thing by means of words: is it not so?

Gorg. It is so.

Socr. Tell me then in reference to what? what is the particular thing about which these words are, which rhetoric uses?

Gorg. The greatest of all human concerns, Socrates, and the best.

Socr. But, Gorgias, what you say is questionable, and by no means clear. For I think you must have heard at banquets men singing that song in which the singers enumerate that the best thing is health, the second beauty, and the third, as the author of the song says, riches gained without fraud.

Gorg. I have heard it; but with what object do you mention this?

Socr. Because the artificers of those things which the author of the song has commended, namely, the physician, the master of gymnastics, and the money-getter, will forthwith present themselves, and the physician will say: Socrates, Gorgias deceives you. For his art is not employed about the greatest good to men, but mine is. If, then, I should ask him, Who are you that say this? he would probably answer, I am a physician. What then do you say? that the object of your art is the greatest good? How can it be otherwise, Socrates, he would probably say, since its object is health? and what greater good can men have than health? And if after him again the master of gymnastics should say, I too should wonder, Socrates, if Gorgias could shew you any greater good from his art than I can from mine, I should again say to him, And who are you, Sir, and what is your employment? A master of gymnastics, he would say, and my employment is to make men beautiful and strong in their bodies. After the master of gymnastics, the money-getter would say, as I imagine, despising all others, Consider, I beg, Socrates, whether there is any greater good than riches, either with Gorgias, or any one else?

I should thereupon say to him, What, then, are you the artificer of this good? He would say, I am. Who are you then? A money-getter. What then? Do you consider riches to be the greatest good to men? I shall say. Assuredly, he will answer. However, Gorgias here contends that his art is the cause of greater good than yours. It is clear then that after this he would ask, And what is this good? let Gorgias answer. Come then, Gorgias, suppose that you are asked by them and by me, and answer, What is this, which you say is the greatest good to men, and of which you are the artificer?

Gorg. That which is in reality, Socrates, the greatest good, and is at the same time the cause of liberty to men, and of their being able to rule over others in their several cities.

Socr. What then do you say it is?

Gorg. I say it is the power of persuading by words judges in a court of justice, senators in the senate-house, and the hearers in a public assembly, and in every other convention of a political nature. Moreover, by this power you will make the physician your slave, and the master of gymnastics your slave, and the money-getter will be found to have gained money, not for himself, but for another, for you who are able to speak, and persuade the multitude.

Socr. At length you appear to me, Gorgias, to have shewn as nearly as possible what kind of art you consider rhetoric to be; and if I understand you rightly, you say that rhetoric is the artificer of persuasion, and that its whole employment and the sum of it terminates in this. Can you say that rhetoric has any further power than that of producing persuasion in the minds of the hearers?

Gorg. By no means, Socrates; but you appear to me to have defined it sufficiently. For that is the sum of it.

Socr. Listen then, Gorgias. Be assured that I, as I persuade myself, if there is any one, who in conversing with another, wishes to know the very thing about which the conversation is, be assured, I say, that I am such a person; and I think you are too.

Gorg. What then, Socrates?

Socr. I will now tell you. The persuasion which you speak of as resulting from rhetoric, what it is, and with what particulars it is conversant, be assured I do not clearly understand, not but that I have a suspicion of what I suppose you mean, and about what it is employed: yet I will not the less ask you what persuasion you mean results from rhetoric, and with what particulars it is conversant.
[139-43]

[*Nature of Persuasion Induced by Rhetoric*]

Socr. Come then, with respect to rhetoric, tell me, whether it appears to you that rhetoric alone produces persuasion, or do other arts produce it likewise? My meaning is this: Does he who teaches any thing persuade what he teaches, or not?

Gorg. He does certainly persuade, Socrates.

Socr. Again, if we speak of the same arts of which we just now made mention, does not arithmetic teach us such things as relate to number? and does not an arithmetician the same?

Gorg. Certainly.

Socr. Does it not also persuade?

Gorg. Yes.

Socr. Arithmetic, then, is an artificer of persuasion.

Gorg. It appears so.

Socr. If, then, any one should ask us, What persuasion it produces, and with respect to what? we should answer, That which teaches about the quantity of even and odd. In like manner we may shew, that all the other arts of which we spoke just now, produce persuasion, and what kind of persuasion, and with respect to what: is it not so?

Gorg. Yes.

Socr. Rhetoric then, is not alone an artificer of persuasion.

Gorg. You say truly.

Socr. Since then, it does not alone produce this effect, but other arts do the same, we may justly, as in the case of the painter, next enquire of the speaker; of what kind of persuasion, and of persuasion on what subject rhetoric is the art? Does it not appear to you that this question may fairly be asked?

Gorg. It does.

Socr. Answer then, Gorgias, since this appears to you to be the case.

Gorg. I speak then, Socrates, of that persuasion which is produced in courts of justice, and in other public assemblies, as I just now mentioned, and with respect to matters that are just and unjust.

Socr. I suspected, Gorgias, that you meant that persuasion, and on such matters. But do not be surprised if I shortly ask you a question that may appear to be evident, but which I shall notwithstanding repeat, for, as I before observed, I ask it for the sake of carrying on the discussion in an orderly manner, and not on your account, but that we may not be in the habit of catching up each other's words on suspicion; but do you finish what you have to say according to your own plan, just as you please.

GORG. You appear to me to act rightly, Socrates.

SOCR. Come then, let us examine this too. Do you admit that to learn is any thing?

GORG. I do admit it.

SOCR. Again? to believe?

GORG. I do.

SOCR. Whether, therefore, does it appear to you, that to learn and to believe, and learning and belief are the same, or different?

GORG. I think, Socrates, that they are different.

SOCR. You think rightly; and you may know from this, if any one should ask you, Is there, Gorgias, a false and true belief? I think you would say there is.

GORG. I should.

SOCR. Well then, is there a false and true science?

GORG. Certainly not.

SOCR. It is clear, therefore, that they (belief and science) are not the same.

GORG. You say truly.

SOCR. Yet both those who learn are persuaded, and those who believe.

GORG. Such is the case.

SOCR. Are you willing, therefore, that we lay down two kinds of persuasion, one that produces belief without knowledge, but the other science?

GORG. Certainly.

SOCR. Which kind of persuasion, then, does rhetoric produce in courts of justice and other public assemblies, respecting what is just and unjust? is it that from which belief springs without knowledge, or that from which knowledge arises?

GORG. It is evident, Socrates, that it is that from which belief springs.

SOCR. Rhetoric, then, as it seems, Gorgias, is the artificer of a persuasion which produces belief, and not of that which teaches respecting the just and unjust.

GORG. It is so.

SOCR. A rhetorician, therefore, does not profess to teach courts of justice, and other public assemblies, respecting things just and unjust, but only to produce belief. For surely he could not teach so great a multitude in a short time things of such great importance.

GORG. Certainly not.

SOCR. Come then, let us see now what we ought to say of rhetoric. [144-6]

[*Concerning the Power of Rhetoric*]

Socr. It is because I wonder at this, Gorgias, that I have been for some time asking you, what is the power of rhetoric. For when I consider it in this manner, it appears to me almost divine in its magnitude.

Gorg. If you knew all, Socrates, that it comprehends under itself almost all powers! And I will give you a strong proof of this. For I have often, ere now, gone with my brother and other physicians to various sick persons, who would neither drink their medicine, nor suffer themselves to be cut or cauterized by the physician, and when the physician was unable to persuade them, I have done so by no other art than rhetoric. I say too, that if a rhetorician and a physician should go to any city you please, and it were necessary to contend by argument in a general assembly, or any other convention, which should be chosen, a rhetorician or a physician, the physician would be held in no account, but he that has the power of speaking would be chosen, if he pleased. And if he should contend with any other artist whatever, the rhetorician would persuade that he himself should be chosen in preference to any one else. For there is no subject on which a rhetorician will not speak to the multitude more persuasively than any other artist whatever. Such, then, and so great is the power of this art. It is right however, Socrates, to use rhetoric in the same way as any other exercise employed in contests: for it is not right to use other exercises against all men alike; nor, because any one has learnt pugilism, and the pancratium, and to fight with arms, so as to be superior both to friends and enemies, is it therefore proper to strike, or pierce, or slay one's friends. Nor, by Jupiter, if some one who, by having frequented the palaestra, has made his body robust, and become a pugilist, should afterwards strike his father or mother, or any other of his relatives or friends, would it on that account be proper to hate, and expel from cities, the training masters and those who teach how to fight with arms. For they instructed their pupils in these exercises, in order that they might make a proper use of them against enemies, and those that do wrong, for self-defence, and not for attack; but they contrariwise, use their strength and skill improperly. The teachers, therefore, are not wicked, nor is their art either to be blamed, or for this reason wicked, but they, I think, who do not use it properly. The same may be said of rhetoric. For a rhetorician is able to speak against all men, and on every subject; so that he can best persuade the multitude, in a word, on whatever subject he pleases: but he ought not any the more on this account to detract from the reputation of physicians, because he is able to do it, nor of other artificers; but he should use rhetoric justly, as well as other exercises. In my opinion, however, if any one having become a rhetorician abuses this power and art, it is not proper to hate the teacher and expel him from cities, for he imparted the knowledge of it for just purposes, but the other makes a contrary use of it. It is just, therefore, to hate, banish, and slay him who does not make a right use of it, but not the teacher.

Socr. I think, Gorgias, that you as well as I, have been present at many discussions, and that you have observed this in them, that it is not easy for men, on whatever subject they undertake to converse, having propounded their ideas to each other, both learning themselves and teaching one another, then to put an end to the conference; but if they have a controversy about any thing, and one says that the other does not speak correctly or clearly, they are indignant, and each thinks that the other is speaking out of envy, from a love of contention, and not seeking what was proposed in the discussion: and some, at length, depart in a most disgraceful manner, having reviled each other, and spoken and heard such things that even the bystanders are vexed at themselves for having deigned to listen to such men. But why do I say this? Because you now appear to me to say what does not follow from, or accord with, what you first said respecting rhetoric. I am afraid, therefore, to proceed with my refutation, lest you should suppose that I do not speak with zeal for the subject, that it may be made clear, but out of opposition to you. If, then, you are of that class of men to which I belong, I should gladly question you: but if not, I would forbear to do so. But to what class of men do I belong? To those who are willingly refuted, if they say any thing that is not true, and who willingly refute if any one says any thing that is not true; and who are not less pleased to be refuted than to refute. For I consider the former to be the greater good, inasmuch as it is a greater good one's-self to be delivered from the greatest evil than to deliver another. For I think no evil so great to man as false opinion on the subjects we are now discussing. If, then, you say that you are such a man, let us continue our discussion; but if you think we ought to desist, let us give it up, and put an end to the argument. [147-9]

[*Rhetoric—and a Knowledge of the Just and Unjust*]

Socr. Hear then, Gorgias, what I wonder at in what you said. For, perhaps, you spoke correctly, and I did not rightly apprehend you. You say that you can make any one a rhetorician, who is willing to be instructed by you?

Gorg. Yes.

Socr. So that he can speak persuasively on any subject to the multitude, not teaching, but persuading?

Gorg. Exactly so.

Socr. You said too, that a rhetorician is able to speak more persuasively than a physician, on the subject of health.

Gorg. I did say so, at least to a multitude.

Socr. Does not, then, this expression "to a multitude" mean to the ignorant? for, surely, among the well-informed he will not be better able to persuade than the physician.

Gorg. You say truly.

Socr. If then he shall be better able to persuade than the physician, he is better able to persuade than one who possesses knowledge?

Gorg. Certainly.

Socr. Although he is not a physician? is it not so?

Gorg. Yes.

Socr. But he who is not a physician must, surely, be unskilled in those things in which a physician is skilled.

Gorg. Clearly so.

Socr. He, therefore, who is ignorant will be more capable than one who possesses knowledge of persuading the ignorant, since a rhetorician is better able to persuade than a physician. Is this the result, or something else?

Gorg. That is the result in this instance.

Socr. The case therefore is the same as concerns a rhetorician and rhetoric with respect to all other arts: I mean, there is no need for it to know the subjects themselves, how they are circumstanced, but only to discover some means of persuasion, so as to appear to the ignorant to know more than those who possess knowledge. [150]

. . . . .

Socr. Whether from this being the case, a rhetorician is inferior, or not inferior to others, we will presently consider, if our argument requires it. But first let us consider this: Whether a rhetorician is in the same condition with reference to the just and the unjust, the base and the honourable, the good and the evil, as he is with reference to health, and other things with which other arts are concerned; I mean, that he does not know them, what is good, or what is evil, what is honourable or what is base, what is just, or what is unjust, but is able to devise some means of persuasion respecting them, so that, though he is ignorant, he appears to the ignorant to know more than one who possesses knowledge; or is it necessary that he should know these, and is it requisite that he who is about to learn rhetoric should have acquired these things before he comes to you; if not, will you, who are a teacher of rhetoric, teach him who comes to you none of these things (for it is not your province), but make him appear to the multitude to know these things, though he does not know them, and to seem to be a good man when he is not so? or shall you be unable to teach him rhetoric at all, unless he knows beforehand the truth respecting these things? What is the case in this respect, Gorgias? And, by Jupiter, as you just now promised, unfold the whole power of rhetoric.

GORG. I think, Socrates, that any one, if he did not know, would learn these things from me.

SOCR. Stay; for you say well. If then you make any one a rhetorician, it is necessary that he should know what is just and unjust, either before, or afterwards from your instruction.

GORG. Certainly.

SOCR. What then? Is he who has learnt carpentering, a carpenter, or not?

GORG. He is.

SOCR. And is not he who has learnt music, a musician?

GORG. Yes.

SOCR. And he who has learnt medicine, a physician? And so, in the same way, with regard to other things, is not he who has learnt any particular art such a person as each science respectively makes its proficient?

GORG. Certainly.

SOCR. By the same reason, then, does it not follow, that he who has learnt just things is just?

GORG. Assuredly.

SOCR. And he who is just surely performs just actions.

GORG. Yes.

SOCR. Is it not, therefore, necessary that the just man should wish to do just actions?

GORG. It appears so.

SOCR. The just man, therefore, will never wish to act unjustly.

GORG. Necessarily.

SOCR. And it follows from the argument that the rhetorician should be just?

GORG. Yes.

SOCR. A rhetorician, therefore, will never wish to act unjustly?

GORG. It appears not.

Socr. Do you remember that you said a little before that we ought not to accuse the trainers of youth, nor expel them from cities, if a pugilist does not make a good use of the pugilistic art, and acts unjustly? And so, likewise, if a rhetorician make an unjust use of rhetoric, that we should not accuse the teacher, nor expel him from the city, but the person who acts unjustly, and does not make a proper use of rhetoric? Were these things said, or not?

Gorg. They were said.

Socr. But now this very same rhetorician appears incapable of ever acting unjustly: Is it not so?

Gorg. It appears so.

Socr. And it was said, Gorgias, at the commencement of our discussion, that rhetoric is conversant with words, not those respecting the even and the odd, but those respecting the just and the unjust. Was it not so?

Gorg. It was.

Socr. When, therefore, you spoke thus, I supposed that rhetoric could never be an unjust thing, since it always discourses concerning justice. But when you said shortly afterwards that a rhetorician might use rhetoric unjustly, then, wondering, and thinking that the two statements did not accord, I made that remark, that if you should think it a gain to be confuted, as I do, it was worth while to continue the discussion, but if not, to give it up. Afterwards, however, when we were investigating the matter, you see yourself that it is again allowed to be impossible for a rhetorician to make an unjust use of rhetoric, and to be willing to act unjustly. How the case really stands, by the dog, Gorgias, requires no little discussion to examine it thoroughly. [151-3]

[Nature of the Rhetorical Skills]

Pol. Does rhetoric, then, appear to you to be skill?

Socr. To me it does, unless you say otherwise.

Pol. Of what is it the skill?

Socr. Of procuring a certain gratification and pleasure.

Pol. Does not rhetoric, then, appear to you to be a beautiful thing, since it is able to gratify mankind?

Socr. What, Polus? Have you already heard from me what I say it is, that you afterwards ask me, if it does not appear to me to be beautiful?

Pol. Did I not hear you say that it is a certain skill?

Socr. Since, then, you prize giving pleasure, are you willing to give me a little pleasure?

Pol. I am.

Socr. Ask me, then, what kind of art cookery appears to me to be.

Pol. I do ask you; what kind of an art is cookery?

Socr. None at all, Polus.

Pol. What is it? say.

Socr. I say, then, it is a certain skill.

Pol. Of what? say.

Socr. I say, of procuring gratification and pleasure, Polus.

Pol. Are cookery and rhetoric the same thing?

Socr. By no means, but a part of the same study.

Pol. Of what study are you speaking?

Socr. I fear it would be too rude to speak the truth, for I hesitate to speak on account of Gorgias, lest he should think that I ridicule his profession. But I know not whether this is the rhetoric which Gorgias studies: for it was not at all clear from our late discussion what his opinion is. But what I call rhetoric is a part of a certain thing which does not rank among things beautiful.

Gorg. Of what thing, Socrates? say, without fear of offending me.

Socr. It appears to me, then, Gorgias, to be a certain study, that does not belong to art, but to a soul that is sagacious and manly, and naturally powerful in its intercourse with men. The sum of it I call flattery. Of this study there appears to me to be many other divisions, and one of them is that of cookery; which, indeed, appears to be an art, but, as I maintain, is not an art, but skill and practice. I also call rhetoric a division of this, and personal decoration, and sophistry, these four divisions relating to four particulars. If, therefore, Polus wishes to enquire, let him enquire, for he has not yet heard what division of flattery I assert rhetoric to be: but he did not observe that I had not yet finished my answer, nevertheless he asks me, if I do not think that it is beautiful. But I shall not answer him, whether I think rhetoric is beautiful or base, till I have first answered what it is. For that would not be right, Polus. If then you wish to enquire, ask me what division of flattery I assert rhetoric to be.

Pol. I ask, then, and do you answer, what division it is.

Socr. Will you understand me when I answer? For rhetoric, in my opinion, is a semblance of a division of the political art. [154-5]

. . . . .

Socr. That I may not, then, be prolix, I wish to tell you, after the manner of geometricians, (for perhaps you can now follow me,) that what personal decoration is to gymnastics, that is cookery to medicine: or rather thus, that what personal decoration is to gymnastics, that is sophistry to legislation, and that what cookery is to medicine, that is rhetoric to justice. [157]

[*Uses of Rhetoric*]

Socr. Well then, if these things are true, Polus, what is the great utility of rhetoric? For, from what has been now agreed on, every one ought especially to beware of acting unjustly, for that, *if he does so act*, he will sustain great evil. Is it not so?

Pol. Certainly.

Socr. And if a man has committed injustice, either himself, or any one else for whom he has regard, he ought of his own accord to betake himself thither, where as soon as possible he will be punished, to a judge as to a physician, taking every pains lest the disease of injustice becoming inveterate should render the soul corrupt and incurable; or what must we say, Polus, if our former admissions are to stand? Do not these things necessarily harmonize with the former in this, but in no other way?

Pol. For what else can we say, Socrates?

Socr. For the purpose, then, of excusing injustice, our own, or that of our parents, or friends, or children, or country, when it acts unjustly, rhetoric is of no use to us at all, Polus, unless on the contrary, any one supposes that he ought especially to accuse himself, and afterwards his relatives, and any other of his friends, who may have acted unjustly, and not conceal the crime, but bring it to light, in order that he may be punished, and restored to health; moreover, that he should compel both himself and the others to lay aside fear, and with his eyes shut, and in a manly way, deliver himself up, as to a physician, to be cut and cauterised, pursuing the good and the beautiful, without paying any regard to what is painful; if he has committed a wrong worthy of stripes, delivering himself up to be beaten, if of bonds, to be bound, if of a fine, to pay it, if of exile, to be banished, if of death, to die, being himself the first accuser of himself, and others his relatives, not sparing either himself or them, but employing rhetoric for this very purpose, that, the crimes being exposed, they may be freed from the greatest of evils, injustice. Shall we say thus, Polus, or not?

Pol. These things appear to me, Socrates, to be absurd; but it must be admitted, they accord with what was before said.

Socr. Must not, therefore, either our former conclusions be done away with, or these results necessarily follow?

Pol. Yes; such is the case.

Socr. Contrariwise, if it is requisite to do ill to any one, whether to an enemy, or any other person, provided only that he is not himself injured by his enemy; for this is to be guarded against; but if an enemy injures another, we should endeavour by all possible means, both by actions and words, that he may not be punished, nor brought before a judge: but, if he is brought before him, we should contrive so that our enemy may escape, and not suffer punishment: and if he has robbed us of a great quantity of gold, that he should not restore it, but should retain it and spend it on himself and his associates unjustly and impiously; and if he has committed an injustice worthy of death, we should contrive that he may not die, if possible never, but that he may be immortal in depravity, or if this cannot be, that he may live in this state for as long a period as possible. For such purposes, Polus, rhetoric appears to me to be useful, since to him who does not intend to act unjustly, its utility does not appear to me to be great, if indeed it is of any utility at all, as in the former part of our discussion it appeared in no respect to be. [177-8]

[Use of Rhetoric in Body Politic]

Socr. Well then. But as to the rhetoric addressed to the Athenian people, and the people in other cities consisting of freemen, what shall we say as to that? Do the rhetoricians appear to you always to speak with a view to what is best, aiming at this, that the citizens may be made as good as possible by their discourses? or do they, too, endeavour to gratify the citizens, and neglecting the public interest for the sake of their own private advantage, do they treat the people as children, trying only to gratify them, without being in the least concerned whether they shall become better or worse by these means?

Cal. This is not a simple question that you ask me. For there are some who, looking to the interest of the citizens, say what they do; but others are such as you describe.

Socr. That is enough. For, if this also is twofold, one part of it will be flattery, and a base popular speaking, but the other will be honourable, namely, that which endeavours to make the souls of the citizens as good as possible, and strives to speak what is best, whether it be pleasant or unpleasant to the hearers. But you have never yet seen this kind of rhetoric. Or, if you can mention any one of the rhetoricians who is of this stamp, why do you not tell me who he is? [204-5]

[Sophists and Orators]

Socr. My good man, a sophist and an orator are the same thing, or nearly so, and very like, as I said to Polus. But you, through ignorance, think that rhetoric is something exceedingly beautiful, and despise the other. But, in truth, the sophist's art is as much more beautiful than rhetoric, as the legislative is than the judicial, and the gymnastic art than medicine. But I for my part think that public speakers and sophists alone ought not to complain of the very thing that they teach, as being mischievous to themselves, or that in the very same charge they should at the same time accuse themselves for not having at all benefited those whom they profess to have benefited. Is it not so? [224]

PHAEDRUS [2]

[Knowledge of Truth Essential to Speaking]

Socr. When an orator, therefore, who is ignorant of good and evil, having found a city that is likewise so, endeavours to persuade it, not by celebrating the praises of an ass's shadow, as if it were a horse, but of evil, as if it were good, and having studied the opinions of the multitude should persuade them to do evil instead of good, what kind of fruit do you suppose rhetoric will afterwards reap from such a sowing?

Phae. By no means a good one.

Socr. But have we not, my good friend, reviled the art of speaking more roughly than is proper? for she may, perhaps, say: "Why, sirs, do you talk so foolishly? For I compel no one who is ignorant of the truth to learn how to speak: but if my advice is worth any thing, when he has acquired that, he then has recourse to me. This, then, I insist on, that without me one who knows the truth will not for all that be able to persuade by art."

Phae. Will she not speak justly, in asserting this?

[2] From the translation by Henry Cary. *The Works of Plato*, vol. I, London, Henry G. Bohn, 1854.

Socr. I admit it, at least if the arguments that assail her testify that she is an art. For I think I have heard some arguments coming up and insisting that she lies and is not an art, but an inartistic trick. But a genuine art of speaking, says the Spartan, without laying hold of truth, neither exists, nor ever can exist hereafter.

Phae. We must have these arguments, Socrates; so bring them forward and examine what they say, and in what manner.

Socr. Come hither then, ye noble creatures, and persuade Phaedrus with the beautiful children, that, unless he has sufficiently studied philosophy, he will never be competent to speak on any subject whatever. Let Phaedrus answer then.

Phae. Put your questions.

Socr. Must not then rhetoric in general be an art that leads the soul by means of argument, not only in courts of justice, and other public assemblies, but also in private, equally with respect to trivial and important matters? and is its right use at all more valued when employed about grave than about trifling things? What have you heard said about this?

Phae. By Jupiter, nothing at all of this kind; but it is for the most part spoken and written according to art in judicial trials, and it is spoken also in popular assemblies; but I have never heard any thing further.

Socr. What, have you heard only of the rhetorical arts of Nestor and Ulysses, which they composed during their leisure in Ilium, and have you never heard of those by Palamedes?

Phae. And, by Jupiter, I have not even heard of those by Nestor, unless you make Gorgias a Nestor, or Thrasymachus and Theodorus a Ulysses.

Socr. Perhaps I do. But let us pass over these; do you say however; in courts of justice what do adversaries do? do they not contradict each other? or what shall we say?

Phae. That very thing.

Socr. And respecting the just and unjust?

Phae. Yes.

Socr. Will not he, then, who accomplishes this by art, make the same thing appear to the same persons, at one time just, and, when he pleases, unjust?

Phae. How not?

Socr. And in a popular assembly the same things seem to the state at one time good, and at another the contrary?

Phae. Just so.

Socr. And do we not know that the Eleatic Palamedes spoke by art in such a manner that the same things appeared to his hearers similar and dissimilar, one and many, at rest and in motion?

Phae. Assuredly.

Socr. The art, then, of arguing on both sides has not only to do with courts of justice and popular assemblies, but as it seems, it must be one and the same art, if it is an art, with respect to all subjects of discourse, by which a man is able to make all things appear similar to each other so far as they are capable of being made appear so, and to drag them to light, when another attempts to make them appear similar and conceals his attempt.

Phae. What mean you by this?

Socr. I think it will be evident if we enquire as follows: Does deception more frequently occur in things that differ much or little?

Phae. In things that differ little.

Socr. But by changing your position gradually, you will more easily escape detection in going to the opposite side, than by doing so rapidly.

Phae. How not?

Socr. It is necessary, then, that he who means to deceive another, but not be deceived himself, should be able to distinguish with accuracy the similarity and dissimilarity of things.

Phae. It is indeed necessary.

Socr. Will he be able, then, if ignorant of the truth of each particular thing, to discern the smaller or greater similarity of the thing of which he is ignorant, in other things?

Phae. Impossible.

Socr. It is clear, therefore, that in the case of those who have formed opinions contrary to the truth and are deceived, this error has found its way in by means of certain resemblances.

Phae. It doubtlessly does happen so.

Socr. Is it possible, then, that one, who is ignorant of what is the nature of each particular thing, should have sufficient art to bring over any one by degrees by leading him through means of resemblances, from each several truth to its opposite, or himself to escape from being so led?

Phae. Never.

Socr. He therefore, my friend, who does not know the truth, but hunts after opinions, will, as it appears, produce but a ridiculous and inartistic art of speaking. [337-40]

. . . . .

RHETORIC AND PUBLIC SPEAKING

Socr. When any one pronounces the word iron or silver, do we not understand the same thing?
Phae. Assuredly.
Socr. When any one pronounces the word just, or good? are we not carried different ways, and do we not differ both with one another and with ourselves?
Phae. Certainly.
Socr. In some things, therefore, we agree, in others not.
Phae. Just so.
Socr. In which class of things, then, are we more easily deceived? and in which of the two has rhetoric greater power?
Phae. Clearly in that in which we are easily led astray.
Socr. He, therefore, who means to pursue the art of rhetoric, ought first of all to have distinguished these methodically, and to have discovered a certain character of each species, both of that in which the generality of men must necessarily be led astray, and of that in which that is not the case. [341]

[Need for Organization of Speech Materials]

Socr. But this at least I think you will allow, that every speech ought to be put together like a living creature, with a body of its own, so as to be neither without head, nor without feet, but to have both a middle and extremities, described proportionately to each other and to the whole. [342-3]

[Observations on Various Methods of Speaking]

Phae. There are indeed very many things, Socrates, which you will find in the books written on the art of speaking.
Socr. You have reminded me very opportunely. The exordium, I think, must first be spoken at the beginning of the speech. You mean these, do you not? the refinements of the art?
Phae. Yes.
Socr. And secondly a kind of narration, and evidence to support it; thirdly, proofs; fourthly, probabilities; and I think that a famous Byzantian tricker-out of speeches mentions confirmation and after-confirmation.
Phae. Do you mean the excellent Theodorus?
Socr. I do. He says, too, that refutation and after-refutation must be employed both in accusation and defence. And must we not adduce the most illustrious Parian, Evenus, who first discovered subordinate intimations and bye-praises? and some say that he put into

metre bye-censures, to assist the memory: for he is a wise man. But shall we suffer Tisias and Gorgias to sleep, who found out that probabilities were more to be valued than truths, and who by force of words make small things appear great, and great things small, and new things old, and the contrary new, and who discovered a concise method of speaking and an infinite prolixity on all subjects? When Prodicus once heard me tell this, he laughed, and said that he alone had discovered what speeches are required by art; that we require them neither long nor short, but of a moderate length.

PHAE. Most wisely, Prodicus.

SOCR. But do we not mention Hippias? for I think our Elean friend was of the same opinion with him.

PHAE. Why not?

SOCR. But how shall we describe Polus's new-fangled method of speaking, as his reduplication of words, his sentences, his similitudes, and the words which Licymnius made him a present of, in order to produce a graceful diction.

PHAE. But was not the system of Protagoras, Socrates, something of this kind?

SOCR. His was a correctness of diction, my boy, and many other fine things besides, but in the art of dragging in speeches to excite commiseration for old age and poverty, the Chalcedonian hero appears to me to have carried off the palm. He was moreover a powerful man to rouse the anger of the multitude, and again, when enraged, to soothe them by enchantment, as he used to say; he was most skilful in raising and removing calumnies, on any ground whatever. But all seem to agree in the same opinion with respect to the conclusion of speeches, to which some have given the name of recapitulation, others a different name.

PHAE. You mean the summarily reminding the hearers, at the conclusion, of the several things that have been said.

SOCR. I mean that, and now consider if you have any thing else to say about the art of speaking. [345-6]

[Rhetoric Compared with Medicine]

SOCR. The ability, Phaedrus, to become a perfect proficient, probably, or rather necessarily, depends on the same things as in other cases: for, if you naturally possess rhetorical abilities, you will be a distinguished orator by adding science and practice; but in whichever of these you are deficient, in that respect you will be imperfect.

But so far as it is an art, its method, I think, will not be found in the way that Lysias and Thrasymachus are proceeding.

PHAE. In what way then?

SOCR. Pericles, my excellent friend, appears, with good reason, to have been the most perfect of all men in rhetoric.

PHAE. How so?

SOCR. All the great arts require a subtle and speculative research into the law of nature: for that loftiness of thought and perfect mastery over every subject seems to be derived from some such source as this; which Pericles possessed in addition to a great natural genius. For meeting, I think, with Anaxagoras, who was a person of this kind, and being filled with speculative research, and having arrived at the nature of intelligence and want of intelligence, about which Anaxagoras made that long discourse, he drew from thence to the art of speaking whatever could contribute to its advantage.

PHAE. What mean you by this?

SOCR. The method of the art of rhetoric is, in a manner, the same as that of medicine.

PHAE. How so?

SOCR. In both it is requisite that nature should be thoroughly investigated, the nature of the body in the one, and the soul in the other, if you mean not only by practice and experience, but by art, to give health and strength to the former by applying medicine and diet, and to impart such persuasion as you please and virtue to the latter, by means of speeches and legitimate employments. [348-9]

[Skill in Speaking Depends upon Knowledge of Soul]

SOCR. The method, then, that neglected these, would resemble the walk of a blind man. He however who proceeds by art, ought on no account to be compared either to a blind or a deaf man; but it is clear that whosoever teaches another speaking by art, should accurately shew the real nature of the things to which he will have to apply his speeches; and this surely is the soul.

PHAE. How not?

SOCR. His whole endeavour, therefore, must be directed to this; for in this he attempts to produce persuasion. Is it not so?

PHAE. Yes.

SOCR. It is clear, therefore, that Thrasymachus, and any one else who seriously endeavours to teach the art of rhetoric, will in the first place describe with all possible accuracy, and make it be seen whether the soul is naturally one and similar, or, like the form of the body, composed of different elements; for this we say is to make known nature.

PHAE. Most assuredly.

SOCR. And, in the second place, in what respect it naturally acts or is acted upon by any thing.

PHAE. How not?

SOCR. In the third place, having set in order the different kinds of speech and of soul, and the different manners in which these are affected, he will go through the several causes, adapting each to each, and teaching what kind of soul is necessarily persuaded, and what not persuaded, by particular kinds of speech, and for what reason.

PHAE. It will assuredly be best done in this way, as it seems.

SOCR. Never then, my dear friend, will any thing that is otherwise explained or spoken, be spoken or written by art, either in any other case or in this. But the modern writers on the art of speech-making, whom you yourself have heard, are dissemblers, and conceal the very admirable knowledge they have of the soul. Until, then, they both speak and write according to this method, let us never be persuaded that they write artistically.

PHAE. What method is this?

SOCR. It is not easy to mention the very words themselves; but how it is proper to write, if a man means to be as artistic as he possibly can, I am willing to tell you.

PHAE. Tell me then.

SOCR. Since the power of speech is that of leading the soul, it is necessary that he who means to be an orator should know how many kinds of soul there are: but they are so many, and of such and such kinds; whence some men are of this character and some of that character. These then being thus divided, there are again so many kinds of speech, each of a certain character. Now men of such a character are for this particular reason easily persuaded by certain speeches, and persons of a different character are for these reasons with difficulty persuaded. It is necessary, therefore, that he, after having sufficiently understood all this, when he afterwards perceives these very things taking place in actions, and being done, should be able to follow them rapidly by perception, otherwise he will know nothing more than the very things which he formerly heard from his preceptor. But when he is sufficiently competent to say, what kind of person is persuaded by what kind of speeches, and is able, when he sees him before him, to point out to himself that this is the person and this the nature for which those speeches were formerly made now actually present before me, and to which these particular speeches are to be addressed, in order to persuade him to these particular things,— when he has acquired all this, and has learnt moreover the proper seasons for speaking and being silent, and again has made himself master of the seasonable and unseasonable occasions for brevity, plaintiveness, and vehemence, and all the other several kinds of speech which he has learnt, then his art will be beautifully and perfectly accomplished, but not before. But whoever is deficient in any of these particulars, either in speaking, or teaching, or writing, and yet asserts that he speaks by art, is overcome by the person who will not be persuaded. "What then," perhaps the writer on rhetoric will say, "does it appear to you, Phaedrus and Socrates, that the art of speaking, as it is called, must be obtained in this or some other way? [350-1]

[*Use of Probability in Speaking*]

SOCR. Having made, then, as it seems, this wise and artistic discovery, he has written, that if a weak but brave man should be brought to trial for having knocked down a strong and cowardly one, and having robbed him of his clothes or any thing else, then that neither of them ought to speak the truth, but the coward should say that he was not knocked down by the brave man alone, and the latter should prove this, that they were alone, and then urge this; "How could a man like me ever attack a man like him?" But the other will not admit his own cowardice, but, in attempting to tell some other falsehood, will perhaps supply his adversary with the means of refuting him. And in other cases, such things as these are said according to art. Is it not so, Phaedrus?

PHAE. How not?

SOCR. Wonderfully clever seems to have been the inventor of this abstruse art, whether Tisias or whoever else he was, and by whatever name he delights to be called. But, my friend, shall we say to him or not?

PHAE. What?

SOCR. Tisias, long since before your arrival, we happened to say, that this probability of yours derives its influence with the multitude from its resemblance to truth; and we just now concluded that in all cases he knows best how to discover resemblances who is best acquainted with the truth. So that, if you have any thing else to say about the art of speaking, we will listen to you; but if not, we shall hold to the conclusions we have lately come to, that unless a man has reckoned up the different natures of those who will have to hear him, and is able to divide things themselves into species, and to comprehend the several particulars under one general idea, he will never be skilled in the art of speaking so far as it is possible for a man to be so. But this he can never acquire without great labour, which a wise man ought not to bestow for the purpose of speaking and acting amongst men, but that he may be able to speak such things as are acceptable to the gods, and act acceptably to them, to the utmost of his power. For, as wiser men than we say, Tisias, a man of understanding ought not to make it his principal study to gratify his fellow-servants, except by the way, but good masters and of good extraction. If therefore the circuit be long, wonder not; for it is to be undertaken for the sake of great ends, not such as you think. And even these, as our argument proves, if any one is willing, will be best attained by those means. [353-4]

SUGGESTED READINGS

Atkins, John William Hey
    Literary Criticism in Antiquity: A Sketch of Its Development. London. Cambridge University Press. 1934. I, p33-70

Cary, Henry, ed.
    Gorgias. In *The Works of Plato.* Vol. I. London. Henry G. Bohn. 1854. p128-232
    Phaedrus. In *The Works of Plato.* Vol. I. London. Henry G. Bohn. 1854. p295-360

Cooper, Lane, tr.
    Phaedrus, Ion, Gorgias, and Symposium, with Passages from the Republic and Laws. London. Oxford University Press. 1938. lviii,436p

Cope, E. M.
    On the Sophistical Rhetoric. *Journal of Classical and Sacred Philology.* 2:129-69 May 1855; 3:34-80 March 1856; 3:253-88 December 1856

Hunt, Everett Lee
    Plato on Rhetoric and Rhetoricians. *Quarterly Journal of Speech Education.* 6:33-53 June 1920
    Plato and Aristotle on Rhetoric and Public Speaking. In *Studies in Rhetoric and Public Speaking in Honor of James Albert Winans.* New York. Century Co. 1925. p3-60

Jevons, Frank B.
    Oratory. In *A History of Greek Literature.* 4th ed. London. Charles Griffin and Co. 1908. p367-464

ARISTOTLE

(384 B. C.-322 B. C.)

In his *Lectures Concerning Oratory,* John Lawson remarks that in reading Aristotle's *Rhetoric* a person is "in the State of one travelling through a strange Country, always pleased, because every step opens a new Prospect. . . ." The *Rhetoric* of Aristotle is generally regarded one of the most significant contributions to the field of public speaking. Its basic principles can be found in one form or another in practically every textbook of the present day.

The *Rhetoric* is both a treatise on the speaking art and a philosophy of discourse. From many points of view it offers as sound a rationale of the art of speaking as any work in the literature of the subject. In the main, Aristotle's contributions rest upon four basic postulates, all of which have been recognized through the years as valid. (1) The *Rhetoric* deals with speaking as a useful art, as an instrument having functional value in the social order. Consequently, the work contains a minimum of material dealing with display, or with glorification of form to the neglect of substance. (2) Rhetoric is considered an interrelated art, relying heavily upon ethics, politics, psychology, and law. (3) Aristotle believes that rhetoric can be taught, that the random performances of speakers can be improved through the study and application of systematized principles of speaking. (4) Aristotle believes that a sound projection of rhetorical theory is based upon the Doctrine of the Mean. This doctrine permeates both the *Rhetoric* and the *Nicomachean Ethics.* As applied to speaking, it simply urges the avoidance of both excess and deficiency. The quality of a speech is directly related to its quantitative proportions; there must be neither too much nor too little, be it of narrative content, length of argument, or amount of introductory detail.

The *Rhetoric* is concise, generally clear, free from pedantry. It stresses invention as over against the other traditional parts of rhetoric; emphasizes deliberative speaking above other types; and (although professing to look upon pathetic proof as a mere accessory) develops an unusually complete analysis of the emotional behavior of human beings.

THE RHETORIC [1]

[*Nature of Rhetoric*]

Rhetoric is a counterpart of Dialectic. For both are concerned with such subjects as fall in a sense within the cognizance of all men, and neither is limited to any definite science. Accordingly we are all in a sense dialecticians and rhetoricians; for everybody essays up to a certain point the criticism and support of a thesis, defence and ac-

[1] From the translation by J. E. C. Welldon. *The Rhetoric of Aristotle,* London and New York, Macmillan and Company, 1886. By permission of The Macmillan Company, publishers.

cusation. It is true that most people do this either without any method at all or by familiarity which is the result of habit. But the possibility of proceeding in both these ways is itself a proof that the processes may be systematized; for it is possible to investigate the causes of such success as is attained by familiarity or at random, and such an investigation will be universally admitted to be essentially a function of an art. [1]

[Uses of Rhetoric]

It is valuable, firstly, because truth and justice possess a natural superiority to their opposites, and therefore, if judgments are not given as they should be, it must be the speakers themselves who are responsible for the defeat; and this is itself a state of things which is reprehensible. Secondly, there are audiences which, even if we possess the most exact scientific knowledge, it is not easy to persuade by scientific arguments. [6-7]

Again, in Rhetoric no less than in syllogistic reasoning it is right to be capable of arguing on both sides of a case, not for the sake of doing both (as we have no right to argue in favour of anything that is wrong), but that the true state of the case may not escape us and that, if another party makes an unfair use of his arguments, we may be able in our turn to refute them. [7]

Lastly, it would be a paradox that there should be something disgraceful in the inability to defend oneself by bodily strength, and not in the inability to defend oneself by speech, when speech is more characteristic of man than the use of the body. [8]

[Definition of Rhetoric]

Rhetoric may be defined as a faculty of discovering all the possible means of persuasion in any subject. For this is exclusively the function of Rhetoric, as every other art, whether instructive or persuasive, deals with a subject-matter peculiar to itself, Medicine e. g. with the conditions of health and disease, Geometry with the properties of magnitudes, Arithmetic with number, and so on through the list of arts and sciences. Rhetoric on the other hand may be said to possess the faculty of discovering the means of persuasion in any given subject; and accordingly we hold that the rules of the rhetorical art are not limited in their application to a certain special definite class of subjects. [10]

[Kinds of Rhetorical Proofs]

Rhetorical proofs are either artistic or inartistic. By "inartistic proofs" I mean all such as are not provided by our own skill but existed before and independently, e. g. witnesses, tortures, contracts and the like; by "artistic," such as admit of being constructed systematically and by our own skill; in fine, the former we have only to apply and the latter we have to invent. [10]

[Modes of Persuasion]

The proofs provided through the instrumentality of the speech are of three kinds, consisting either in the moral character of the speaker or in the production of a certain disposition in the audience or in the speech itself by means of real or apparent demonstration. The instrument of proof is the moral character, when the delivery of the speech is such as to produce an impression of the speaker's credibility; for we yield a more complete and ready credence to persons of high character not only ordinarily and in a general way, but in such matters as do not admit of absolute certainty but necessarily leave room for difference of opinion, without any qualification whatever. (It is requisite however that this result should itself be attained by means of the speech and not of any antecedent conception of the speaker's character.) For so far from following the example of some authors of rhetorical handbooks, who in their "art" of Rhetoric regard the high character of the speaker as not being itself in any sense contributory to his persuasiveness, we may practically lay it down as a general rule that there is no proof so effective as that of the character. *Secondly,* proof may be conveyed through the audience, when it is worked up by the speech to an emotional state. For there is a wide difference in our manner of pronouncing decisions, according as we feel pleasure or pain, affection or hatred; and indeed *the power of working upon the emotions* is, as we assert, the one end or object to which our present professors of the rhetorical art endeavour to direct their studies. This is a part of the subject which will be elucidated in detail, when we come to discuss the emotions. *Lastly,* the instrument of proof is the speech itself, when we have proved a truth or an apparent truth from such means of persuasion as are appropriate to a particular subject. [10-12]

[Modes of Proof]

. . . *We find that,* as in Dialectics there are three modes of proof, viz. induction, syllogism and apparent syllogism, so in Rhetoric there is the example corresponding to induction, the enthymeme to syllogism and the apparent enthymeme to apparent syllogism. I call an enthymeme a rhetorical syllogism and an example a rhetorical induction. [12-13]

[*Materials of Enthymemes*]

It is evident then from these considerations that the propositions which form the materials of enthymemes, although sometimes they are necessary, are for the most part only generally true. For the materials of enthymematic reasoning are probabilities and signs; and it follows that these are respectively identical with the propositions which are generally and necessarily true. A probability is something that usually happens, although the definition must not be stated, as it sometimes is, without qualification, but something that usually happens in such matters as are indeterminate; and it stands to the thing which is to be proved in the relation of the universal to the particular. A sign on the other hand bears *to the thing which is to be proved* the relation either of an individual to the universal or of an universal to the particular. Such signs as are necessary *or conclusive* are called demonstrations; the others have no distinctive name. By "necessary signs" I mean the propositions of which a syllogism *in its strict sense* is composed. Hence a sign of this kind is called a demonstration; for it is when we suppose the statement we make to be irrefutable that we think we adduce a demonstration, meaning that it has been *logically* proved and concluded, as demonstration and conclusion are in old parlance identical. [17-18]

. . . . .

". . . A woman is giving milk; therefore she has lately become a mother," is an instance of a necessary sign. This is the only kind of sign which is a demonstration, as it is the only one which, if true, is irrefutable. As an instance of a sign which stands *to the thing to be proved* in the relation of the universal to the particular, one may say, "It is a sign that so-and-so has a fever; his breathing is hard." This again however admits of refutation, even if it is true; for a person may breathe heavily without having a fever. . . .

As to the example, we have stated that it is an induction and have described the character of the subjects with which it deals. It stands *to the thing which is to be proved* in the relation not of part to whole nor of whole to part nor of whole to whole, but of part to part, of similar to similar, *and is employed* when both the example and the thing exemplified fall under the same general head, but the one is more familiar than the other. Thus, *if we are arguing* that Dionysius in asking for his bodyguard has a design of attempting to gain tyrannical power, *we may urge that* Pisistratus once asked for a bodyguard with this design and, as soon as he had obtained it, made himself tyrant, and that the same was true of Theagenes at Megara.... [18-19]

[*Topics*]

I mean that the proper subjects of dialectical and rhetorical syllogisms are the topics, as we call them *par excellence,* i.e. such as are equally suitable to questions of justice, physics or politics, and to many questions of many different kinds. Such is e. g. the topic of "the more or less," *or of degree,* which will serve equally well to construct a syllogism or enthymeme about justice, physics or anything else, although these are subjects differing in kind. Special topics on the other hand are such as spring from the propositions appropriate to a particular species or class of subjects. Thus there are propositions in physics from which it is impossible to form an enthymeme or syllogism upon ethics, ethical propositions again from which it is impossible to form an enthymeme or syllogism upon physics, and so on through the whole range of subjects. [20-1]

[*Kinds of Speeches*]

There are three kinds of Rhetoric, corresponding to the three kinds of audience to which speeches are naturally addressed. For a speech is composed of three elements, viz. the speaker, the subject of the speech and the persons addressed; and the end *or object* of the speech is determined by the last, viz. by the audience. Audiences are necessarily either critics or judges; and if the latter, they may be judges of things lying either in the past or in the future. A member of the Public Assembly may be taken as an instance of a judge of the future, a member of the Courts of Law as an instance of a judge of the past; while one who judges merely of the ability *displayed in a speech* is the critic. It follows that there must necessarily be three kinds of rhetorical speeches, the deliberative, the forensic and the epideictic. [22]

. . . . .

Deliberative Rhetoric is partly hortatory and partly dissuasive; for people who counsel their friends deliberatively on private affairs and people who address popular meetings on matters of State are alike in this, that they always exhort or dissuade. Forensic Rhetoric may be divided into accusation and defence; for the parties to any legal action necessarily adopt either one or other of these lines. To the epideictic orator belong eulogy and censure. Again, there are times belonging to the several kinds of Rhetoric; to deliberative Rhetoric the future, as deliberative counsel, whether hortatory or dissuasive, has reference to things which lie in the future; to forensic Rhetoric the past, as the subject of accusation or defence is always something which has been already done; and to epideictic Rhetoric most properly the present, as it is always existing facts which form the grounds of eulogy or censure, although epideictic orators often amplify their resources by appealing to the past in the way of reminiscence and to the future in the way of anticipation. There are three ends too appropriate respectively to the three kinds of Rhetoric. The end which the deliberative orator has in view is expediency or injury; for if he exhorts to a particular line of action, he recommends it as being better, *i.e. more advantageous,* if he dissuades from it, he does so on the ground that it is worse, and every other consideration, whether justice or injustice, honour or disgrace, he embraces merely as something secondary and subservient to this. The end of the parties to a legal action *or in other words of forensic orators* is justice and injustice; and if they too introduce other considerations, it is always as subordinate to these. Orators of the panegyrical and depreciatory style take honour and disgrace as their end and again refer all other considerations to these. [22-3]

. . . . .

The most important subjects of general deliberation and deliberative oratory are practically five, viz. finance, war and peace, the defence of the country, imports and exports, and legislation. [27]

[*The Ends of Human Action*]

It may be said that all men both individually and collectively have a certain object at which they aim in all that they choose and in all that they avoid. This object may be summarily defined as happiness and the constituents of happiness. [30-1]

[*Constituents of Happiness*]

Such then being the definition of happiness, it follows that its constituent parts are nobility, the possession of many and excellent friends, wealth, a goodly and numerous family and a happy old age; also such physical excellences as health, beauty, strength, stature, and athletic power, and *finally* fame, honour, good fortune and virtue. [31]

[Nature of the Good]

But as in deliberative Rhetoric it is expediency which is the end proposed, the subject of deliberation being not the end but the means to the end or in other words whatever is expedient in actions, and as what is expedient is good, it is necessary to apprehend certain elementary propositions respecting what is good or expedient in general.

Good then may be defined as that which is desirable for its own sake and for the sake of which we desire or choose something else, and which is sought by all things or by all sentient or intelligent things or *would be sought by them,* if they should acquire intelligence. Again, whatever intelligence would assign to each individual or the intelligence of each individual assigns to himself, this is good relatively to him. Or again, that which by its presence produces a good condition and a state of independence, or independence *in the abstract,* or that which is productive or preservative of such things, or that upon which they are consequent, or that which tends to hinder or destroy their opposites *is also a good.* Consequence however may be either subsequent or simultaneous; knowledge e. g. is consequent upon learning subsequently but life upon healthiness simultaneously. Also a cause may be productive in three senses; as healthiness e. g. is productive of health in one sense, food is productive of it in another and gymnastic exercise, as generally producing health, in a third. [39-40]

[Necessity of Knowing the Forms of Polity]

The proper sources of proofs in exhortation and dissuasion have been now pretty exhaustively described. But the greatest and most authoritative of all, as a means of persuasion and good counsel, is an acquaintance with all the various forms of polity and an analysis of their several customs, institutions and interests. For it is self-interest which is the dominant force in the world, and whatever is preservative of a particular polity is its interest. Further, it is the expressed will of the supreme authority which is supreme *in any State,* and the supreme authorities are different in the different polities, being as numerous as the polities themselves. There are four polities, viz., Democracy, Oligarchy, Aristocracy and Monarchy; consequently the supreme or decisive authority in each case is either some particular part of these polities or the whole. [57-8]

[*The Eulogy*]

We have next to discuss virtue and vice, or what is noble and shameful, as these are the objects of eulogy and censure. For the discussion of them will incidentally serve to indicate the means by which we shall ourselves be regarded as persons of a certain moral character, (which, as we saw, is a second species of proof), since the same means will enable us to represent both ourselves and others as deserving of confidence in respect of virtue. [59-60]

. . . . .

Eulogy is speech setting forth magnitude of virtue. It is the business then *of an orator in eulogy* to demonstrate that the actions of his hero are virtuous. But a panegyric has reference to accomplished results, and the attendant circumstances, such as rank and education, are merely confirmatory from the natural presumption that the children of virtuous parents will be virtuous, and that the recipient of a good education will be good. Hence when we pronounce a panegyric upon anyone, we pronounce it for something that he has already done. But the accomplished results are *praised as being* indications of the moral state; for we should eulogize a person even without his actual performance of the deeds, if we believed him to be capable of performing them. Felicitation and congratulation, *it may be observed,* although themselves identical, are not identical with eulogy and panegyric; still, as virtue is included in happiness, so are these included in congratulation. [67-8]

[*Styles Appropriate to the Three Kinds of Speaking*]

It may be laid down as a general rule that, of the characteristics which are common to the three styles of Rhetoric, exaggeration is most appropriate to the epideictical style—for as the facts are taken for granted *in this style,* it only remains to invest them with grandeur and dignity—examples to the deliberative style, as in this we divine and infer the future from the past; and enthymemes to the forensic style, as in this the obscurity of the facts leaves the largest room for deduction and demonstration. [70]

[*Forensic Speaking*]

Coming now to accusation and defence, we have next to describe the number and nature of the materials proper for the construction of the syllogisms. There are three points which we have to ascer-

RHETORIC AND PUBLIC SPEAKING

tain, viz. (1) the nature and number of the objects of crime, (2) the dispositions of the criminals, and (3) the character and condition of the victims. [70]

. . . . .

To sum up then; all our actions are necessarily due to seven causes, viz. chance, nature, compulsion, habit, reasoning, passion and desire. [72-3]

. . . . .

Having now determined the comparative magnitude of crimes, we have next to take a rapid survey of the inartistic proofs as they are called. *We consider them last,* as they belong exclusively to forensic Rhetoric. They are five in number, viz. laws, witnesses, contracts, tortures and the oath. [100-101]

[Pathetic Proof]

As Rhetoric is intended to be judged—*for in deliberative oratory* we pass judgment on the counsel given, and every legal decision is a judgment—it must necessarily be our object not only to render our speech demonstrative and credible, but also to produce a particular disposition in our judges. [112]

[Ethical Proof]

The sources of personal credibility in orators are three; or in other words there are three things, apart from demonstrative proofs, which inspire belief, viz. sagacity, high character and good will. It is *the want* of all these qualities or of one of them that occasions great errors in matters of discussion or deliberation; for either people are so foolish that they entertain erroneous opinions, or, although their opinions are right, they are so corrupt that they do not express their true sentiments, or, although they are persons of sagacity and high character, they are not well-disposed to their audience, and perhaps in consequence do not recommend the best policy, although they understand it. These are the three sources of credibility, and there is no other. The necessary inference is that, if a person is supposed to command them all, he will be deserving of credit in the eyes of his audience. [113-14]

. . . . .

This being so, the means of getting credit for sagacity and high character must be ascertained from our analysis of the virtues, as it is by the same means that we shall succeed in establishing our own character and the character of others; goodwill or a friendly disposition on the other hand must be discussed now under the head of the emotions. And by the emotions I mean all such states as are attended by pain and pleasure and produce a change or difference in our attitude as judges, e.g. anger, compassion, fear and the like and their opposites. [114]

[*Method of Describing Emotions*]

It is proper to consider each emotion under three heads; if we take e.g. anger, to consider (1) the conditions under which people are irascible, (2) the usual objects, and (3) the usual causes of anger; for the knowledge of one or two of these points without the third will not enable us to excite the passion of anger, and the same is true of any other emotion. [114]

[*Analysis of Emotion of Envy*]

Nor is it difficult to see what are the occasions and objects of envy and the conditions under which we feel envious, envy being defined as a species of pain felt at conspicuous prosperity on the part of persons like ourselves in respect of such goods as have been already described, and this not with any view to our own personal advantage but *solely* because they are prosperous.

For people will be envious, if there are or if they think there are persons like themselves, like, I mean, in race, family, age, habit of mind, reputation or possessions. Or if they only just fall short of having everything *which men can desire*; hence the envious disposition of persons who are engaged in important affairs or who are highly prosperous, as they fancy all the world is robbing them of their due. Or again if they have a permanent reputation for something, and especially for wisdom or happiness. Ambitious persons too are more liable to envy than the unambitious. Pretenders to wisdom are envious, as being ambitious of the credit of wisdom; and in general persons who are eager for reputation in a particular subject are envious in regard to it. Lastly, mean-minded persons are envious; for everything appears important to them.

As regards the occasions of envy, the goods which provoke it have been already stated; for all achievements or possessions of which we covet the reputation or are ambitious, all things which arouse in us a longing for reputation, as well as all the various gifts of Fortune are practically without exception natural objects of envy, and of these such especially as we ourselves either desire or imagine we have a right to possess, or as by their acquisition confer a slight superiority or inferiority.

It is clear too who are the natural objects of envy, as they are implied in the statement which has just been made; they are persons who are near to us in time, place, age or reputation. Hence the saying,

"For to be kin is to be envious."

We are envious too of people whom we are ambitious of rivalling, i.e. of such people as have been mentioned, but not of those who lived many ages ago or who are yet unborn or dead or at the ends of the world. Nor again, where there are people to whom we think we are far inferior or far superior, whether we depend upon our own opinion only or upon that of the world at large, have we the same feeling of rivalry in regard to them and in cases like theirs. But as this rivalry extends to those who are our antagonists in any competition or in love and indeed to all who aspire to the same things as ourselves, these will necessarily be the principal objects of envy; whence the proverb "Two of a trade never agree."

Again, we are envious of people who have attained a rapid success, if we have succeeded with difficulty or have not succeeded at all. Or of people whose possession of a thing or whose success is a reproach to us, such people again being near and similar to ourselves; for as it is evidently our own fault that we fail to obtain the good *which they obtain*, it is the annoyance of this fact which produces in us the feeling of envy. Or again of people who either naturally or by acquisition possess anything which naturally belonged to us or had been acquired by us; this is the reason why seniors are envious of their juniors. Lastly, people who have spent a large sum upon a particular thing are envious of those who have spent little upon it *with an equal result*.

We see now clearly the occasions upon which envious people experience a feeling of pleasure, the persons whose cases give rise to such a feeling and the conditions under which people experience it; for, whatever be the conditions the absence of which produces pain *at certain things*, their presence will produce pleasure at the opposite things. Hence if the audience has been brought to an envious condition of mind and the persons on whose behalf a claim to compassion or to good of any kind is advanced are such as have been described, *i.e. proper objects of envy*, it is evident that they will not meet with compassion at the hands of those who are masters of the position. [158-61]

[*Division and Characteristics of People According to Age*]

The young are in character prone to desire and ready to carry any desire they may have formed into action. Of bodily desires it is the sexual to which they are most disposed to give way, and in regard to sexual desire they exercise no self-restraint. They are changeful too and fickle in their desires, which are as transitory as they are vehement; for their wishes are keen without being permanent, like a sick man's fits of hunger and thirst. They are passionate, irascible and apt to be carried away by their impulses. They are the slaves too of their passion, as their ambition prevents their ever brooking a slight and renders them indignant at the mere idea of enduring an injury. And while they are fond of honour, they are fonder still of victory; for superiority is the object of youthful desire, and victory is a species of superiority. Again, they are fonder both of honour and of victory than of money, the reason why they care so little for money being that they have never yet had experience of want, as the saying of Pittacus about Amphiaraus puts it. They are charitable rather than the reverse, as they have never yet been witnesses of many villainies; and they are trustful, as they have not yet been often deceived. They are sanguine too; for the young are heated by Nature as drunken men *by wine*, not to say that they have not yet experienced frequent failures. Their lives are lived principally in hope, as hope is of the future and memory of the past, and while the future of youth is long, its past is short; for on the first day of life it is impossible to remember anything, but all things must be matters of hope. For the same reason they are easily deceived, as being quick to hope. They are inclined to be valorous; for they are full of passion, which excludes fear, and of hope, which inspires confidence, as anger is incompatible with fear, and the hope of something good is itself a source of confidence. They are bashful too, having as yet no independent standard of honour and having lived entirely in the school of conventional law. They have high aspirations; for they have never yet been humiliated by the experience of life, but are unacquainted with the limiting force of circumstances; and a great idea of one's own deserts, such as is characteristic of a sanguine disposition, is itself a form of high aspiration. Again, in their actions they prefer honour to expediency, as it is habit rather than calculation which is the rule of their lives, and, while calculation pays regard to expediency, virtue pays regard *exclusively* to honour. Youth is the age when people are most devoted to their friends or relations or companions, as they are then extremely fond of social intercourse and have not yet learnt to judge their friends or indeed anything else by the rule of expediency. If the young commit a fault, it is always on the side of excess and exaggeration in defiance of Chilon's maxim; for they carry everything too far, whether it be their love or hatred or anything else. They regard themselves as omniscient and are positive in their assertions; this is in fact the reason of their carrying everything too far. Also their offences take the line of insolence and not of meanness. They are compassionate from supposing all people to be virtuous or *at least* better *than they really are*; for as they estimate their neighbours by their own guilelessness, they regard the evils which befall them as undeserved. Finally, they are fond of laughter and consequently facetious, facetiousness being disciplined insolence.

Such being the character of the young, it may be said generally that elder men who have passed their prime have characters mostly composed of the qualities opposite to these. For as they have lived many years and have been often the victims of deception and error, and as vice is the rule rather than the exception in human affairs, they are never positive about anything and always err on the side of too little excess. They "suppose," they never "know" anything; and in discussion they always add "perhaps" or "possibly," expressing themselves invariably in this guarded manner, but never positively. They are uncharitable too, i.e. they are ready to put the worst construction upon everything. Again, they are suspicious of evil from not trusting anybody, and they do not trust anybody from having had experience of human wickedness. Hence too they have no strong loves or hatreds; but according to the precept of Bias their love is such as may some day be converted into hatred and their hatred such as may some day be converted into love. Their temper of mind is neither grand nor generous; not the former, for they have been so much humiliated by the experience of life as to have no desire of any great or striking object or of anything but the mere appliances of life; nor the latter, for property is a necessity of life, and they have learnt by experience the difficulty of acquiring it and the facility with which it may be lost. They are cowards and perpetual alarmists, their disposition being exactly contrary to that of the young; for as they are not fervent like the young, but have cooled down, their old age has in consequence paved the way for cowardice, fear itself being a sort of cooling process. They are fond of life, and never so fond of it as on their last day; for it is the absent which is the object of all desire, and that which we *most* lack we are most desirous to possess. They are selfish to a fault, selfishness again being a species of mean-mindedness. And from their selfishness it follows that their standard of life is too apt to be expediency rather than honour; for expediency is what is good to the individual, and honour what is good in an absolute sense. They are apt to be shameless rather than the contrary; for as they pay less regard to honour than to expediency, they are able to disregard appearances. They are despondent too partly from their experience of life—for the generality of things which occur in the world are bad or at least do not turn out so well as they might—and partly from their cowardly disposition. Again, they live by memory rather than by hope; for while the remainder of their life is *necessarily* short, its past is long, and the future is the sphere of hope, the past the sphere of memory. This too is the explanation of their garrulity; they are perpetually talking over what has happened in the past because of the pleasure they feel in recollection. Their fits of passion, although violent, are feeble; their sensual desires have either died away or become enfeebled, so that they are not prone either to desire or to action regulated by their desires but are rather guided in their actions by self-interest. The consequence is that people at this time of life are capable of self-control, as the strength of their desires has abated and self-interest is their mastering passion. Again, it is calculation rather than character which regulates their lives; for while calculation is directed to expediency, morality is directed to virtue *as its end*. The offences which they commit take the line of petty meanness rather than of insolence. The old are compassionate as well as the young, not however for the same reason; for in the one case the reason is humanity, and in the other infirmity, as the old suppose all manner of suffering to be at their door, and this is a state of mind which, as we have said, excites compassion. Hence they are querulous, not facetious nor fond of laughter; for querulousness is opposed to the love of laughter. Such then are the characteristics of youth and age. And as everybody approves such speeches as are framed according to his own character or reflect it, it is easy to see the proper way of treating our speeches in order that we and the speeches we make may assume the requisite character.

As to persons who are in the prime of life, it is evident that in character they will occupy a position intermediate between the young and the old. They will be exempt from the excess of either; they will be neither excessively confident, as excess of confidence is fool-hardiness, nor excessively fearful, but will preserve a proper balance of confidence and fear; they will be neither universally trustful nor universally distrustful, but will rather form their judgment in accordance with the facts; their rule of life will be neither honour only nor expediency only but both, and neither parsimony nor extravagance but a proper mean. The same will be true in regard to passion and desire. They will combine temperance with valour and valour with temperance, these being qualities which are distributed separately among the young and the old; for the young are brave and licentious and the old are temperate and cowardly. It may indeed be said generally that, wherever there are advantages distributed between youth and age, persons in the prime of life enjoy both, and that, wherever there are excesses or defects inherent in youth and age, they observe moderation and propriety in respect to them. The body, I may say, is at its prime from 30 to 35, and the soul about 49. [164-70]

[*The Common Topics*]

If there are two opposites, and the existence or production of one of them is possible, so presumably is the existence or production of the other. For instance, if a human being can be cured, he can also fall ill, inasmuch as the potentiality of opposites, *qua* opposites, is identical. Again, if there are two similar things, and one of them is possible, so is the other. Of if the more difficult of two things is possible, so is the easier. Or if the production of a thing in an excellent and noble form is possible, its production generally is possible, as the making of a fine house is harder than the making of a house. Again, if the beginning of a thing is possible, so is the completion of it, as no impossibility ever comes or begins to come into being; the commensurability e.g. of the diagonal of a square with its side cannot begin to come, nor ever does come, into being. Or if the completion of a thing is possible, so is its beginning; for whatever comes into being originates from a beginning. Or if the posterior in essence or in generation is capable of coming into being, so is the prior; thus if a man can come into being, so can a boy, the boy being prior in generation, and if a boy can come into being, so can a man, the man being *essentially* a beginning. Again, the objects of natural love or desire are possible, as in general nobody is enamoured or desirous of impossibilities. Again, the existence of any science or art implies the possibility of the existence or production of the objects with which it deals. The same is true of anything, if the origin of its production depends upon things which we can influence

by force or persuasion, i.e. upon persons whose superiors or masters or friends we are. Again, if the parts of a thing are possible, so is the whole, and if the whole is possible, so in general are the parts; thus if it is possible to produce an instep, toe-cap and body of a shoe, it is possible also to produce shoes, and if it is possible to produce shoes, it is possible also to produce an instep, toe-cap and body. Again, the possibility of producing the genus as a whole implies the possibility of producing the species, and *vice versa*; the possibility e.g. of producing a vessel implies the possibility of producing a trireme, and the possibility of producing a trireme implies the possibility of producing a vessel. And of two things which are naturally inter-dependent if one is possible, so is the other; if double e.g. is possible, so is half, and if half, so is double. Again, if a thing can be produced without art and preparation, it can *a fortiori* be produced by means of art and careful pains; whence the lines of Agathon
"Of some must art be mother, some accrues
To us of fortune or necessity."
Lastly, if a thing is possible to inferior, weaker and less intelligent people, it is possible *a fortiori* to their opposites, according to the saying of Isocrates that it was strange, if he should himself be unable to discover what a person like Euthynus had learnt.

On the subject of the impossible, it is evident that *the orator* has a stock *of topics* ready to hand in the opposites of those which have been mentioned.

The fact of a thing having occurred or not in the past is to be examined by the light of the following considerations. In the first place, if that which is less likely to have occurred has occurred, it would appear that that which is more likely has also occurred. Or if that which is usually subsequent has occurred, *it may be argued that* that which is usually antecedent has occurred, as e.g., if a person has forgotten something, that he had once learnt it. Or if a person had at once the power and the will to do a certain act, *it may be argued that* he has done it; for everybody acts, when he has the power to do what he wishes, as there is then no impediment to his action. The same is true, if he had the wish and there was no external obstacle, or if he had the power and was in an angry mood, or if he had the power and with it the desire; for it is a general rule that people, when they are eager to do a thing, actually do it, as soon as they have the power, if they are bad people from the lack of self-control, and if they are good, because the objects of their desire are honourable. Again, if it was a person's intention to do a thing, *it may be argued that he did it*, as there is always a probability that the intention was carried out. Or if all the natural preliminaries or means to a thing have occurred, *it may be argued that the thing itself occurred*, as e.g., if it lightened that it thundered too, and if a thing was attempted, that it was done. Similarly, if the natural sequel or end of anything has occurred, *it may be argued that* the preliminaries and means to it have occurred also, as e.g., if it thundered, that it lightened, and if a thing was done, that it was attempted. In all these cases the rule is sometimes one of necessity, and sometimes one of only general validity.

Arguments against the occurrence of an event in the past may evidently be derived from the topics opposite to these.

As *to arguments* in regard to the future, it is clear *that they may be derived* from the same sources. *It may be argued* that a thing will be done, if there is both the power and the wish to do it or if there is desire, anger and calculation combined with power. Accordingly it will be done, if one has an immediate impulse or an intention to do it; for what is intended is generally more likely to happen than what is not; or if it has been preceded by all its former natural antecedents; if e.g. the sky is clouded, there is a probability of rain. Finally, if the means to an end have happened, there is a probability of the end itself happening; thus the foundation of a house implies the house itself.

The topic of the greatness and smallness of things, in themselves and in comparison with each other and of great and small things generally is evident from the remarks we have already made, for in our chapters upon deliberative Rhetoric we have discussed the greatness of goods and comparative greatness or smallness in the abstract. Hence as in each of the three kinds of Rhetoric the end proposed is a good, whether expediency, honour or justice, it is evident that these must be the means of supplying the materials of amplification in each case. It is idle to look for anything more than this in regard to abstract greatness and superiority, particular facts being more important than general truths to the purpose *which we have now in hand*. [176-80]

[The Common Proofs]

It remains then to speak of the proofs which are common to the three kinds of Rhetoric, as the special proofs have already been discussed. These are two in kind, viz. example and enthymeme; for the maxim is part of an enthymeme. It will be proper to begin with example, as example corresponds to induction, and induction is a beginning *or principle of knowledge*. [180-1]

[*Examples and Their Use*]

It is proper in default of enthymemes to make use of examples as logical proofs, these being the natural means of producing conviction, but otherwise to make use of them as testimonies by way of a supplement to our enthymemes. For if we put them first, they resemble an induction, and induction is something inappropriate to Rhetoric unless in exceptional cases; but if we put them last, they resemble testimonies, and testimony is invariably persuasive. And from this it follows that, if we put them first, it is necessary to employ a considerable number of them, but if last, a single one is sufficient, as even a single credible witness is of service. [184]

[*Maxims and Their Use*]

A maxim is a declaration, not however relating to particulars, as e.g. to the character of Iphicrates, but to universals; nor yet again to all universals indiscriminately, as e.g. that straight is the opposite of crooked, but to all such as are the objects of human action and are to be chosen or eschewed in that regard. [184]

. . . . .

The maxim, as has been said, is a general statement, and people are pleased by a general statement of anything of which they already entertain a partial conviction; thus anybody who has been unfortunate in his neighbours or his children will be glad to hear it said that there is nothing which is so troublesome as a pack of neighbours or nothing so foolish as the procreation of children. It is proper, therefore, to conjecture what are the manner and character of their prepossessions, and, having done so, to put forward a general statement in regard to them. This is one advantage in the use of maxims; but there is another which is more important, as they impart an ethical character to our speeches. A speech is ethical, if its moral purpose is apparent. But this is the invariable effect of maxims; for a speaker who gives utterance to a maxim makes a statement in general terms about the object of his moral predilection, and hence, if the maxims are virtuous, they give the appearance of a virtuous character to the speaker. [189-90]

[*Materials of Enthymemes*]

It follows that the proper materials of enthymemes must be not all opinions indiscriminately, but certain definite opinions, defined,

I mean, either by our audience or by persons in whom they believe, and *in the latter case* the fact of such an opinion being entertained must be well known to all or the great majority of our audience. Again, the premises from which our conclusions are drawn must be not only such as are necessary, but such also as are only generally true. [191]

[*Species of Enthymemes*]

There are two species of enthymemes, viz. demonstrative enthymemes which prove that a thing is or is not so and so, and refutative enthymemes, the difference between the two being the same as between a refutation and a syllogism in dialectics. The demonstrative enthymeme consists in drawing conclusions from admitted propositions, the refutative in drawing conclusions which are inconsistent *with the conclusions of one's adversary.* [194]

[*Topics of Enthymemes*]

One topic of demonstrative enthymemes may be derived from a consideration of opposites. *If we take any two things, of which one is said to be predicable of the other,* we have to consider whether the opposite of the one is predicable of the opposite of the other, upsetting *the original proposition*, if it is not predicable, and confirming *the original proposition*, if it is, as e.g. arguing that self-restraint is expedient on the ground that licentiousness is injurious. [194-5]

. . . . .

A second topic is derived from the inflexions of the same stem, as that which is or is not predicable of one is or is not predicable of another. Thus *we may argue* that justice is not always good; else the word "justly" would always have a good sense, whereas to be justly put to death is the reverse of desirable. [195]

. . . . .

There is another arising from relative terms. *It may be argued that,* if "honourably" and "justly" are terms which are predicable of the action of the agent, they are predicable also of the suffering of the patient, and that if they are predicable of the command, they are predicable of its execution. [196]

. . . . .

Another topic is the argument from degree. Thus *it may be argued that,* if the Gods themselves are not omniscient, much less are men, meaning that if a condition is not realized, where it would be more natural, it will evidently not be realized, where it would be less so. [197]

. . . . .

There is another topic depending upon a consideration of the time. Thus Iphicrates in defending himself against Harmodius said "Suppose that before the action I had demanded the statue in case of doing it, you would have granted it; now that the action has been done, will you refuse it? Do not then make a promise in anticipation, and defraud me of it, when you have received the benefit." [198-9]

. . . . .

Another topic consists in applying to our adversary's case anything that he has said about ourselves. It is a topic of singular force as may be seen in the *Teucer*. It was employed by Iphicrates in his reply to Aristophon, when he asked him if he would take a bribe to betray the fleet. "No" said Aristophon. "Well, then" he replied "if you an Aristophon would refuse the bribe, shall I an Iphicrates accept it?" [199]

. . . . .

There is another topic arising from definition, as e.g. *the argument* that the supernatural must be either God or the work of God; but anybody who believes in the existence of a work of God necessarily believes also in the existence of Gods. [200]

. . . . .

Another topic springs from the various senses of a word; . . . [201]

. . . . .

Another from division, as e.g. if there are three possible causes of a crime, and while two of these are out of the question, the third is not alleged even by the prosecution. [201]

. . . . .

Another topic depends upon induction; and of this the Peparethian case supplies an example. It was argued in it that the decision of women about their children is everywhere correct; for in one instance at Athens, in the dispute between Mantias the rhetorician and his son, the declaration of the mother *was regarded as final*, and in another at Thebes, in the dispute between Ismenias and Stilbon, Dodonis *the mother* affirmed that Ismenias was the father of the child, and accordingly *the child* Thettaliscus was always considered to be his son. [201]

. . . . .

There is another topic derivable from a judgment already pronounced upon the same or similar or an opposite question, especially if it is the judgment of all men and all times, or, failing that, of a large majority or of all or nearly all the wise or good or again of the judges themselves or of those whose authority they admit or whose judgment admits of no contradiction, as e.g. if they are those who are masters of the situation or who cannot be opposed without impropriety, such as the Gods or a parent or one's teachers. [202-3]

. . . . .

Another topic consists in *taking separately* the parts *of a subject, in considering e.g.,* as is done in *Topics*, what sort of motion the soul is, as it must be this or that. [204]

. . . . .

Also, as it happens in the great majority of cases that the same thing has consequences partly good and partly bad, another topic consists in using the attendant circumstances as means of exhortation or dissuasion, accusation or defence, eulogy or censure. Thus education is attended by envy, which is an evil, and by wisdom, which is a good; hence it is possible to argue against education on the ground that envy is a thing to be avoided, and in its favour on the ground that wisdom is a thing to be desired. [204]

. . . . .

There is another topic when in reference to two opposite things it is necessary to employ exhortation or dissuasion and to apply to both the method already described, the difference being that, whereas in the last case it was any two things, it is here two opposites that are contrasted. [204-5]

. . . . .

Again, as there is a difference between the objects which people praise in public and in secrecy, and, while they make a show of lauding justice and honour above everything else, they prefer expediency in their hearts, another topic consists in trying to use *an adversary's premisses, whichever mode of sentiment he adopts,* to infer the opposite *of his conclusion;* for there is no topic of paradoxes so entirely effective as this. [205]

. . . . .

Another topic is derived from analogy of results. Iphicrates, for instance, resisted an effort to impose a public burden upon his son because of his size, although he was under the legal age, by saying,

"If you reckon tall boys men, you will have to vote short men boys." [206]

* * * * *

Another topic consists in arguing identity of cause from identity of effect. Xenophanes, for instance, contended that it was as impious to affirm the birth of the Gods as to affirm their death; for in either case it follows that there is a time when they do not exist. [206]

* * * * *

There is another topic depending upon the fact that people do not always make the same choice at a later as at an earlier time, but often reverse it. [207]

* * * * *

Another topic consists in treating the conceivable as the actual reason of a thing existing or having come into existence, as in the supposition that a person would make a present in order to inflict the pain of taking it away. [207]

* * * * *

There is another topic common to forensic and deliberative oratory, viz. to consider the inducements and discouragements and the motives of acting or abstaining from action; for these are the conditions, the presence or the absence of which renders action desirable or the reverse. [208]

* * * * *

There is yet another topic in the case of things which are supposed to happen but are difficult to believe. [208]

* * * * *

Another topic, which is proper to refutation, consists in examining whether there is any contradiction in the series of dates, actions or words, and this under three separate heads, viz. firstly in reference to your adversary, as e.g. *if you can say*, "Although he pretends to be your friend, he took part in the conspiracy of the Thirty," secondly in reference to yourself, as "Although he calls me litigious, it is beyond his power to prove that I have ever been party to a suit," thirdly in reference to yourself and your adversary, as "While he has never lent you a farthing, there are actually many of you whom I have ransomed." [209]

* * * * *

RHETORIC AND PUBLIC SPEAKING

Another topic, where there is or appears to be a prejudice against particular persons or things, is to state the explanation of the circumstance which is unaccountable, as there is always something which accounts for the appearance. . . . [209]

. . . . .

Another topic consists in arguing from the presence or absence of the cause the existence or non-existence of the effect; for cause and effect go always hand in hand, and there is nothing which has not a cause. [209-10]

. . . . .

Another topic is to consider whether it was or is possible to take a better course than that which the person either recommends or takes or has taken in action; for if this course has not been taken, it is evident that he has not done the deed, as nobody voluntarily and intentionally chooses what is bad. [210]

. . . . .

Again, if an intended action is inconsistent with some action already performed, there is another topic which consists in viewing them side by side. Thus when the inhabitants of Elea inquired of Xenophanes whether they should sacrifice to Leucothea and lament for her, he gave them as his advice, if they regarded her as a goddess, not to lament, if as a mortal, not to offer sacrifice. [210]

. . . . .

Another topic is to discover a ground of accusation or defence in any mistake that has been made. In the *Medea* of Carcinus for example, Medea is accused of having murdered her children; at all events (it is urged) they have disappeared, the fact being that Medea made a mistake in sending her children away; and Medea's reply is that it is not her children but Jason whom she would have murdered, as assuming her to have been capable of the other crime, it would have been a mistake in her not to have committed this. This is the topic or species of enthymeme which constitutes the entire earlier system of Theodorus. [211]

. . . . .

Another topic is derivable from a play on names, . . . [211]

[*Topics of Apparent Enthymemes*]

Among topics of apparent enthymemes the first is that which arises from the use of language, and of this there are two divisions.

The first is when, as in Dialectic, we make a final statement as if it were the conclusion of a syllogism without having gone through the process of reasoning, *saying,* "It follows that this is not so and so." [212]

. . . . .

Secondly, there is the topic of equivocation, as if one should assert that the mouse is an estimable creature, because it gives its name to the most venerable of all religious rites, viz. the mysteries, or if in a panegyric of a dog one includes the heavenly dog, *viz. the dogstar,* or Pan. . . . [213]

. . . . .

Another topic consists in combining what is separate or separating what is combined; for as a thing appears the same *when so treated,* although it is often not the same, we must represent it in whichever way best serves our purpose. [214]

. . . . .

Another topic is that of indignant asseveration whether in a constructive or destructive sense, as when, without having proved the perpetration of a certain act, we exaggerate the horror of it; for by so doing we produce the impression either that the act has not been perpetrated, if it is the defendant who employs the exaggeration, or the reverse, if it is the prosecutor who is in a passion. [215]

. . . . .

Another topic is the use of a mere sign *or single instance as an argument,* the conclusion here again not being logically complete. [215-16]

. . . . .

There is another topic, dependent upon accidental circumstances. [216]

. . . . .

There is another topic, which arises from the consequences of an action. In the *Alexander* e.g. it is argued that the hero was a man of elevated mind, because he disdained the society of numbers and remained on Mount Ida by himself; for as this is conduct natural to persons of elevated minds, he would appear to possess such elevation. [216-17]

. . . . .

Another topic is to treat that which is not a cause as the cause, because e.g. it has occurred simultaneously or subsequently. ... [217]

* * * * *

There is another topic arising from the omission of the time or manner, as *when it is urged* that Alexander had a right to take Helen, because her father allowed her her choice *of a husband.* [217]

* * * * *

Again, it is possible here, as well as in eristical discussions, to derive an apparent syllogism from the interchange of the absolute with that which is not absolute but particular. Such a case in Dialectic is the argument that the non-existent is, on the ground that the non-existent *is* non-existent; or that the unknown is knowable, because the unknown is known to be unknown. Similarly in Rhetoric an apparent enthymeme may be derived from a probability which is not absolute but particular. [218]

[Methods of Refutation]

There are two ways of refuting an argument, viz. either by a counter-syllogism or by adducing an objection. It is clear that the counter-syllogisms may be constructed out of the same topics as the syllogisms *of which we have spoken;* for it is the common opinions of the world which form the materials of syllogisms, and opinions are often contradictory. Objections on the other hand, as in the *Topics,* may be adduced in four different ways, viz. either from the enthymeme of your adversary himself, or from analogy, or from antithesis, or from a previous decision. [219]

[Materials of Enthymemes]

The materials of enthymemes are four, viz. probabilities, examples, demonstrations and signs. They are probabilities, when the conclusion is derived from such facts as either are or are supposed to be generally true; examples, when it is reached by induction from an analogy of one or several instances, the universal rule being first ascertained and the particulars afterwards inferred from it; demonstrations, when it depends upon a rule which is necessary and absolute; signs, when upon general or particular statements which may be either true or false. [220-1]

[Declamation or Delivery]

The art consists in understanding (1) the proper use of the voice for the expression of the several emotions, i.e. when it should be loud or low or intermediate, (2) the proper use of the accents, i.e. when the tone should be acute or grave or intermediate, and (3) the rhythms suitable to each emotion. [225]

. . . . .

... And *declamation* is still popularly considered, and indeed is rightly supposed, to be something vulgar. Still as the entire study of Rhetoric has regard to appearance, it is necessary to pay due attention to declamation, not that it is right to do so but because it is inevitable. Strict justice indeed, if applicable to Rhetoric, would confine itself to seeking such a delivery as would cause neither pain nor pleasure. For the right condition is that the battle should be fought out on the facts of the case alone; and therefore everything outside the *direct* proof is *really* superfluous, although extraneous matters are highly effective, as has been said, owing to the depraved character of the audience. [226]

[Characteristics of Style: Perspicuity]

We may rest content then with our study of that question, and may take it as settled that one virtue of style is perspicuity. There is an evidence of this in the fact that our speech, unless it makes its meaning clear, will fail to perform its proper function. Again, style should be neither mean nor exaggerated, but appropriate; for a poetical style, although possibly not mean, is still not appropriate to prose. [228]

[Metaphor]

Again, if it is your wish to adorn a subject, the proper means is to borrow your metaphor from things superior to it which fall under the same genus; if to disparage it, from such things as are inferior. [232]

[Purity]

Such then being the component elements of the speech, the basis of style is purity of language. But purity of language falls under five heads; and of these the first is *the proper use of* connecting words or clauses, i.e. when they are made to correspond in the natural relation of priority or posteriority to one another, as some of them require.... [241]

. . . . .

A second point of purity of style consists in calling things by their own proper names rather than by *general or* classnames. A third consists in the avoidance of ambiguous terms, but this only if your purpose is not opposed *to perspicuity.* [241]

[*Classification of Words*]

A fourth point is to observe Protagoras's classification of nouns generically as masculine, feminine and neuter; for it is important that the genders should be properly assigned. . . . A fifth is the correct expression *of number, i.e.* many, few or unity. . . . [242-3]

[*Dignity of Style*]

We will pass now to dignity of style. The following are the causes which contribute to it. *Firstly,* to use a definition instead of the simple name of a thing, *to say* e.g. not "a circle" but "a plane figure which is at all points equidistant from the centre." [244]

. . . . .

Secondly, where the subject is one that is foul or indecorous, if the foulness lies in the definition, to use the name, and if in the name, to use the definition. *Thirdly,* to employ metaphors and epithets as means of elucidating the subject, being on your guard at the same time against a poetical style. *Fourthly,* to put the plural for the singular. . . . [244]

. . . . .

Fifthly, not to combine *two cases by a single article but* to give each case its own article. . . . [244]

. . . . .

Sixthly, to use connecting particles or, if for brevity's sake you omit the connecting particle, to preserve the connexion. . . . [244-5]

[*Propriety*]

The conditions of propriety in a speech are that the style should be emotional and ethical, and *at the same time* proportionate to the subject-matter. By a proportionate style I mean that the manner of the composition should not be slovenly if the subject is pompous, or dignified if it is humble; and that there should be no ornamental epithets attached to unimportant words. . . . [245]

[Structure]

The structure of the style should be neither metrical nor wholly unrhythmical. If it is the former, it lacks persuasiveness from its appearance of artificiality, and at the same time diverts the minds of the audience from the subject by fixing their attention upon the return of the similar cadence. . . . [248]

. . . . .

If on the other hand the composition is wholly unrhythmical, it has no definiteness, whereas it ought to be definitely limited, although not by metre, as what is indefinite is disagreeable and incapable of being known. [249]

[Kinds of Style]

The style must be either jointed, i.e. united only by its connecting particles, after the manner of *modern* dithyrambic preludes, or compact, like the antistrophes of the ancient poets. [251]

. . . . .

By a "jointed style" I mean one which has no end in itself except the completion of the subject under discussion. It is disagreeable from its *endlessness or* indefiniteness, as everybody likes to have the end clearly in view. This is the reason why *people in a race* do not gasp and faint until they reach the goal; for while they have the finishing-point before their eyes, they are insensible of fatigue. The compact style on the other hand is the periodic; and I mean by a "period" a sentence having a beginning and an end in itself, and a magnitude which admits of being easily comprehended at a glance. [251-2]

[Adaptation of Style to Type of Speaking]

The style of political oratory is precisely similar to scene-painting. For the greater the crowd, the more distant is the view: hence it is that in both a finished style appears superfluous and unsuccessful. The forensic style on the other hand is more finished, especially when addressed to a single judge; for he is least subject to rhetorical influences, as he can take a more comprehensive view of what is germane to the case or alien to it and, as there is no actual contest, is not prejudiced in his judgment. Accordingly it is not the same orators who succeed in all the different styles of Rhetoric; but, where there is most opportunity for declamation, there is the least possibility of finish. And this is the case where voice, and especially where a loud voice, is required.

RHETORIC AND PUBLIC SPEAKING

The epideictic style is best suited to literary purposes, as its proper function is to be read; and next to it the forensic style. [273]

[*Organization of Speeches*]

A speech has two parts. It is necessary first to state the case and then to prove it. It is impossible therefore to state your case without proceeding to prove or to prove it without having first stated it; for a proof is *necessarily* a proof of something, and a preliminary statement is not made except in order to be proved. [274]

. . . . .

It appears then that the only indispensable parts *of a speech* are the statement of the case and the proof.

These are the only proper or *characteristic* parts; but if more are added, they must not exceed four, viz. exordium, exposition, proof and peroration. [275]

. . . . .

The exordium is the beginning of a speech and corresponds to a prologue in poetry and a prelude in a musical performance, all the three being beginnings and, as it were, preparations for what follows. [276]

. . . . .

For the art of exciting attention is one that belongs equally to all the parts of a speech, if it is needed, *and perhaps especially to the other parts*; for people are apt to become inattentive at any other part rather than at the beginning. It is absurd then to speak of the beginning as its proper place, when every one is listening most attentively. [280-1]

. . . . .

There are four elements or *objects* of the peroration, viz. to inspire the audience with a favourable opinion of yourself and an unfavourable one of your adversary, to amplify or depreciate the subject, to excite the emotions of the audience and to recall the facts to their memory. [301]

SUGGESTED READINGS

Baldwin, Charles Sears
    Ancient Rhetoric and Poetic. New York. Macmillan Co. 1924. p6-36

Cooper, Lane, tr.
    The Rhetoric of Aristotle. New York. D. Appleton and Co. 1932. xlviii,259p

Cope, E. M.
An Introduction to Aristotle's Rhetoric. London. Macmillan and Co. 1867. xvi,464p

Freese, John Henry, ed.
The Rhetoric of Aristotle. London. William Heinemann. 1926. xlvii,491p

Hunt, Everett Lee
Plato and Aristotle on Rhetoric and Public Speaking. In *Studies in Rhetoric and Public Speaking in Honor of James Albert Winans.* New York. Century Co. 1925. p3-60

Loukas, Christ
The Psychology of Aristotle: a Logical Arrangement of His De Anima and Allied Treatises. *Journal of General Psychology.* 6:157-89 January 1932

Roberts, W. Rhys, ed.
Rhetorica. In *The Works of Aristotle Translated into English.* Ed. by W. D. Ross. Oxford. Clarendon Press. 1924. XI, 1354a-1420b

Utterback, William E.
Aristotle's Contribution to the Psychology of Argument. *Quarterly Journal of Speech Education.* 11:218-25 June 1925

Welldon, J. E. C., tr.
The Rhetoric of Aristotle. London. Macmillan and Co. 1886. xlvii,306p

CICERO

(106-B. C.-43 B. C.)

Like many treatises on rhetoric, Cicero's *De Oratore* is written in the form of a dialogue. In Book I Crassus comments on the qualifications of the Ideal Orator, while in Book III he develops the Ciceronian conception of oratorical style. Antonius, serving as the protagonist in Book II, discourses on invention and disposition. Incidental remarks on humor are also introduced by Caesar.

Cicero bases his theory upon the assumption that rhetoric and philosophy are closely related. This inter-relation accounts in some measure for the relative scarcity of great orators, since accomplishment in speaking presupposes great learning. "A knowledge of a vast number of things is necessary," says Cicero, "without which volubility of words is empty and ridiculous...."

The five parts of rhetoric receive systematic treatment in *De Oratore*, and incidental consideration in the minor works. Consistent with the close relation between oratory and Roman education for public life, the emphasis throughout is upon forensic and deliberative speaking. A certain appeal to copiousness in the use of language permeates the entire rhetorical scheme. "For the proper concern of an orator,... is language of power and elegance accommodated to the feelings and understanding of mankind."

De Oratore is less concise than Aristotle's *Rhetoric,* less profound in its analysis of the art of speaking, but more consistently developed from the point of view of the orator himself. Despite the fact that, as John Lawson remarked, "Cicero hath little new, [he] so embellishest the old as to give it the Charms of Novelty."

Cicero's most important works on rhetoric are *De Oratore, Orator,* and *Brutus; or Remarks on Eminent Orators.*

DE ORATORE [1]

[*Qualifications of the Orator*]

A knowledge of a vast number of things is necessary, without which volubility of words is empty and ridiculous; speech itself is to be formed, not merely by choice, but by careful construction of words; and all the emotions of the mind, which nature has given to man, must be intimately known; for all the force and art of speaking must be employed in allaying or exciting the feelings of those who listen. To this must be added a certain portion of grace and wit, learning worthy of a well-bred man, and quickness and brevity in replying as well as attacking, accompanied with a refined decorum

[1] From the translation by J. S. Watson (1855). The bracketed numerals indicate the book and chapter references.

and urbanity. Besides, the whole of antiquity and a multitude of examples is to be kept in the memory; nor is the knowledge of laws in general, or of the civil law in particular, to be neglected. And why need I add any remarks on delivery itself, which is to be ordered by action of body, by gesture, by look, and by modulation and variation of the voice, the great power of which, alone and in itself, the comparatively trivial art of actors and the stage proves, on which though all bestow their utmost labor to form their look, voice, and gesture, who knows not how few there are, and have ever been, to whom we can attend with patience? What can I say of that repository for all things, the memory, which, unless it be the keeper of the matter and words that are the fruits of thought and invention, all the talents of the orator, we see, though they be of the highest degree of excellence, will be of no avail? Let us then cease to wonder what is the cause of the scarcity of good speakers, since eloquence results from all those qualifications. ... [I, 5]

. . . . .

In my opinion, indeed, no man can be an orator possessed of every praiseworthy accomplishment, unless he has attained the knowledge of everything important, and of all liberal arts, for his language must be ornate and copious from knowledge, since, unless there be beneath the surface matter understood and felt by the speaker, oratory becomes an empty and almost puerile flow of words. [I, 6]

[Speech the Distinguishing Mark of Man]

For it is by this one gift that we are most distinguished from brute animals, that we converse together, and can express our thoughts by speech. Who therefore would not justly make this an object of admiration, and think it worthy of his utmost exertions, to surpass mankind themselves in that single excellence by which they claim their superiority over brutes? But, that we may notice the most important point of all, what other power could either have assembled mankind, when dispersed, into one place, or have brought them from wild and savage life to the present humane and civilized state of society; or, when cities were established, have described for them laws, judicial institutions, and rights? [I, 8]

[Knowledge Necessary for Good Speaking]

But if you allow nothing to belong to the orator but to speak aptly, ornately, and copiously, how can he even attain these qualities without that knowledge which you do not allow him? for there can be no true merit in speaking, unless what is said is thoroughly understood by him who says it. [I, 11]

* * * * *

For what savors so much of madness, as the empty sound of words, even the choicest and most elegant, when there is no sense or knowledge contained in them? Whatever be the subject of a speech, therefore, in whatever art or branch of science, the orator, if he has made himself master of it, as of his client's cause, will speak on it better and more elegantly than even the very originator and author of it can. [I, 12]

* * * * *

For the proper concern of an orator, as I have already often said, is language of power and elegance accommodated to the feelings and understandings of mankind. [I, 12]

* * * * *

. . . But the accomplished and complete orator I shall call him who can speak on all subjects with variety and copiousness. [I, 14]

* * * * *

If, therefore, any one desires to define and comprehend the whole and peculiar power of an orator, that man, in my opinion, will be an orator, worthy of so great a name, who, whatever subject comes before him, and requires rhetorical elucidation, can speak on it judiciously, in set form, elegantly, and from memory, and with a certain dignity of action. [I, 15]

[*Nature and Art Contribute to Good Speaking*]

"I am, then, of opinion," said Crassus, "that nature and genius in the first place contribute most aid to speaking; and that to those writers on the art, to whom Antonius just now alluded, it was not skill and method in speaking, but natural talent that was wanting; for there ought to be certain lively powers in the mind and understanding, which may be acute to invent, fertile to explain and adorn, and strong and attentive to remember; and if any one imagines that these powers may be acquired by art, (which is false, for it is very well if they can be animated and excited by art; but they certainly cannot by art be ingrafted or instilled, since they are all the gifts of nature,) what will he say of those qualities which are certainly born with the man himself, volubility of tongue, tone of voice, strength of lungs, and a peculiar conformation and aspect of the whole countenance and body? I do not say, that art cannot improve in these particulars, (for I am not ignorant that what is good may be made better by education, and what is not very good may be in some degree polished and amended;) but there are some persons so hesitating in their speech, so inharmonious in their tone of voice, or so unwieldly and rude in the air and movements of their bodies, that, whatever power they possess either from genius or art, they can never be reckoned in the number of accomplished speakers; while there are others so happily qualified in these respects, so eminently adorned with the gifts of nature, that they seem not to have been born like other men, but moulded by some divinity." [I, 25]

[Timidity in Speaking]

To me, those who speak best, and speak with the utmost ease and grace, appear, if they do not commence their speeches with some timidity, and show some confusion in the exordium, to have almost lost the sense of shame, though it is impossible that such should not be the case; for the better qualified a man is to speak, the more he fears the difficulties of speaking, the uncertain success of a speech, and the expectation of the audience. But he who can produce and deliver nothing worthy of his subject, nothing worthy of the name of an orator, nothing worthy the attention of his audience, seems to me, though he be ever so confused while he is speaking, to be downright shameless; for we ought to avoid a character for shamelessness, not by testifying shame, but by not doing that which does not become us. [I, 26]

[General Business of the Orator]

In the first place, I will not deny that, as becomes a man well born and liberally educated, I learned those trite and common precepts of teachers in general; first, that it is the business of an orator to speak in a manner adapted to persuade; next, that every speech is either upon a question concerning a matter in general, without specification of persons or times, or concerning a matter referring to certain persons and times. But that, in either case, whatever falls under controversy, the question with regard to it is usually, whether such a thing has been done, or, if it has been done, of what nature it is, or by what name it should be called; or, as some add, whether it seems to have been done rightly or not. That controversies arise also on the interpretation of writing, in which anything has been expressed ambiguously, or contradictorily, or so that what is written is at variance with the writer's evident intention; and that there are certain lines of arguments adapted to all these cases. But that of such subjects as are distinct from general questions, part come under the head of judicial proceedings, part under that of deliberations; and that there is a third kind which is employed in praising or censuring particular persons. That there are also certain commonplaces on which we may insist in judicial proceedings, in which equity is the object; others, which we may adopt in deliberations, all which are to be directed to the advantage of those to whom we give counsel; others in panegyric, in which all must be referred to the dignity of the persons commended. That since all the business and art of an orator is divided into five parts, he ought first to find out what he should say; next, to dispose and arrange his matter, not only in a certain order, but with a sort of power and judgment; then to clothe and deck his thoughts with language; then to secure them in his memory; and lastly, to deliver them with dignity and grace. I had learned and understood also, that before we enter upon the main subject, the minds of the audience should be conciliated by an exordium; next, that the case should be clearly stated; then, that the point in controversy should be established; then, that what we maintain should be supported by proof, and that whatever was said on the other side should be refuted; and that, in the conclusion of our speech, whatever was in our favor should be amplified and enforced, and whatever made for our adversaries should be weakened and invalidated.

I had heard also what is taught about the costume of a speech; in regard to which it is first directed that we should speak correctly and in pure Latin; next, intelligibly and with perspicuity; then gracefully; then suitably to the dignity of the subject, and as it were becomingly; and I had made myself acquainted with the rules relating to every particular. Moreover, I had seen art applied to those things which are properly endowments of nature; for I had gone over some precepts concerning action, and some concerning artificial memory, which were short indeed, but requiring much exercise; matters on which almost all the learning of those artificial orators is employed; and if I should say that it is of no assistance, I should say what is not true; for it conveys some hints to admonish the orator, as it were, to what he should refer each part of his speech, and to what points he may direct his view, so as not to wander from the object which he has proposed to himself. But I consider that with regard to all precepts the case is this, not that orators by adhering to them have obtained distinction in eloquence; but that certain persons have noticed what men of eloquence practised of their own accord, and formed rules accordingly; so that eloquence has not sprung from art, but art from eloquence; not that, as I said before, I entirely reject art, for it is, though not essentially necessary to oratory, yet proper for a man of liberal education to learn. [I, 31-2]

[*Writing Helps To Improve Speaking*]

Writing is said to be *the best and most excellent modeller and teacher of oratory*; and not without reason; for if what is meditated and considered easily surpasses sudden and extemporary speech, a constant and diligent habit of writing will surely be of more effect than meditation and consideration itself; since all the arguments relating to the subject on which we write, whether they are suggested by art, or by a certain power of genius and understanding, will present themselves, and occur to us, while we examine and contemplate it in the full light of our intellect; and all thoughts and words, which are the most expressive of their kind, must of necessity come under and submit to the keenness of our judgment while writing; and a fair arrangement and collocation of the words is effected by writing, in a certain rhythm and measure, not poetical, but oratorical. [I, 33]

[*Studies Essential to Speaking*]

The poets must also be studied; an acquaintance must be formed with history; the writers and teachers in all the liberal arts and sciences must be read, and turned over, and must, for the sake of exercise, be praised, interpreted, corrected, censured, refuted; you must dispute on both sides of every question; and whatever may seem maintainable on any point, must be brought forward and illustrated. The civil law must be thoroughly studied; laws in general must be understood; all antiquity must be known; the usages of the senate, the nature of our government, the rights of our allies, our treaties and conventions, and whatever concerns the interests of the state, must be learned. [I, 34]

[*Province of Oratory*]

For almost all other arts can support themselves independently, and by their own resources; but to speak well, that is, to speak with learning, and skill, and elegance, has no definite province within the limits of which it is enclosed and restricted. Everything that can possibly fall under discussion among mankind, must be effectively treated by him who professes that he can practise this art, or he must relinquish all title to eloquence. [II, 2]

[Kinds of Subjects Assigned to Orator]

Under this head, too, there is an infinite field of matter; for (as Crassus observed) most writers assign to the orator two kinds of subjects on which he may speak; the one *concerning stated and defined questions,* such as are treated in judicial pleadings or political debates, to which he that will may add panegyrics; the other, what all authors term, (though none give any explanation,) *questions unlimited in their kind, without reference to time or person.* When they speak of this sort of subjects, they do not appear to know the nature and extent of it; for if it is the business of an orator to be able to speak on whatever subject is proposed *without limitation,* he will have to speak on the magnitude of the sun, and on the shape of the earth; nor will be able, when he has undertaken such a task, to refuse to speak on mathematical and musical subjects. In short, for him who professes it to be his business to speak not only on those questions which are confined to certain times and persons, (that is, on all judicial questions,) but also on such as are unlimited in their kinds, there can be no subject for oratory to which he can take exception. [II, 15]

[Role of Imitation]

Let this, then, be the first of my precepts, to point out to the student whom he should imitate, and in such a manner that he may most carefully copy the chief excellencies of him whom he takes for his model. Let practice then follow, by which he may represent in his imitation the exact resemblance of him whom he chose as his pattern; ... [II, 22]

[Kinds of Causes]

There are in all, therefore, three sorts of matters, which may possibly fall under doubt and discussion; what is now done, or what is to be done; what the nature of a thing is, or how it should be designated; for as to the question which some Greeks add, whether a thing be rightly done, it is wholly included in the inquiry, what the nature of the thing is. [II, 26]

[*Requisites for Success in Persuasion*]

But to return to my own method. When, after hearing and understanding the nature of a cause, I proceed to examine the subject matter of it, I settle nothing until I have ascertained to what point my whole speech, bearing immediately on the question and case, must be directed. I then very diligently consider two other points; the one, how to recommend myself, or those for whom I plead; the other, how to sway the minds of those before whom I speak to that which I desire. Thus the whole business of speaking rests upon three things for success in persuasion; that we prove what we maintain to be true; that we conciliate those who hear; that we produce in their minds whatever feeling our cause may require. For the purpose of proof, two kinds of matter present themselves to the orator; one, consisting of such things as are not invented by him, but, as appertaining to the cause, are judiciously treated by him, as deeds, testimonies, covenants, contracts, examinations, laws, acts of the senate, precedents, decrees, opinions of lawyers, and whatever else is not found out by the orator, but brought under his notice by the cause and by his clients; the other, consisting entirely in the orator's own reasoning and arguments: so that, as to the former head, he has only to handle the arguments with which he is furnished; as to the latter, to invent arguments likewise. [II, 27]

[*Constituents of Persuasion*]

The supports of my whole eloquence, and that power of speaking which Crassus just now extolled to the skies, are, as I observed before, three processes; the first, that of conciliating my hearers; the second, that of instructing them; and the third, that of moving them. The first of these divisions requires mildness of address; the second penetration; the third energy; for it is impossible but that he, who is to determine a cause in our favour, must either lean to our side from propensity of feeling, or be swayed by the arguments of our defence, or be forced by action upon his mind. [II, 29]

. . . . .

First, then, let him examine the nature of his cause, which is never obscure so far as the inquiry "whether a thing has been done or not;" or "of what nature it is;" or "what name it should receive;" and when this is ascertained, it immediately occurs, with the aid of natural good sense, and not of those artifices which teachers of rhetoric inculcate, "what constitutes the cause," that is, the point without which there would be no controversy; then, "what is the matter for trial," which they direct you to ascertain in this manner: .... [II, 30]

[*Requisites for Finding Arguments*]

Since, then, in speaking, three things are requisite for finding argument; genius, method, (which, if we please, we may call art,) and diligence, I cannot but assign the chief place to genius; yet diligence can raise even genius itself out of dullness; diligence, I say, which, as it avails in all things, is also of the utmost moment in pleading causes. [II, 35]

[*Sources of Arguments and Commonplaces*]

But if we argue from what is intimately connected with the subject, there are many sources of arguments and common-places; for we shall look to adjuncts, to general views, to particulars falling under general views, to things similar and dissimilar, contrary, consequential; to such as agree with the case, and are, as it were, forerunners of it, and such as are at variance with it; we shall investigate the causes of circumstances, and whatever has arisen from those causes; and shall notice cases that are stronger, or similar, or weaker. [II, 39]

[*Technique in Speaking*]

We now see, that it is by no means sufficient to find out what to say, unless we can handle it skilfully when we have found it. This treatment ought to be diversified, that he who listens may neither discover any artifice, nor be tired and satiated with uniformity. Whatever you advance, should be laid down as a proposition, and you should show why it is so; and, from the same premises, you should sometimes form a conclusion, and sometimes leave it to be formed by the hearer, and make a transition to something else. Frequently, however, you need make no proposition, but show, by the reasoning which you shall use, what proposition might have been made. If you produce a comparison to anything, you should first confirm what you offer as a comparison; and then apply to it the point in question. [II, 41]

[*Audience Analysis*]

For there is nothing, Catulus, of more importance in speaking than that the hearer should be favourable to the speaker, and be himself so strongly moved that he may be influenced more by impulse and excitement of mind, than by judgment or reflection. For mankind make far more determinations through hatred, or love, or desire, or anger, or grief, or joy, or hope, or fear, or error, or some other affection of mind, than from regard to truth, or any settled maxim, or principle of right, or judicial form, or adherence to the laws. [II, 42]

. . . . .

It contributes much to success in speaking, that the morals, principles, conduct, and lives of those who plead causes, and of those for whom they plead, should be such as to merit esteem; and that those of their adversaries should be such as to deserve censure; and also that the minds of those before whom the cause is pleaded should be moved as much as possible to a favourable feeling, as well towards the speaker as towards him for whom he speaks. The feelings of the hearers are conciliated by a person's dignity, by his actions, by the character of his life; particulars which can more easily be adorned by eloquence, if they really exist, than be invented, if they have no existence. But the qualities that attract favour to the orator are a soft tone of voice, a countenance expressive of modesty, a mild manner of speaking; so that if he attacks any one with severity, he may seem to do so unwillingly and from compulsion. It is of peculiar advantage that indications of good nature, of liberality, of gentleness, of piety, of grateful feelings, free from selfishness and avarice, should appear in him; and every thing that characterizes men of probity and humility, not acrimonious, nor pertinacious, nor litigious, nor harsh, very much conciliates benevolence, and alienates the affections from those in whom such qualities are not apparent. The contrary qualities to these, therefore, are to be imputed to your opponents. This mode of address is extremely excellent in those causes in which the mind of the judge cannot well be inflamed by ardent and vehement incitation; for energetic oratory is not always desirable, but often smooth, submissive, gentle language, which gains much favor for *rei*, or defendants, a term by which I designate not only such as are accused, but all persons about whose affairs there is any litigation; for in that sense people formerly used the word. To describe the character of your clients in your speeches, therefore, as just, full of integrity, religious, unpresuming, and patient of injuries, has an extraordinary effect; and such a description, either in the commencement, or in your statement of facts, or in the peroration, has so much influence, if it is agreeably and judiciously managed, that it often prevails more than the merits of the cause. Such influence, indeed, is produced by a certain feeling and art in speaking, that the speech seems to represent, as it were, the character of the speaker; for, by adopting a peculiar mode of thought and expression, united with action that is gentle and indicative of amiableness, such an effect is produced, that the speaker seems to be a man of probity, integrity, and virtue. [II, 43]

. . . . .

To this mode of speaking we may subjoin the opposite method, which moves the minds of the judges by very different means, and impels them to hate, or love, or envy, or benevolence, or fear, or hope, or desire, or abhorrence, or joy, or grief, or pity, or severity; or leads them to whatever feelings resemble and are allied to these and similar emotions of mind. It is desirable, too, for the orator, that the judges may voluntarily bring to the hearing of the cause some feelings in their breasts favourable to the object of the speaker. For it is easier, as they say, to increase the speed of him that is already running, than to excite to motion him that is torpid. [II, 44]

. . . . .

. . . So I, for my part, when I undertake a cause of such doubt and importance as is likely to excite the feelings of the judges, employ all my sagacity on the care and consideration of ascertaining, as skilfully as I can, what their sentiments and opinions are, what they expect, to which side they incline, and to what conclusion they are likely to be led, with the least difficulty, by the force of oratory. If they yield themselves up, and, as I said before, voluntarily incline and preponderate to the side to which I would impel them, I embrace what is offered, and turn my sails to that quarter from whence any breath of wind is perceived to blow. But if the judge is unbiassed, and free from all passion, it is a work of greater difficulty; for every feeling must then be moved by the power of oratory, without any assistance from nature. [II, 44]

. . . . .

Nor is it possible that the judge should feel concern, or hate, or envy, or fear in any degree, or that he should be moved to compassion and tears, unless all those sensations which the orator would awaken in the judge shall appear to be deeply felt and experienced by the orator himself. [II, 45]

[*Pathetic Proof*]

The first thing I generally consider is, whether the cause requires that the minds of the audience should be excited; for such fiery oratory is not to be exerted on trivial subjects, nor when the minds of men are so affected that we can do nothing by eloquence to influence their opinions, lest we be thought to deserve ridicule or dislike, if we either act tragedies about trifles or endeavour to pluck up what cannot be moved. For as the feelings on which we have to work in the minds of the judges, or whoever they may be before whom we may plead, are *love, hatred, anger, envy, pity, hope, joy, fear, anxiety*, we are sensible that *love* may be gained if you seem to advocate what is advantageous to the persons before whom you are speaking; or if you appear to exert yourself in behalf of good men, or at least for such as are good and serviceable to them; for the latter case more engages favour, the former, the defence of virtue, esteem; and if a hope of future advantage is proposed, it has a greater effect than the mention of past benefits. You must endeavour to show that in the cause which you defend, either their dignity or advantage is concerned; and you should signify that he for whom you solicit their love has referred nothing to his own private benefit, and done nothing at all for his own sake; for dislike is felt for the selfish gains of individuals, while favour is shown to their desires to serve others. But we must take care, while we are on this topic, not to appear to extol the merit and glory of those whom we would wish to be esteemed for their good deeds, too highly, as these qualities are usually the greatest objects of envy. From these considerations, too, we shall learn how to draw *hatred* on our adversaries, and to avert it from ourselves and our friends. The same means are to be used, also, either to excite or allay *anger*; for if you exaggerate every fact that is hurtful or disadvantageous to the audience, their hatred is excited; but if anything of the kind is thrown out against men of worth, or against characters on whom no one ought to cast any reflection, or against the public, there is then produced, if not so violent a degree of hatred, at least an unfavourable feeling, or displeasure near akin to hatred. *Fear* is also inculcated either from people's own dangers or those of the public. Personal fear affects men more deeply; but that which is common to all is to be treated by the orator as having similar influence.

Similar, or rather the same, is the case with regard to *hope, joy,* and *anxiety;* but I know not whether the feeling of *envy* is not by far the most violent of all emotions; nor does it require less power to

RHETORIC AND PUBLIC SPEAKING

suppress than to excite it. Men envy chiefly their equals or inferiors when they perceive themselves left behind, and are mortified that the others have outstripped them; but there is often a strong unfavourable feeling toward superiors, which is the stronger if they are intolerably arrogant, and transgress the fair bounds of common justice through super-eminence in dignity or fortune. If such advantages are to be made instruments to kindle dislike, the chief thing to be said is, "that they are not the acquisitions of virtue, that they have been gained perhaps by vice and crime; and that, however honourable or imposing they may appear, no merit was ever carried so high as the insolence of mankind and their contumelious disdain." To allay envy, it may be observed, "that such advantages have been gained by extreme toil and imminent perils; that they have not been applied to the individual's own private benefit, but that of others; that he himself, if he appear to have gained any glory, although it might not be an undue reward for danger, was not elated with it, but wholly set it aside and undervalued it;" and such an effect must by all means be produced (since most men are envious, and it is a most common and prevalent vice, and envy is felt towards all supereminent and flourishing fortune), that the opinion entertained of such characters be lowered, and that their fortunes, so excellent in people's imaginations, may appear mingled with labour and trouble.

Pity is excited, if he who hears can be induced to apply to his own circumstances those unhappy particulars which are lamented in the case of others, particulars which they have either suffered or fear to suffer; and while he looks at another, to glance frequently at himself. Thus, as all the circumstances incident to human suffering are heard with concern, and if they are pathetically represented, so virtue in affliction and humiliation is the most sorrowful of all objects of contemplation; and as that other department of eloquence which, by its recommendation of goodness, ought to give the picture of a virtuous man, should be in a gentle and (as I have often observed) a submissive strain, so this, which is adopted by the orator to effect a change in the minds of the audience, and to work upon them in every way, should be vehement and energetic. [II, 51-2]

[*Technique in Use of Pathetic Proof*]

But in both modes of speaking, as well that in which spirit and force are required as that which is brought down to ordinary life and manners, the beginning should be slow, but the sequel full and diffuse. For you must not spring at once into the pathetic portion of your speech, as it forms no part of the question, and men are first desirous to learn the very point that is to come under their judgment; nor, when you have entered upon that track, are you suddenly to diverge from it; for you are not to suppose that as an argument is understood as soon as it is stated, and a second and a third are then desired, so you can with the same ease move compassion, or envy, or anger, as soon as you make the attempt. Reason itself confirms an argument which fixes itself in the mind as soon as it is delivered; but that sort of eloquence does not aim at instructing the judge, but rather at agitating his mind by excessive emotion, which no one can produce unless by fulness and variety and even copiousness of language, and a proportionate energy of delivery. Those, therefore, who speak either with brevity, or in a low submissive strain, may indeed inform the judge, but can never move him, an effect on which success altogether depends. [II, 53]

[*Use of Wit and Humor*]

A jocose manner, too, and strokes of wit, give pleasure to an audience, and are often of great advantage to the speaker; qualities which, even if everything else can be taught by art, are certainly peculiar gifts of nature, and require no aid from instruction. [II, 54]

. . . . .

As there are two kinds of wit, one running regularly through a whole speech, the other pointed and concise; the ancients denominated the former humour, the latter jesting. [II, 54]

. . . . .

But, to come to the third point, it certainly becomes the orator to excite laughter; either because mirth itself attracts favour to him by whom it is raised; or because all admire wit, which is often comprised in a single word, especially in him who replies, and sometimes in him who attacks; or because it overthrows the adversary, or hampers him, or makes light of him, or discourages, or refutes him; or because it proves the orator himself to be a man of taste, or learning, or polish; but chiefly because it mitigates and relaxes gravity and severity, and often, by a joke or a laugh, breaks the force of offensive remarks, which cannot easily be overthrown by arguments. [II, 58]

. . . . .

Such is the caution that must be principally observed in joking. Those subjects accordingly are most readily jested upon which are neither provocative of violent aversion, nor of extreme compassion. [II, 59]

[Technique in Pleading]

In pleading, my usual method is, to fix on whatever strong points a cause has, and to illustrate and make the most of them, dwelling on them, insisting on them, clinging to them; but to hold back from the weak and defective points, in such a way that I may not appear to shun them, but that their whole force may be dissembled and overwhelmed by the ornament and amplification of the strong parts. If the cause turn upon arguments, I maintain chiefly such as are the strongest, whether they are several or whether there be but one; but if the cause depend on the conciliation or excitement of the feelings of the judges, I apply myself chiefly to that part which is best adapted to move men's minds. Finally, the principal point for consideration on this head is, that if my speech can be made more effective by refuting my adversary, than by supporting my own side of the question, I employ all my weapons against him; but if my own case can be more easily supported, than that on the other side can be confuted, I endeavour to withdraw the attention of the judges from the opposite party's defence, and to fix it on my own. In conclusion, I adopt, on my own responsibility, two courses which appear to me most easy (since I cannot attempt what is more difficult): one, that I make, sometimes, no reply at all to a troublesome or difficult argument or point (and at such forbearance perhaps somebody may reasonably laugh; for who is there that cannot practise it? But I am now speaking of my own abilities, not those of others; and I confess that, if any particular press very hard upon me, I usually retreat from it, but in such a manner as not only to appear to flee with my shield thrown away, but even with it thrown over my shoulders; adopting, at the same time, a certain pomp and parade of language, and a mode of flight that resembles fighting; and keeping upon my guard in such a way, that I seem to have retired, not to avoid my enemy, but to choose more advantageous ground;) the other is one which I think most of all worthy of the orator's precaution and foresight, and which generally occasions me very great anxiety: I am accustomed to study not so much to benefit the causes which I undertake, as not to injure them; not but that an orator must aim at both objects; but it is however a much greater disgrace to him to be thought to have damaged a cause, than not to have profited it. [II, 72]

[Ways of Prejudicing a Cause]

Antonius mentions seven ways by which the indiscretion of the orator may be of prejudice to the cause, to illustrate his last observation:— 1. By irritating a witness, who would not have injured his client without provocation. 2. By not giving way when the arguments press too hard upon him, he may lose his cause. 3. By extolling those qualities in his client which ought to be extenuated, he may do mischief. 4. By throwing invectives upon those who are entitled to the esteem and favour of the judges. 5. By upbraiding his adversary with the same defects that are in some of the judges; of which Philip's derision of a dwarfish evidence, before Lucius Aurifex, who was still lower in stature, was an instance mentioned before. 6. He may plead his own cause rather than that of his client; which blame Cicero seems to have incurred in his oration for Publius Sextius, a cause in which he was warmly and specially interested. . . . 7. By the use of false or repugnant arguments, or such as are foreign to the usage of the bar and judicial proceedings. [Note II, 74]

[Arrangement of Material]

I now return therefore to that point, Catulus, on which you a little while ago accorded me praise; the order and arrangement of facts and topics of argument. On this head, two methods may be observed; one, which the nature of causes dictates; the other, which is suggested by the orator's judgment and prudence. For, to premise something before we come to the main point; then to explain the matter in question; then to support it by strengthening our own arguments, and refuting those on the other side; next, to sum up, and come to the peroration; is a mode of speaking that nature herself prescribes. But to determine how we should arrange the particulars that are to be advanced in order to prove, to inform, to persuade, more peculiarly belongs to the orator's discretion. For many arguments occur to him; many, that seem likely to be of service to his pleading; but some of them are so trifling as to be utterly contemptible; some, if they are of any assistance at all, are sometimes of such a nature, that there is some defect inherent in them; while that which appears to be advantageous, is not of such import that it need be advanced in conjunction with anything prejudicial. And as to those arguments which are to the purpose, and deserving of trust, if they are (as it often happens) very numerous, I think that such of them as are of least weight, or as are of the same tendency with others of greater force, ought to be set aside, and excluded altogether from our pleading. I myself, indeed, in collecting proofs, make it a practice rather to weigh than to count them.

Since, too, as I have often observed, we bring over people in general to our opinions by three methods, by instructing their understandings, conciliating their benevolence, or exciting their passions, one only of these three methods is to be professed by us, so that we may appear to desire nothing else but to instruct; the other two, like blood throughout the body, ought to be diffused through the whole of our pleading; for both the beginning, and the other parts of a speech, on which we will by-and-by say a few words, ought to have this power in a great degree, so that they may penetrate the minds of those before whom we plead, in order to excite them. But in those parts of the speech which, though they do not convince by argument, yet solicitation and excitement produce great effect, though their proper place is chiefly in the exordium and the peroration, still, to make a digression from what you have proposed and are discussing, for the sake of exciting the passions, is often advantageous. Since, after the statement of the case has been made, an opportunity often presents itself of making a digression to rouse the feelings of the audience; or this may be properly done after the confirmation of our own arguments, or the refutation of those on the other side, or in either place, or in all, if the cause has sufficient copiousness and importance; and those causes are the most considerable, and most pregnant with matter for amplification and embellishment, which afford the most frequent opportunities for that kind of digression in which you may descant on those points by which the passions of the audience are either excited or calmed. In touching on this matter, I cannot but blame those who place the arguments to which they trust least in the front; and, in like manner, I think that they commit an error, who, if ever they employ several advocates, (a practice which never had my approbation,) will have him speak first in whom they confide least, and rank the others also according to their abilities. For a cause requires that the expectations of the audience should be met with all possible expedition; and if nothing to satisfy them be offered in the commencement, much more labour is necessary in the sequel; for that case is in a bad condition which does not at the commencement of the pleading at once appear to be the better. For this reason, as, in regard to pleaders, he who is the most able should speak first, so in regard to a speech, let the arguments of most weight be put foremost; yet so that this rule be observed with respect to both, that some of superior efficiency be reserved for the peroration; if any are but of moderate strength, (for to the weak no place should be given at all,) they may be thrown into the main body and into the midst of the group. All these things being duly considered, it is then my custom to think last of that which is to be spoken first, namely, what exordium I shall adopt. For whenever I have felt inclined to think of that first, nothing occurs to me but what is jejune, or nugatory, or vulgar and ordinary.

The beginnings of speeches ought always to be accurate and judicious, well furnished with thoughts, and happy in expression, as well as peculiarly suited to their respective causes. For our earliest acquaintance with a speech as it were, and the first recommendation of it to our notice, is at the commencement; which ought at once to propitiate and attract the audience. [II, 76-8]

. . . . .

Nor is the exordium of a speech to be sought from without, or from anything unconnected with the subject, but to be derived from the very essence of the cause. [II, 78]

. . . . .

But every exordium ought either to convey an intimation of the whole matter in hand, or some introduction and support to the cause, or something of ornament and dignity. But, like vestibules and approaches to houses and temples, so the introductions that we prefix to causes should be suited to the importance of the subjects. [II, 79]

. . . . .

From those before whom we plead we may draw such considerations, as to procure their benevolence and good opinion; an object better attained in the course of pleading than by direct entreaty. This object indeed is to be kept in view throughout the whole oration, and especially in the conclusion; but many exordia, however, are wholly based upon it; for the Greeks recommend us to make the judge, at the very commencement, attentive and desirous of information; and such hints are useful, but more proper for the exordium than for other parts; but they are indeed easier to be observed in the beginning, because the audience are then most attentive, when they are in expectation of the whole affair, and they may also, in the commencement, be more easily informed, as the particulars stated in the outset are generally of greater perspicuity than those which are spoken by way of argument, or refutation, in the body of the pleading. [II, 79]

. . . . .

Let the exordium, also, be so connected with the sequel of the speech, that it may not appear, like a musician's prelude, to be something attached merely from imagination, but a coherent member of the whole body; ... [II, 80]

* * * * *

For the narrative parts of a speech, as well as the other parts, ought to be perspicuous, and we ought to take the more pains with that part, because it is more difficult not to be obscure in stating a case, than either in an exordium, in argumentation, in refuting of an accusation, or in a peroration: and obscurity in this part of a speech is attended with greater danger than in other parts; both because, if anything be obscurely expressed in any other part, only that is lost which is so expressed; but obscurity in the narrative part spreads darkness over the whole speech; and because, as to other parts, if you have expressed anything obscurely in one place, you may explain it more clearly in another; while for the narrative part of a speech there is but one place. [II, 80]

* * * * *

But when we ought to introduce a statement of facts, and when we ought not, requires judicious consideration. For we ought to make no such statement, either if the matter is notorious, or if the circumstances are free from doubt, or if the adversary has related them, unless indeed we wish to confute his statement; and whenever we do make a statement of facts, let us not insist too eagerly upon points which may create suspicion and ill-feeling, and make against us, but let us extenuate such points as much as possible; ... [II, 81]

* * * * *

What follows is, that the matter in question be laid down, when we must settle what is the point that comes under dispute; then the chief grounds of the cause are to be laid down conjunctively, so as to weaken your adversary's supports, and to strengthen your own; for there is in causes but one method for that part of your speech, which is of efficacy to prove your arguments; and that needs both confirmation and refutation; but because what is alleged on the other side cannot be refuted unless you confirm your own statements, and your own statements cannot be confirmed unless you refute the allegations on the opposite side, these matters are in consequence united both by their nature, by their object, and by their mode of treatment. The whole speech is then generally brought to a conclusion by some amplification on the different points, or by exciting or mollifying the judge; and every particular, not only in the former parts of the speech, but more especially towards the conclusion, is to be adapted to excite as much as possible the feelings of the judges, and to incline them in our favour. [II, 81]

[*Panegyrical Speeches*]

Nor does there now appear to be any reason, indeed, why we should make a distinct head of these precepts which are given concerning suasory or panegyrical speeches; for most of them are common to all kinds of oratory; . . . [II, 81]

[*Speeches before the Popular Assembly*]

Speeches are to be made in the senate with less display; for it is an assembly of wise men; and opportunity is to be left for many others to speak. All suspicion, too, of ostentation of ability is to be avoided. A speech to the people, on the other hand, requires all the force, weight, and various coloring of eloquence. [II, 82]

. . . . .

But it happens that, because a popular assembly appears to the orator to be his most enlarged scene of action, he is naturally excited in it to a more magnificent species of eloquence; for a multitude has such influence, that, as the flute-player cannot play without his flutes, so the orator cannot be eloquent without a numerous audience. [II, 83]

[*Memory*]

For Simonides, or whoever else invented the art, wisely saw, that those things are the most strongly fixed in our minds, which are communicated to them, and imprinted upon them, by the senses; that of all the senses that of seeing is the most acute; and that, accordingly, those things are most easily retained in our minds which we have received from the hearing or the understanding, if they are also recommended to the imagination by means of the mental eye; so that a kind of form, resemblance, and representation might denote invisible objects, and such as are in their nature withdrawn from the cognisance of the sight, in such a manner, that what we are scarcely capable of comprehending by thought we may retain as it were by the aid of the visual faculty. By these imaginary forms and objects, as by all those that come under our corporeal vision, our memory is admonished and excited; but some place for them must be imagined; as bodily shape cannot be conceived without a place for it. [II, 87]

[Style]

Those matters, therefore, of which Antonius has treated so explicitly, are to be endowed with action and elocution by the orator in some certain manner. What manner of elocution can be better ... than that of speaking in pure Latin, with perspicuity, with gracefulness, and with aptitude and congruity to the subject in question? [III, 10]

. . . . .

Whom do they consider as a deity, if I may use the expression, amongst mortals? Him who speaks distinctly, explicitly, copiously, and luminously, both as to matter and words; who produces in his language a sort of rhythm and harmony; who speaks, as I call it, *gracefully*. Those who treat their subject as the importance of things and persons requires, are to be commended for that peculiar kind of merit, which I term *aptitude* and *congruity*. [III, 14]

. . . . .

A speech, then, is to be made becoming in its kind, with a sort of complexion and substance of its own; for that it be weighty, agreeable, savoring of erudition and liberal knowledge, worthy of admiration, polished, having feeling and passion in it, as far as is required, are qualities not confined to particular members, but are apparent in the whole body; but that it be, as it were, strewed with flowers of language and thought, is a property which ought not to be equally diffused throughout the whole speech, but at such intervals, that, as in the arrangement of ornaments, there may be certain remarkable and luminous objects disposed here and there. [III, 25]

. . . . .

But the greatest glory of eloquence is to exaggerate a subject by embellishment; which has the effect not only in amplifying and extolling anything in a speech to an extraordinary degree, but also in extenuating it, and making it appear comtemptible. This is required on those points which Antonius said must be observed in order to gain credit to our statements, when we explain anything, or when we conciliate the feelings, or when we excite the passions of our audience; but in the particular which I mentioned last, amplification is of the greatest effect; and excellence in it the peculiar and appropriate praise of the orator. [III, 26-7]

. . . . .

As the orator therefore has liberty to expatiate in so large and immense a field, and, wherever he stops, can stand upon his own territory, all the furniture and embellishments of eloquence readily offer themselves to him. For copiousness of matter produces copiousness of language; and, if there be an inherent dignity in the subjects on which he speaks, there must be, from the nature of the thing, a certain splendour in his expression. If the speaker or writer has but been liberally instructed in the learning proper for youth, and has an ardent attachment to study, and is assisted by natural endowments, and exercised in those indefinite questions on general subjects, and has chosen, at the same time, the most elegant writers and speakers to study and imitate, he will never, be assured, need instruction from such preceptors how to compose or embellish his language; so readily, in an abundance of matter, will nature herself, if she be but stimulated, fall without any guide into all the art of adorning eloquence. [III, 31]

[*Philosophers vs. Orators*]

Now, if anyone desires either to call that philosopher, who instructs us fully in things in words, an *orator,* he may do so without opposition from me; or if he prefer to call that orator, of whom I speak as having wisdom united with eloquence, a *philosopher,* I shall make no objection, provided it be allowed that neither *his* inability to speak, who understands his subject but can not set it forth in words, nor *his* ignorance, to whom matter is wanting though words abound, can merit commendation; and if I had to choose one of the two, I should prefer uneloquent good sense to loquacious folly. But if it be inquired which is the more eminent excellence, the palm is to be given to the learned orator; and if they allow the same person to be a philosopher, there is an end of controversy; but if they distinguish them, they will acknowledge their inferiority in this respect, that all their knowledge is inherent in the *complete orator;* but in the knowledge of the *philosophers* eloquence is not necessarily inherent; which, though it may be undervalued by them, must of necessity be thought to give a finishing grace to their sciences." [III, 35]

[*Style*]

All speech, then, is formed of words, which we must first consider singly, then in composition; for there is one merit of language which lies in single words, another which is produced by words joined and compounded. [III, 37]

. . . . .

There are three qualities, then, in a simple word, which the orator may employ to illustrate and adorn his language; he may choose either an *unusual* word, or one that is *new* or metaphorical. [III, 38]

. . . . .

A metaphor is a brief similitude contracted into a single word; which word being put in the place of another, as if it were in its own place, conveys, if the resemblance be acknowledged, delight; if there is no resemblance, it is condemned. [III, 39]

. . . . .

However, such an arrangement of words is to be observed, as that of which I was speaking; such a one as may give a compactness and coherence to the language, and a smooth and equal flow; this you will attain if you join the extremities of the antecedent words to the commencements of those that follow in such a manner that there be no rough clashing in the consonants, nor wide hiatus in the vowels. [III, 43]

. . . . .

Next to diligent attention to this particular, follows modulation and harmonious structure of the words;.... [III, 44]

. . . . .

In what manner, then, shall we pursue so important an object, so as to entertain hopes of being able to acquire this talent of speaking in harmonious numbers? It is not a matter of so much difficulty as it is of necessity; for there is nothing so pliant, nothing so flexible, nothing which will so easily follow whithersoever you incline to lead it, as language; out of which verses are composed; out of which all the variety of poetical numbers; out of which also prose of various modulation and of many different kinds; for there is not one set of words for common discourse, and another for oratorical debate; nor are they taken from one class for daily conversation, and from another for the stage and for display; but, when we have made our selection from those that lie before us, we form and fashion them at our pleasure like the softest wax. According, therefore, as we ourselves are grave, or subtle, or hold a middle course between both, so the form of our language follows the nature of our thoughts, and is changed and varied to suit every method by which we delight the ear or move the passions of mankind. [III, 45]

. . . . .

It happens likewise in all parts of language, that a certain agreeableness and grace are attendant on utility, and, I may say, on necessity; for the stoppage of the breath, and the confined play of the lungs, introduced periods and the pointing of words. This invention gives much gratification, that, if unlimited powers of breath were granted to a person, yet we could not wish him to speak without stopping; for the invention of stops is pleasing to the ears of mankind, and not only tolerable, but easy, to the lungs. [III, 46]

. . . . .

For the dwelling on a single circumstance has often a considerable effect; and a clear *illustration* and *exhibition* of matters to the eye of the audience, almost as if they were transacted before them. This has wonderful influence in giving a representation of any affair, both to illustrate what is represented, and to amplify it, so that the point which we amplify may appear to the audience to be really as great as the powers of our language can represent it. Opposed to this is *rapid transition* over a thing, which may often be practiced. There is also *signification* that more is to be understood than you have expressed; distinct and concise *brevity;* and *extenuation,* and, what borders upon this, *ridicule,* not very different from that which was the object of Caesar's instructions; and *digression* from the subject, and when gratification has thus been afforded, the return to the subject ought to be happy and elegant; *proposition* of what you are about to say, *transition* from what has been said, and *retrogression;* there is *repetition;* apt *conclusion* of reasoning; *exaggeration,* or surpassing of the truth, for the sake of amplification or diminution; *interrogation,* and, akin to this, as it were, *consultation* or seeming inquiry, followed by the delivery of your own opinion; and *dissimulation,* the humour of saying one thing and signifying another, which steals into the minds of men in a peculiar manner, and which is extremely pleasing when it is well managed, not in a vehement strain of language, but in a conversational style; also *doubt;* and *distribution;* and *correction* of yourself, either before or after you have said a thing, or when you repel anything from your self; there is also *premonition,* with regard to what you are going to prove; there is the *transference of blame* to another person; there is *communication,* or consultation, as it were, with the audience before whom you are speaking; *imitation* of manners and character, either with names of persons or without, which is a great ornament to a speech, and adapted to conciliate the feelings even in the utmost degree, and often also to rouse them; the introduction of fictitious characters, the most heightened figure of exaggeration; there is *description; falling into a wilful mistake; excitement of the audience to cheerfulness; anticipation; comparison* and *example,* two figures which have a very great effect; *division; interruption; contention; suppression; commendation;* a certain *freedom and even uncontrolledness of language,* for the purpose of exaggeration; *anger; reproach; promise; deprecation; beseeching;* slight *deviation* from your intended course, but not like digression, which I mentioned before; *expurgation; conciliation; attack; wishing; execration.* Such are the figures with which thoughts give lustre to a speech. [III, 53]

. . . . .

Of words, themselves, as of arms, there is a sort of threatening and attack for use, and also a management for grace. For the *reiteration* of words has sometimes a peculiar force, and sometimes eloquence; as well as the *variation* or deflexion of a word from its common signification; and the frequent *repetition* of the same word in the beginning, and *recurrence* to it at the end, of a period; *forcible emphasis* on the same words; *conjunction; adjunction; progression;* a sort of *distinction* as to some word often used; the *recal* of a word; the use of words, also, which end similarly, or have similar cadences, or which balance one another, or which correspond to one another. There is also a certain *gradation,* a *conversion,* an elegant *exaggeration* of the sense of words; there is *antithesis, asyndeton, declination, reprehension, exclamation, diminution;* the use of the *same word in different cases;* the *referring* of what is derived *from many particulars to each particular singly; reasoning* subservient to your *proposition,* and *reasoning* suited to the order of *distribution; concession;* and again another kind of *doubt;* the introduction of something *unexpected; enumeration;* another *correction; division; continuation; interruption; imagery; answering your own questions; immutation; disjunction; order; relation; digression;* and *circumspection.* These are the figures, and others like these, or there may even be more, which adorn language by peculiarities in thought or structure of style. [III, 54]

. . . . .

On this head [propriety], therefore, no direction seems possible to be given but this, that we adopt a character of style, fuller, plainer, or middling, suited to the subject on which we are to speak; the same ornaments we may use almost constantly, but sometimes in a higher, sometimes in a lower strain; and it is the part of art and nature to be able *to do* what is becoming on every occasion; *to know* what is becoming, and when, is an affair of judgment. [III, 55]

[*Delivery*]

But all these parts of oratory succeed according as they are delivered. Delivery, I say, has the sole and supreme power in oratory; without it, a speaker of the highest mental capacity can be held in no esteem; while one of moderate abilities, with this qualification, may surpass even those of the highest talent. [III, 56]

. . . . .

On all these emotions a proper gesture ought to attend; not the gesture of the stage, expressive of mere words, but one showing the whole force and meaning of a passage, not by gesticulation, but by emphatic delivery, by a strong and manly exertion of the lungs, not imitated from the theatre and the players, but rather from the camp and the palaestra. The action of the hand should not be too affected, but following the words rather than, as it were, expressing them by mimicry; the arms should be considerably extended, as one of the weapons of oratory; the stamping of the foot should be used only in the most vehement efforts, at their commencement or conclusion. But all depends on the countenance; and even in that the eyes bear sovereign sway;.... [III, 59]

. . . . .

It is the eyes, by whose intense or languid gaze, as well as by their quick glances and gaiety, we indicate the workings of our mind with a peculiar aptitude to the tenor of our discourse; for action is, as it were, the speech of the body, and ought therefore the more to accord with that of the soul. [III, 59]

. . . . .

To effectiveness and excellence in delivery the voice doubtless contributes most; the voice, I say, which, in its full strength, must be the chief object of our wishes; and next, whatever strength of voice we have, to cherish it. [III, 60]

. . . . .

And what is more adapted to delight the ear, and produce agreeableness of delivery, than change, variety, and alteration of tone? [III, 60]

. . . . .

There is in every voice, a certain middle key; but in each particular voice that key is peculiar. For the voice to ascend from this key is advantageous and pleasing; since to bawl at the beginning of a speech is boorish, and gradation is salutary in strengthening the voice. There is also extreme in the highest pitch, (which, however, is lower than the shrillest cry,) to which the pipe will not allow you to ascend, but will recal you from too strained an effort of voice. There is also, on the other hand, an extreme in the lowest notes, to which, as being of a full sound, we by degrees ascend. This variety and this gradual progression of the voice throughout all the notes, will preserve its powers, and add agreeableness to delivery. [III, 61]

ORATOR [2]

[The Plain Style]

But first of all we must give a sketch of the man whom some consider the only orator of the Attic style.

He is a gentle, moderate man, imitating the usual customs, differing from those who are not eloquent in fact rather than in any of his opinions. Therefore those who are his hearers, even though they themselves have no skill in speaking, still feel confident that they could speak in that manner. For the subtlety of his address appears easy of imitation to a person who ventures on an opinion, but nothing is less easy when he comes to try it; for although it is not a style of any extraordinary vigour, still it has some juice, so that even though it is not endowed with the most extreme power, it is still, if I may use such an expression, in perfect health. First of all, then, let us release it from the fetters of rhythm. For there is, as you know, a certain rhythm to be observed by an orator, proceeding on a regular system; but though it must be attended to in another kind of oratory, it must be entirely abandoned in this. This must be a sort of easy style, and yet not utterly without rules, so that it may seem to range at freedom, not to wander about licentiously. He should also guard against appearing to cement his words together; for the hiatus formed by a concourse of open vowels has something soft about it, and indicates a not unpleasing negligence, as if the speaker were anxious more about the matter than the manner of his speech. But as to other points, he must take care, specially as he is allowed more licence in these two,—I mean the rounding of his

[2] From the translation by C. D. Yonge. *The Orations of Marcus Tullius Cicero*, Vol. IV, London, Henry G. Bohn, 1852.

periods, and the combination of his words; for those narrow and minute details are not to be dealt with carelessly. [403-4]

. . . . .

The language will be pure and Latin; it will be arranged plainly and clearly, and great care will be taken to see what is becoming. [404]

. . . . .

There will be a moderate use of what I may call oratorical furniture; for there is to a certain degree what I may call our furniture, consisting of ornaments partly of things and partly of words. [404]

. . . . .

He will have besides this, action, not tragic, nor suited to the stage, but he will move his body in a moderate degree, trusting a great deal to his countenance; not in such a way as people call making faces, but in a manner sufficient to show in a gentlemanlike manner in what sense he means what he is saying to be understood.

Now in this kind of speech sallies of wit are admissible, and they carry perhaps only too much weight in an oration. Of them there are two kinds,—facetiousness and raillery,—and the orator will employ both; but he will use the one in relating anything neatly, and the other in darting ridicule on his adversaries. [406]

. . . . .

The orator must also avoid using jests ready prepared, such as do not arise out of the occasion, but are brought from home; for they are usually frigid. And he must spare friendships and dignities. He will avoid such insults as are not to be healed; he will only aim at his adversaries, and not even always at them, nor at all of them, nor in every manner. [407]

[*The Moderate Style*]

There is another style more fertile, and somewhat more forcible than this simple style of which we have been speaking; but nevertheless tamer than the highest class of oratory, of which I shall speak immediately. In this kind there is but little vigour, but there is the greatest possible quantity of sweetness; for it is fuller than the plain style, but more plain than that other which is highly ornamented and copious.

Every kind of ornament in speaking is suitable to this style; and in this kind of oratory there is a great deal of sweetness. It is a style in which many men among the Greeks have been eminent; but Demetrius Phalereus, in my opinion, has surpassed all the rest; and while his oratory proceeds in calm and tranquil flow, it receives brilliancy from numerous metaphors and borrowed expressions, like stars. [407-8]

. . . . .

The same kind of oratory, (I am speaking of the moderate and temperate kind), admits of all sorts of figures of expressions, and of many also of ideas. Discussions of wide application and extensive learning are explained in it, and common topics are treated without any impetuosity. In a word, orators of this class usually come from the schools of philosophers, and unless the more vigorous orator, whom I am going to speak of presently, is at hand to be compared with them, the one whom I am now describing will be approved of. [408-9]

[*The Grand Style*]

The third kind of orator is the sublime, copious, dignified, ornate speaker, in whom there is the greatest amount of grace. For he it is, out of admiration for whose ornamented style and copiousness of language nations have allowed eloquence to obtain so much influence in states; but it was only this eloquence, which is borne along in an impetuous course, and with a mighty noise, which all men looked up to, and admired, and had no idea that they themselves could possibly attain to. It belongs to this eloquence to deal with men's minds, and to influence them in every imaginable way. This is the style which sometimes forces its way into and sometimes steals into the senses; which implants new opinions in men, and eradicates others which have been long established. But there is a vast difference between this kind of orator and the preceding ones. A man who has laboured at the subtle and acute style, in order to be able to speak cunningly and cleverly, and who has had no higher aim, if he has entirely attained his object, is a great orator, if not a very great one; he is far from standing on slippery ground, and if he once gets a firm footing, is in no danger of falling. But the middle kind of orator, whom I have called moderate and temperate, if he has only arranged all his own forces to his satisfaction, will have no fear of any doubtful or uncertain chances of oratory; and even if at any time he should not be completely successful, which may often be the case, still he will be in no great danger, for he cannot fall far. But this orator of ours, whom we consider the first of orators, dignified, vehement, and earnest, if this is the only thing for which he appears born, or if this is the only kind of oratory to which he applies himself, and if he does not combine his copiousness of diction with those other two kinds of oratory, is very much to be despised. For the one who speaks simply, inasmuch as he speaks with shrewdness and sense, is a wise man; the one who employs the middle style is agreeable; but this most copious speaker, if he is nothing else, appears scarcely in his senses. For a man who can say nothing with calmness, nothing with gentleness; who seems ignorant of all arrangement and definition and distinctness, and regardless of wit, especially when some of his causes require to be treated in that manner entirely, and others in a great degree; if he does not prepare the ears of his hearers before he begins to work up the case in an inflammatory style, he seems like a madman among people in their senses, or like a drunken man among sober men. [409-10]

[*Rhythm in Oratory*]

And all this, which is also contained in Aristotle, is said by Theophrastus and Theodectes about the paeon. But my opinion is, that all feet ought to be jumbled together and confused, as it were, in an oration; and that we could not escape blame if we were always to use the same feet; because an oration ought to be neither metrical, like a poem, nor inharmonious, like the conversation of the common people. The one is so fettered by rules that it is manifest that it is designedly arranged as we see it; the other is so loose as to appear ordinary and vulgar; so that you are not pleased with the one, and you hate the other.

Let oratory then be, as I have said above, mingled and regulated with a regard to rhythm; not prosaic, nor on the other hand sacrificed wholly to rhythm; composed chiefly of the paeon, (since that is the opinion of the wisest author on the subject,) with many of the other feet which he passes over intermingled with it.

But what feet ought to be mingled with others, like purple, must be now explained; and we must also show to what kind of speech each sort of foot and rhythm is the best adapted. For the iambic is most frequent in those orations which are composed in a humble and lowly style; but the paeon is suited to a more dignified style; and the dactyl to both. Therefore, in a varied and long-continued speech these feet should be mingled together and combined. And in this way the fact of the orator aiming at pleasing the senses, and the careful attempt to round off the speech, will be the less visible, and they will at all times be less apparent if we employ dignified expressions and sentiments. For the hearers observe these two things, and think them agreeable: (I mean, expressions and sentiments.) And while they listen to them with admiring minds, the rhythm escapes their notice; and even if it were wholly wanting they would still be delighted with those other things. [442-3]

. . . . .

For there is in both oratory and poetry, first of all the material, then the execution. The material consists in the words, the execution in the arrangement of the words. But there are three divisions of each,—of words there is the metaphorical, the new, and the old-fashioned; for of appropriate words we say nothing at present; but of arrangement there are those which we have mentioned, composition, neatness, and rhythm. But the poets are the most free and frequent in the use of each; for they use words in a metaphorical sense not only more frequently, but also more daringly; and they use old-fashioned words more willingly, and new ones more freely. And the case with respect to rhythm is the same; in which they are obliged to comply with a kind of necessity: but still these things must be understood as being neither too different, nor yet in any respect united. Accordingly we find that rhythm is not the same in an oration as in a poem; and that that which is pronounced to be rhythmical in an oration is not always effected by a strict attention to the rules of rhythm; but sometimes either by neatness, or by the casual arrangement of the words.

Accordingly, if the question is raised as to what is the rhythm of an oration, it is every sort of rhythm; but one sort is better and more suitable than another. If the question is, what is the place of this rhythm? it is in every portion of the words. If you ask where it has arisen; it has arisen from the pleasure of the ears. If the principle is sought on which the words are to be arranged; that will be explained in another place, because that relates to practice, which was the fourth and last division which we made of the subject. If the question is, when; always: if, in what place; it consists in the entire connexion of the words. If we are asked, What is the circumstance which causes pleasure? we reply, that it is the same as in verse; the method of which is determined by art; but the ears themselves define it by their own silent sensations, without any reference to principles of art. [444-5]

A DIALOGUE CONCERNING ORATORICAL PARTITIONS [3]

[*Rules for the Narration*]

Since narration is an explanation of facts, and a sort of base and foundation for the establishment of belief, those rules are most especially to be observed in it, which apply also, for the most part, to the other divisions of speaking; part of which are necessary, and part are assumed for the sake of embellishment. For it is necessary for us to narrate events in a clear and probable manner; but we must also attend to an agreeable style. Therefore, in order to narrate with clearness, we must go back to those previous rules for explaining and illustrating facts, in which brevity is enjoined and taught. And brevity is one of the points most frequently praised in narration.... Again, our narrative will be probable, if the things which are related are consistent with the character of the persons concerned, with the times and places mentioned,—if the cause of every fact and event is stated,—if they appear to be proved by witnesses,—if they are in accordance with the opinions and authority of men, with law, with custom, and with religion,—if the honesty of the narrator is established, his candour, his memory, the uniform truth of his conversation, and the integrity of his life. Again, a narration is agreeable which contains subjects calculated to excite admiration, expectation, unlooked-for results, sudden feelings of the mind, conversations between people, grief, anger, fear, joy, desires. [495]

SUGGESTED READINGS

Atkins, John William Hey
  Literary Criticism in Antiquity; a Sketch of Its Development. London. Cambridge University Press. 1934. II, p1-46

D'Alton, John Francis
  Roman Literary Theory and Criticism; a Study in Tendencies. London and New York. Longmans, Green and Co. 1931. p141-207, 208-65

Baldwin, Charles Sears
  Ancient Rhetoric and Poetic. New York. Macmillan Co. 1924. p37-61

Watson, J. S., tr.
  Brutus; or, Remarks on Eminent Orators. In *Cicero on Oratory and Orators.* New York. Harper and Bros. 1890. p262-367

[3] From the translation by C. D. Yonge. *The Orations of Marcus Tullius Cicero,* Vol. IV, London, Henry G. Bohn, 1852.

RHETORIC AND PUBLIC SPEAKING 97

De Oratore; or, On the Character of the Orator. In *Cicero on Oratory and Orators*. London. Henry G. Bohn. 1855. p142-401

Yonge, C. D., tr.
A Dialogue concerning Oratorical Partitions. In *The Orations of Marcus Tullius Cicero*. London. G. Bell and Sons. 1913. IV, p486-527

On Rhetorical Invention. In *The Orations of Marcus Tullius Cicero*. London. G. Bell and Sons. 1913. IV, p241-380

On the Best Style of Orators. In *The Orations of Marcus Tullius Cicero*. London. G. Bell and Sons. 1913. IV, p527-33

On Topics. In *The Orations of Marcus Tullius Cicero*. London. G. Bell and Sons. 1913. IV, p458-86

QUINTILIAN

(c. A. D. 35-95)

One of the most ambitious projects ever undertaken by a rhetorician, Quintilian's *Institutes of Oratory* trace the development and prescribe the pedagogical treatment of the prospective orator from birth to retirement in old age. In twelve books Quintilian develops exhaustively, but with due regard for economy in the use of detail, the complete course of training adequate to mould the orator into "a good man skilled in speaking." The *Institutes* represent the most comprehensive analysis of oratorical training in print.

Quintilian's contributions derive from the fact that in one work he (1) sets forth a systematic treatise on the principles of speaking, embracing a full discussion of the five traditional parts of rhetoric; (2) develops a progressive plan for the training of speakers; and (3) presents in Book X and elsewhere a body of observations on Greek and Roman literature which stamps him as a critic of unusual discernment. All this resulted from the protest, as embodied in the *Institutes,* against the tastes of the time; against the false show and exhibitionism which characterized certain aspects of the period between Cicero and Quintilian.

Quintilian believes that nature and training cooperate in forming the orator; that the making of the orator is "an arduous task, even when nothing is deficient for the formation of his character;" that it is more important for the orator to be a *good man* than *skilled in speaking;* that teachers should always strive for the ideal in the training program; and that safeguards should be set up to prevent oratory from becoming a support of evil.

While admitting the possibility for its misuse and insisting upon its proper pedagogical application, Quintilian emphasizes the importance of the declamation as a teaching tool. Thus he accepts as sound and essential the rhetorical device which Tacitus, under its broader term *declamatio,* condemned vigorously as a deterrent of cultural advancement.

INSTITUTES OF ORATORY [1]

[*The Orator As a Good Man*]

We are to form, then, the perfect orator, who cannot exist unless as a good man; and we require in him, therefore, not only consummate ability in speaking, but every excellence of mind. [Pref., 9]

[*No Formal Rules in Rhetoric*]

But let no man require from me such a system of precepts as is laid down by most authors of *books of rules,* a system in which I

---

[1] From the translation by J. S. Watson (1856). The bracketed numerals indicate the book, chapter, and paragraph references.

should have to make certain laws, fixed by immutable necessity, for all students of eloquence, commencing with the *prooemium,* and what must be the character of it, saying that the *statement of facts* must come next, and what rule must be observed in stating them; that after this must come the *proposition,* or as some have preferred to call it, the *excursion;* and then that there must be *a certain order of questions;* adding also other precepts, which some speakers observe as if it were unlawful to do otherwise, and as if they were acting under orders; for rhetoric would be a very easy and small matter, if it could be included in one short body of rules, but rules must generally be altered to suit the nature of each individual case, the time, the occasion, and necessity itself; consequently, one great quality in an orator is discretion, because he must turn his thoughts in various directions, according to the different bearings of his subject. [II, 13, 1-2]

. . . . .

For my part I shall, above all things,
    Direct, enjoin, and o'er and o'er repeat,
that an orator, in all his pleadings, should keep two things in view, *what is becoming,* and *what is expedient;* but it is frequently *expedient,* and sometimes *becoming,* to make some deviations from the regular and settled order, as, in statues and pictures, we see the dress, look, and attitude, varied. [II, 13, 8]

. . . . .

The art of speaking depends on great labour, constant study, varied exercise, repeated trials, the deepest sagacity, and the readiest judgment. [II, 13, 15]

[*The Art of Rhetoric*]

RHETORIC, then, (for we shall henceforth use this term without dread of sarcastic objections,) will be best divided, in my opinion, in such a manner, that we may speak first of the *art,* next of the *artist,* and then of the *work.* The *art* will be that which ought to be attained by study, and is the *knowledge how to speak well.* The *artificer* is he who has thoroughly acquired the art, that is, the orator, whose business is to *speak well.* The *work* is what is achieved by the artificer, that is, *good speaking.* [II, 14, 4]

. . . . .

For I shall say, not what I shall invent, but what I shall approve; as, for instance, that *oratory is the art of speaking well;* since, when the best definition is found, he who seeks for another must seek for a worse. [II, 15, 38]

. . . . .

But if eloquence be the *art of speaking well,* (the definition which I adopt,) so that a true *orator* must be, above all, *a good man,* it must assuredly be acknowledged that it is a useful art. [II, 16, 11]

. . . . .

For, not to mention how beneficial it is, and how becoming in a man of virtue, to defend his friends, to direct a senate or people by his counsels, or to lead an army to whatever enterprise he may desire, is it not extremely honourable to attain, by the common understanding and words which all men use, so high a degree of esteem and glory as to appear to speak or plead, but, as was the case with Pericles, to hurl forth lightning and thunder? [II, 16, 19]

. . . . .

The objection might, perhaps, hold good against those who think that the end of oratory is *to persuade,* but my orator and his art, as defined by me, do not depend upon the result; he indeed who speaks directs his efforts towards victory, but when he *has spoken well,* though he may not be victorious, he has attained the full end of his art. [II, 17, 23]

. . . . .

Need I show that it depends on understanding and practice, like other arts? If logic be an art, as is generally admitted, oratory must certainly be an art, as it differs from logic rather in *species* than in *genus.* Nor must we omit to observe that in whatever pursuit one man may act according to a method, and another without regard to that method, that pursuit is an art; and that in whatever pursuit he who has learned succeeds better than he who has not learned, that pursuit is an art. [II, 17, 42]

[*Nature and Art in Oratory*]

I am aware that it is also a question whether *nature* or *learning* contributes most to oratory. This inquiry, however, has no concern with the subject of my work; for a perfect orator can be formed only with the aid of both. . . . [II, 19, 1]

. . . . .

In a word, nature is the material for learning; the one forms, and the other is formed. Art can do nothing without material; material has its value even independent of art; but perfection of art is of more consequence than perfection of material. [II, 19, 3]

[*Material of Oratory*]

For my part, I consider, and not without authorities to support me, that the material of oratory is *everything that may come before an orator for discussion*. [II, 21, 4]

[*Parts of Oratory*]

The whole *art* of *oratory*, as the most and greatest writers have taught, consists of five parts, *invention, arrangement, expression, memory*, and *delivery* or *action*; for the last is designated by either of these terms. [III, 3, 1]

[*Kinds of Oratory*]

To me it has appeared safest to follow the majority of writers; and so reason seems to direct. There is, then, as I said, one kind of oratory in which praise and blame are included, but which is called, from the better part of its office, the *panegyrical*; others, however, term it the *demonstrative* or *epideictic*. [III, 4, 11-12]

. . . . .

The second kind is the *deliberative*, and the third the *judicial*. [III, 4, 15]

[*Ends of Oratory*]

But every speech consists at once of that which is expressed, and of that which expresses, that is, of *matter* and *words*. Ability in speaking is produced by *nature, art*, and *practice*; to which some add a fourth requisite, namely *imitation*; which I include under art. There are also three objects which an orator must accomplish, to *inform*, to *move*, to *please*. . . . [III, 5, 1-2]

[*Characteristics of Questions*]

All writers admit, however, that questions depend on what *is written* or what is *not written*. Questions about something written concern *legality*; those about something not written concern *fact*. [III, 5, 4]

. . . . .

RHETORIC AND PUBLIC SPEAKING 103

It is also agreed that questions are either *indefinite* or *definite*. The indefinite are those which, without regard to persons, time, place, and other such circumstances, are argued *for* or *against*. [III, 5, 5]

* * * * *

Definite questions embrace particular *circumstances, persons, times*, and other things. [III, 5, 7]

[State of the Cause]

Since every cause, therefore, is comprehended is some *state*, I think that before I proceed to specify how the several kinds of causes are to be managed, I must consider that question which has reference to all of them alike, *what is a state?* as well as *whence it is drawn*, and *how many and what kinds of states* there are? [III, 6, 1]

* * * * *

A simple cause, though it may be defended in various ways, cannot contain more than one point on which a decision is to be pronounced; and hence the *state of the cause* will be that which the pleader regards as the chief object to be gained, and the judge as the chief object of attention; for it is on this that the cause will *take its stand*. [III, 6, 9]

* * * * *

My own opinion has always been, as there are frequently different *states* of questions in a cause, to regard that as the *state of the cause* which is the strongest point in it, and on which the whole matter chiefly turns. [III, 6, 21]

* * * * *

According to the system of most authors, then, I adhered to three *ratiocinatory states*, those of *conjecture, quality*, and *definition*, and one *legal*. These were my general *states*. The legal I divided into five species, those relating to *writing and intention, contradictory laws, induction, ambiguity*, and *exception*. I now see that the fourth of the general *states* may be withdrawn from them; for the primary division is sufficient, by which I pronounced some *states* to be *ratiocinatory*, others *legal*; thus the fourth will not be a *state*, but a species of question; otherwise it would be a *ratiocinatory state*. [III, 6, 66-7]

* * * * *

We must therefore adhere to those writers whose authority Cicero has followed, and who say that there are three points about which there is a question in every cause; *whether a thing is, what it is*, and *of what species it is*; a distinction which even nature herself teaches us; for there must first of all be something which is the object of the question; concerning which it certainly cannot be determined *what* and *of what species it is*, until it be settled that it really exists; and this, therefore, is the first question. But as to that which is proved to exist, it does not immediately appear *what it is*. When this point is also decided, there remains, last of all, the *quality*; and, when all these particulars are settled, nothing further is left. [III, 6, 80-1]

* * * * *

Let students learn, therefore, before all, that there are four modes of proceeding in every cause; which four modes he who is going to plead ought to make it his first business to consider. For, to begin first of all with the defendant, by far the strongest mode of defence is, *if the charge which is made can be denied*; the next, *if an act of the kind charged against the accused can be said not to have been done*; the third, and most honourable, *if what is done is proved to have been justly done*. If we cannot command these methods, the last and only mode of defence is that of eluding an accusation, which can neither be denied nor combated, by the aid of some point of law, so as to make it appear that the action has not been brought in due legal form. [III, 6, 83]

* * * * *

By the accuser nothing more is to be kept in view than that he must prove that *something was done*; that *a particular thing was done*; that *it was done wrongfully*; and that *he brings his action according to law*. [III, 6, 85]

* * * * *

These plans, as it were, and forms, of proceeding, which I then called *general states*, resolve themselves, as I showed, into two general kinds, the one dependent on reasoning, the other on legality. The one dependent on reasoning is the more simple, as it consists merely in the contemplation of the nature of things; and it is sufficient, therefore, in respect to it, to mention *conjecture, definition, quality*. Of legal questions there must necessarily be more species, as laws are numerous, and have various forms. [III, 6, 86-7]

* * * * *

This is agreed among all writers, that in every simple cause there is but one single *state*; but that many questions, which, as secondary points, are referred to that in which the main point for judgment is contained, may be comprised in one and the same cause. [III, 6, 91]

* * * * *

In every kind of legal controversy, too, must be comprehended a *cause*, a *matter for judgment*, and the *containing point*, for there is nothing brought into question in which there is not some reason, something to which judgment is directed, and something which chiefly contains the substance of the matter in question. [III, 6, 103]

[*Panegyric Oratory*]

But the peculiar business of panegyric is to *amplify* and *embellish* its subjects. [III, 7, 6]

* * * * *

This kind of eloquence is devoted chiefly to gods or men; though it is sometimes employed about animals and things inanimate. In praising the gods, we shall, in the first place express a general veneration for the majesty of their nature, and shall then eulogize the peculiar power of each, and such of their inventions as have conferred benefit on mankind. [III, 7, 6-7]

* * * * *

The praise of men is more varied. First of all it is distinguished with respect to time, that which was before them, and that in which they themselves lived; and, in regard to those who are dead, that also which followed their death. Antecedent to the birth of a man will be his *country, parents,* and *ancestors,* to whom we may refer in two ways; for it will be honourable to them either to have equalled the nobility of their forefathers, or to have ennobled a humble origin by their achievements. Other subjects for eulogy may also sometimes be found in the time that preceded a man's birth; such as occurrences, for example, that denoted his future eminence by prophetic indications or auguries; as the oracles are said to have foretold that the son of Thetis would be greater than his father. The praises of a man personally should be derived from the qualities of his mind, body, or external circumstances. [III, 7, 10-12]

* * * * *

Praise of the good qualities of the mind is always just; but more than one way may be pursued in the treatment of it; for sometimes it is more honourable to follow the progress of a person's life and the order of his actions; so that his natural genius, shown in his early years, may be first commended, then his advancement in learning, and then his course of conduct, including not only what he did, but what he said; sometimes it will be better to divide our praises among the several kinds of virtue, fortitude, justice, temperance, and others, and to assign to each the honour of that which has been done under its influence. [III, 7, 15]

. . . . .

The same method will be observed in censure, but so as to set things in a different light; for meanness of origin has been a dishonour to many; and nobility itself has rendered others more conspicuous and more odious for their vices. [III, 7, 19]

. . . . .

Some praise of his audience, too, should always be mingled with his remarks, (for it makes them favourably disposed towards him,) and, whenever it is possible, should be so introduced as to strengthen his cause. [III, 7, 24]

. . . . .

Cities are eulogized in the same way as persons; for their founder is to be considered as their parent; and antiquity confers much dignity on their inhabitants; as we see in regard to people who are said to be sprung from the soil of their country. [III, 7, 26]

. . . . .

Encomiums may also be bestowed on public works, in respect to which magnificence, utility, beauty, and the architect of them, are commonly considered. [III, 7, 27]

. . . . .

Panegyrics on places are also found; . . . [III, 7, 27]

. . . . .

While I do not admit, therefore, that this laudatory department of oratory relates only to questions concerning what is honourable, I think, at the same time, that it is chiefly comprised under *quality*. . . . [III, 7, 28]

. . . . .

But the whole of panegyrical oratory bears some resemblance to deliberative, because, for the most part, that which is recommended in the one is praised in the other. [III, 7, 28]

[Deliberative Oratory]

I am surprised, also, that deliberative oratory is confined by some authors wholly to matters of utility. [III, 8, 1]

* * * * *

Nor is it sufficient to include deliberative oratory in the *state* of quality, in which is comprised the question of what is honourable and what is useful; for often, in respect to these, there is room for conjecture; at times some definition is to be considered; and occasionally, too, legal inquiries may occur, especially in reference to private proceedings, if ever a doubt arises *whether a thing be lawful*. [III, 8, 4]

* * * * *

The deliberative department of oratory, therefore, (which is also called the suasory,) while it consults concerning the future, inquires also into the past. It has two objects, to *persuade* and to *dissuade*.

An exordium, such as is usual in judicial pleadings, it does not require; because whoever consults an orator is already well-disposed to hear him. Yet the commencement, whatever it be, ought to have some resemblance to an exordium; for we must not begin abruptly, or with whatever we may fancy, because in every subject there is something naturally first.

In speaking before the senate, and, indeed, before the people, the same object is to be kept in view as in addressing judges, namely, that of securing the good will of the majority of those to whom we speak. [III, 8, 6-7]

* * * * *

As to a regular statement of facts, a private subject of discussion will never require it, at least a statement of the matter on which an opinion is to be given; for no man is ignorant of the particulars on which he consults others. Statements, however, of many external circumstances relative to the subject of deliberation may be introduced. In deliberative addresses to the people a statement setting forth the order of circumstances is indispensable. Deliberative oratory requires appeals to the feelings more than any other kind of eloquence; for indignation is often to be kindled and allayed; and the minds of the audience are to be moved to fear, eagerness, hatred, benevolence. Sometimes, too, pity is to be excited, whether we have, for example, to recommend what aid be given to a besieged town, or whether we be called upon to lament the overthrow of a people in alliance with us. [III, 8, 10-12]

. . . . .

But what is of most weight in deliberative speeches is authority in the speaker; for he who desires everybody to trust to his opinion about what is expedient and honourable, ought to be, and to be esteemed, a man of the greatest judgment and probity. [III, 8, 13]

. . . . .

In persuading and dissuading, then, three particulars are chiefly to be regarded: *what is the subject of deliberation; who those that deliberate are*; and *what is the character of him that would influence their deliberations.* [III, 8, 15]

. . . . .

As to that which is the subject of deliberation, it is either certain that it may be carried into effect, or uncertain. If it be uncertain, its uncertainty will be the sole point for consideration, or, I should say, the chief point, for it will often happen that we shall assert, first of all, that a thing, even if it could be done, ought not to be done, and, next, that it cannot be done. But when the question is respecting something uncertain, the point is conjectural. . . . [III, 8, 16]

. . . . .

Some have thought that the topics for persuasion are the three considerations *what is honourable, what is useful,* and *what is necessary.* For the introduction of the third I find no motive; for, when any force oppresses us, it may be necessary for us to *suffer* something, but certainly not *to do* anything; but it is about *doing* that deliberation is concerned. [III, 8, 22]

. . . . .

Often, too, we say that advantage is to be disregarded, in order that we may do what is honourable. . . . [III, 8, 30]

. . . . .

Nor is what is advantageous compared only with what is disadvantageous, but things that are advantageous or disadvantageous are compared with one another; as when we try to determine, of two advantageous measures, which is the more advantageous, or of two that are disadvantageous, which is the less so. [III, 8, 33]

. . . . .

A question of advantage may also have reference to time: *it is expedient, but not now*; or to place: *not here*; or to persons: *not for us, or against those*; or to a particular mode of proceeding: *not thus*; or to measure: *not to so great a degree*. [III, 8, 35]

. . . . .

Though examples, therefore, are of the utmost effect in deliberative oratory, because men are most easily led to consent to any measure by instances of similar proceedings, yet it makes a great difference *whose* authority is adduced, and *to whom* it is recommended; for the feelings of those who listen to deliberative speeches are various. [III, 8, 36]

. . . . .

To recommend honourable measures to those who are honourable is extremely easy; but if we ever have occasion to enforce a right course of conduct on the unprincipled, we must be careful not to reproach them with the opposite nature of their life. The minds of such an audience are to be influenced, not by dissertations on the nature of virtue, for which they have no regard, but by allusions to honour, and to the opinion of others, and if such arguments to their vanity do not move them, by showing the advantage likely to follow from what you advise, or rather perhaps, and with more effect, by showing them how much is to be dreaded if they act otherwise. For besides the fact that minds of the lightest principles are most easily alarmed, I know not whether the fear of evil has not naturally more influence with the majority of mankind than the hope of good; to whom also the knowledge of what is vicious comes with greater facility than the knowledge of that which is virtuous. [III, 8, 38-40]

. . . . .

If any one, however, recommend to a good man anything not quite honourable, let him remember not to recommend it *as dishonourable*. . . . [III, 8, 44]

[*Judicial Oratory*]

I am now to speak of the *judicial* kind of oratory, which is extremely varied, but lies in the two duties of *attack* and *defence*. The divisions of it, as most authors are of opinion, are five, the *exordium*, the *statement of facts*, the *proof* of what we advance, the *refutation* of our adversary, and the *peroration*. To these some have added *partition, proposition,* and *digression;* the first two of which evidently fall under *proof;* for you must necessarily *propose* what you are going to prove, as well as *conclude* after you have proved; and, if *proposition* is a division of cause, why is not also *conclusion?* As for *partition,* it is only one of the duties of *arrangement,* which is a portion of oratory in general, equally pervading all its parts and the whole body of each, like invention and delivery. [III, 9, 1-2]

. . . . .

I do not, however, agree with those who, like Aristotle, omit *refutation,* as comprehended under proof; for proof establishes, refutation overthrows. [III, 9, 5]

. . . . .

But with regard to the divisions which I have made, it is not to be understood that that which is to be delivered first is necessarily to be contemplated first; for we ought to consider, before everything else, *of what nature the cause is; what is the question in it; what may profit or injure it;* next, *what is to be maintained or refuted;* and then, *how the statement of facts should be made.* For the *statement* is preparatory to proof, and cannot be made to advantage, unless it be first settled what it ought to promise as to proof. Last of all, it is to be considered how the judge is to be conciliated; for, until all the bearings of the cause be ascertained, we cannot know what sort of feeling it is proper to excite in the judge, whether inclined to severity or gentleness, to violence or laxity, to inflexibility or mercy. [III, 9, 6-7]

. . . . .

Every cause, in which there is one method for a plaintiff, and another for a defendant, consists either in a controversy about one charge or about several. The one is called *simple,* the other *complex.* [III, 10, 1]

. . . . .

There is, however, said to be a third kind, different from these, called *comparative;* and some consideration with regard to comparison frequently happens in some part of a cause; as when, in a case before the centumviri, there arises, after other questions, one of this kind, *which of two persons is better entitled to an inheritance?* But it seldom happens that trials are appointed in the forum merely for that object, and only in cases of *divination,* which take place for the purpose of appointing an accuser, or sometimes between informers to decide *which of two has a better claim to a reward.* [III, 10, 3]

. . . . .

When the nature of the cause has been determined, we shall then have to consider, whether the fact, which is made a charge by the accuser against the defendant, is to be denied, or to be justified, or to be called by another name, or to be excluded from that particular sort of process. By this means the states of causes are determined. [III, 10, 5]

. . . . .

The *mode of defence* is that process by which what is admitted to have been done is justified. [III, 11, 4]

[*The Exordium*]

In giving an exordium at all there is no other object but to prepare the hearer to listen to us more readily in the subsequent parts of our pleading. This object, as is agreed among most authors, is principally effected by three means, by securing his *good will* and *attention*, and by rendering him *desirous of further information*; not that these ends are not to be kept in view throughout the whole pleading, but because they are pre-eminently necessary at the commencement, when we gain admission as it were into the mind of the judge in order to penetrate still farther into it. [IV, 1, 5]

. . . . .

But as the authority of the speaker becomes thus of the highest efficacy, if, in his undertaking the business, all suspicion of meanness, or hatred, or ambition, be far removed from him, so it is a sort of tacit commendation to him, if he represents himself as weak, and inferior in ability to those acting against him, a practice which is adopted in most of the exordia of Messala. [IV, 1, 8]

. . . . .

We must also take care not to appear *insolent, malignant, overbearing,* or *reproachful* towards any man or body of men, especially such as cannot be wounded without exciting an unfavourable feeling in the judge. [IV, 1, 10]

. . . . .

The character of the *advocate for the opposite party* may sometimes afford us matter for an exordium; if we speak of him sometimes with honour, making it appear that we fear his eloquence and influence, so to render them objects of suspicion to the judge; or sometimes, though very rarely, with contempt. . . . [IV, 1, 11]

. . . . .

As to the character of the *prosecutor*, it may be treated in various ways; sometimes his worth may be asserted, sometimes his weakness commended to notice. [IV, 1, 13]

. . . . .

The favour of the *judge* we shall conciliate, not merely by offering him praise, (which ought indeed to be given with moderation, though it is to be remembered at the same time, that the privilege of offering it is common to both parties,) but by turning his praises to the advantage of our cause, appealing, in behalf of the *noble* to his dignified station, in behalf of the *humble* to his justice, in behalf of the *unfortunate* to his pity, in behalf of the *injured* to his severity; and using similar appeals in other cases. [IV, 1, 16]

. . . . .

It also has effect in securing the attention of the audience, if they think that we shall not detain them long, or enter upon matters foreign to the subject. [IV, 1, 34]

. . . . .

Of the old precepts this still remains in force, that *no unusual expression, no highly audacious metaphor, nothing borrowed from what is obsolete and antiquated, or from poetic license, should appear in the exordium.* For we are not as yet admitted to full freedom of speech, and the attention of the audience, being still fresh, keeps us under restraint, but when their minds are propitiated and warmed, greater liberty will be tolerated. . . . [IV, 1, 58-9]

. . . . .

Our style in the exordium ought not to resemble that of the argumentative, or sentimental, or narrative parts of our speech. Nor should our manner be too prolix or circumlocutory, but should wear the appearance of simplicity and unaffectedness, not promising too much either in words or look. [IV, 1, 60]

. . . . .

To be confused in memory, or to lose our fluency of speech, has nowhere a worse effect than at the commencement, as a faulty exordium may be compared to a countenance disfigured with scars; and that pilot is surely one of the worst who runs his vessel aground as it is leaving the harbour. As to the length of an exordium, it must be regulated by the nature of the cause. [IV, 1, 61]

[*Statement of Facts*]

It is most natural, and ought to be most usual, that when the judge has been prepared by the methods which have been noticed above, the matter, on which he is to give judgment, should be stated to him. [IV, 2, 1]

. . . . .

Some have thought that there must always be a statement of facts; but that this notion is unfounded, may be proved by many arguments. [IV, 2, 4]

. . . . .

For my part, besides resting on the authority of eminent rhetoricians, I am myself of opinion that there are two kinds of statements in judicial causes; the one sort being an exposition of the cause itself, and the other of the circumstances connected with it. [IV, 2, 11]

. . . . .

Sometimes a fictitious statement of particulars is introduced; either to rouse the feelings of the judges, as that in the speech for Roscius respecting Chrysogonus, which I mentioned a little above; or to amuse them with a little pleasantry. . . . [IV, 2, 19]

. . . . .

For a statement of facts is not made merely that the judge may comprehend the case, but rather that he may look upon it in the same light with ourselves. [IV, 2, 21]

. . . . .

Sometimes we may pretend to repeat our statement for the information of some new member taking his seat among the judges; sometimes, in order that even the by-standers may be convinced of the iniquity of what is asserted on the opposite side. [IV, 2, 22]

. . . . .

There is another point about which there is still more frequently a question, *Whether the statement of facts is always to be immediately subjoined to the exordium*; and those who hold the affirmative cannot be thought destitute of arguments to support them; for as the exordium is made with the intent that the judge may be rendered more favourable by it, and more willing and attentive to understand the case, and as proof cannot be adduced unless the case be previously understood, it appears right that the judge should at once be made master of the facts. But the nature of a cause sometimes justly changes this order. . . . [IV, 2, 24-5]

. . . . .

I shall now add some remarks on the method of stating a case. A statement of a case is an *account of a thing done, or supposed to have been done; which account is adapted to persuade;* or, as Apollodorus defines it, a *narrative to inform the auditor what the matter in question is.* Most writers, and especially those who are of the school of Isocrates, direct that it should be *lucid, brief,* and *probable.* It is of no consequence if, instead of *lucid,* we say *perspicuous,* or instead of *probable, credible* or *apparently deserving of belief.* [IV, 2, 31]

. . . . .

A statement, then, is either *wholly in our own favour, wholly in that of our opponent,* or *a mixture of both.* If it be *wholly in our own favour,* we may be content with the three qualities of which the effect is that the judge more readily *understands, remembers,* and *believes.* [IV, 2, 33]

. . . . .

Our statement will be sufficiently concise, if, in the first place, we commence the exposition of the case at the point where it begins to concern the judge; next, if we say nothing foreign to the cause; and, lastly, if we retrench everything of which the absence will deduct nothing from the knowledge of the judge or the advantage of our client. [IV, 2, 40]

. . . . .

For myself, I make brevity consist, not in saying less, but in not saying more, than is necessary. . . . [IV, 2, 43]

. . . . .

We must no less be on our guard, however, against that obscurity which attends on those who abbreviate every part too much; and it is better that there should be something superabundant in a statement than that anything should be wanting; for what is unnecessary is attended with weariness, but what is necessary is not withheld without danger. [IV, 2, 44]

. . . . .

We shall make it somewhat less long, if we defer such particulars as we can to another part of our speech, not without specifying, however, what we defer. . . . [IV, 2, 48]

. . . . .

Division also lessens the tediousness of a statement: I *shall relate what took place before the commencement of the affair; I shall relate what occurred during the course of it; I shall relate what happened afterwards.* [IV, 2, 49]

. . . . .

Nor will it be without advantage if we scatter here and there some seeds of proof, but so as not to forget that we are stating a series of facts and not of arguments. [IV, 2, 54]

. . . . .

As to *conjectural* causes, in which the question is about fact, they do not so often require an explanation of the point on which a decision is to be given, as of the circumstances from which a knowledge of it is to be collected. As the prosecutor will represent those circumstances in an unfavourable light, the defendant must try to remove the unfavourable impression produced by him; the circumstances must be laid before the judge by the one in a different way from that in which they are presented to him by the other. But, it may be said, some arguments are strong when advanced in a body, but of less force when separated. This remark, I answer, does not apply to the question *Whether we ought to make a statement,* but *how we ought to make one.* For what hinders us from accumulating a variety of evidence in our statement, and to promise to produce more? Or to divide our statement into portions, to give proofs under each portion as it is brought forward, and so proceed to what follows? For I do not agree with those who think that we must always relate matters in the order in which they occurred: I consider rather that we should relate them in the order which is best for our cause. [IV, 2, 81-3]

. . . . .

The following directions, too, are commonly given respecting the statement of facts; that no *digression* is to be made from it; that we are *to address ourselves constantly to the judge; that we are to speak in no character but our own*; and that we are *to introduce no argumentation*; and some even add that we are *not to attempt to excite the feelings.* These precepts, doubtless, are to be in general observed; or, I may say, never to be departed from, unless the nature of our cause obliges us to disregard them. [IV, 2, 103]

* * * * *

I am the more surprised at those, therefore, who think that we are not to touch the feelings in a statement of facts. If they mean, indeed, that we are not to work on them long, or as in the peroration, they are of the same opinion with myself; for tediousness is to be avoided; otherwise, why should I not move the judge while I am instructing him? [IV, 2, 111]

* * * * *

Nor is the judge in any part more attentive; and consequently nothing that is expressed with effect is lost upon him. Besides he is more inclined, I know not how, to believe what gratifies his ear, and is led by being pleased to being persuaded. [IV, 2, 119]

* * * * *

Nor can I omit to remark how much credit *the authority of the speaker* gives to his statement; an authority which we ought to secure chiefly by our general conduct, but also by our style of oratory; since the more grave and serious it is, the more weight it must give to our assertions. We must especially avoid, therefore, in this part of our speech, all suspicion of artifice, (for nowhere is the judge more on his guard,) so that nothing may appear fictitious or studied, but that all may be thought to emanate rather from the cause than from the advocate. [IV, 2, 125-6]

[*Digression*]

It is the custom of most speakers, when the order of facts is set forth, to make a digression to some pleasing and attractive moral topic, so as to secure as much favourable attention as possible from the audience. [IV, 3, 1]

* * * * *

To this custom there is this objection, that the speakers indulge in it without making due distinction of causes, and what particular causes require, but as if such displays of eloquence were always expedient or even necessary; and in consequence they force into their digression matters taken from other parts to which they properly belong; so that many things must either be said over again, or, as they have been said in a place to which they had no right, cannot be said in their own. [IV, 3, 3]

[*Proof*]

For no part of a speech ought to be more closely attached to any other part, than the proof is to the statement; unless indeed the digression be intended either as the end of the statement or as the beginning of the proof. [IV, 3, 5]

. . . . .

In my opinion the commencement of any proof is a *proposition*, which may be advanced not only in stating the principal question, but sometimes even to introduce particular arguments, ... [IV, 4, 1]

[*Partition*]

Partition is the enumeration, according to their order, of our own propositions, or those of our adversary, or both; an enumeration which some think that we should always make, because, by its aid, the cause is rendered clearer, and the judge more observant and attentive, if he knows exactly on what point we are speaking, and on what points we intend to speak afterwards. [IV, 5, 1]

. . . . .

There are other reasons why we should not always adopt a partition; first, because most observations please better when they appear to be conceived on the moment, and not to be brought from home, but to spring from the subject itself as we are discussing it; and hence the common expressions, *I had almost forgotten, It had escaped me, You aptly remind me.* ... [IV, 5, 4]

. . . . .

In addition, it is to be considered that there is, in every division of a case, some one point of more importance than the rest, and when the judge has become acquainted with it, he is apt to disdain other points as requiring no notice. Consequently, if more charges than one are to be established or overthrown, a partition is both advantageous and agreeable; in order that what we have to say on each head may distinctly be shown; but if we have to combat one charge by various arguments, it is needless. [IV, 5, 8]

. . . . .

But though partition is not always necessary, or even advantageous, yet, when it is seasonably adopted, it contributes great lucidity and agreeableness to a speech; for it not only causes what is stated to become clearer, by drawing certain particulars out of the crowd, as it were, and placing them full in the sight of the judges, but relieves the attention by fixing a definite termination to certain parts, as distances on a road, marked by inscribed stones, appear greatly to diminish the fatigue of travellers. [IV, 5, 22]

. . . . .

The first step in partition is, to distinguish what is admitted and what is disputed. Next, in regard to what is admitted, to distinguish what our adversary admits, and what we admit; and, in respect to what is disputed, to specify what our propositions are, and what those of our opponent. But what is most culpable, is, not to treat of your several points in the order in which you have arranged them. [IV, 5, 28]

[Classification of Proofs]

In the first place, then, the division which has been laid down by Aristotle has gained the approbation of almost all rhetoricians; namely, that there are some proofs which an orator adopts that are *unconnected with the art* of speaking, and others which *he himself extracts,* and, as it were, produces, *from his cause.* Hence they have called the one sort . . . 'inartificial,' and the other . . . 'artificial.' Of the former kind, are *precognitions, public reports, evidence extracted by torture, writings, oaths,* and *the testimony of witnesses,* with which the greater part of forensic pleadings are concerned. [V, 1, 1-2]

. . . . .

All artificial proof, then, depends on *indications,* or *arguments,* or *examples.* I am aware that *indications* are thought by many a species of arguments; and I had, in consequence, two motives for distinguishing them; the *first,* that indications generally, almost always, belong to inartificial proofs; for *a blood-stained garment, a shriek, a livid spot,* and similar particulars, are circumstances of the same nature as *writings, reports,* and *depositions;* they are not invented by the orator, but communicated to him with the cause itself; the *second,* that neither can *indications,* if they are *certain,* be arguments, because, where there are certain indications, there is no question, and there can be no room for argument except upon a controverted point; nor, if they are *uncertain,* can they be arguments, but have themselves need of arguments.

All artificial proofs, then, . . . are distinguished, first of all, into two kinds, one in which the conclusion is *necessary,* the other in which it is not *necessary.* [V, 9, 1-3]

[*Artificial Proofs*]

But before I distinguish the different sorts of artificial proofs, I think it necessary to intimate that there are certain qualities common to all kinds of proof. For there is no question which does not relate either to a *thing* or to a *person*; nor can there be any grounds for argument, except respecting matters that affect things or persons; and these matters are either to be considered by themselves or referred to something else; nor can there be any proof except from things *consequent* or *opposite,* which we must seek either in the time that *preceded* the alleged fact, in the time at which it took place, or in the time that followed it; nor can anything be proved but from some other thing, which must either be greater or less than it, or equal to it. As for *arguments* they arise either from *general questions,* which may be considered in themselves, apart from any connexion with things or persons, or from *the cause.itself,* when anything is found in it not derived from common reasoning, but peculiar to that point on which the decision is to be pronounced. Of all conclusions, moreover, some are *necessary,* some *probable,* some *not impossible.*

Of all proofs, too, there are four forms. Because one thing is, another is not; as *It is day, therefore it is not night;* because there is one thing, there is also another; as, *The sun is above the earth, therefore it is day;* because one thing is not, another is: as *It is not night, therefore it is day;* because one thing is not, another is not: as, *He is not a rational being, therefore he is not a man.* [IV, 8, 4-7]

[*Arguments: Proof*]

Since, then, an *argument* is *a process of reasoning affording a proof, by which one thing is gathered from another, and which establishes what is doubtful by reference to what is certain,* there must assuredly be something in a cause that does not require proof; for unless there be something which is true, or which appears true, and from which support may be gained for what is doubtful, there will be no grounds on which we can prove anything. As certainties, accordingly, we have, in the first place, what is perceived by the senses, as what we see, what we hear, as *signs* or *indications*; next, what is admitted by the general consent of mankind, as, *that there are gods,* and *that respect is to be paid to parents*; also, what is established by the laws, or what is passed into general usage, with the concurrence, if not of the whole world, at least of that community or people among whom we have to plead, as indeed, in what is called legal right, most points are settled, not by positive laws, but by common custom; and, lastly, whatever is agreed between the two parties, whatever is proved, or whatever our adversary does not dispute. . . . But to him who would handle arguments properly, the nature and quality of all things whatever ought to be known, as well as their general effects; for it is by such knowledge that arguments called . . . "probable" are established. Now of *probability* there are three degrees; one, which rests on very strong grounds, because that to which it is applied generally happens, as *that children are loved by their parents*; a second, somewhat more inclined to uncertainty, as *that he who is in good health today will live till tomorrow*; a third, which is only not repugnant to credibility, as *that a theft committed in a house was committed by one of the household*. [V, 10, 11-16]

[*Places of Argument*]

By *places* . . . I mean . . . *the seats of argument, in which they lie concealed, and from which they must be drawn forth.* [V, 10, 20]

. . . . .

First of all, then, arguments are to be drawn from *persons*; there being, as I said, a general division of all arguments into two kinds, those which concern *things,* and those which concern *persons;* and the accidents of things being *cause, time, place, opportunity, instruments, manner,* and the like. As to *persons,* I do not undertake to treat of every particular concerning them, as most rhetoricians have done, but only of those topics from which arguments may be drawn.

These, then, are, *birth,* for people are mostly thought similar in character to their fathers and forefathers, and sometimes derive from their origin motives for living an honourable or dishonourable life; *nation,* for every nation has its peculiar manners, and the same thing will not be alike probable in regard to a Barbarian, a Roman, and a Greek; *country,* for, in like manner, the laws, institutions, and opinions of states have their peculiarities; *sex,* for you would more readily believe a charge of robbery with regard to a man, and poisoning with regard to a woman; *age,* for different modes of action belong to different periods of life; *education* and *discipline,* for it makes a difference by whom, and in what manner a person has been brought up; *bodily constitution,* for beauty is often drawn into an argument for libertinism, and strength for insolence, and the contrary qualities for contrary conduct; *fortune,* for the same charge is not equally credible in reference to a rich and a poor man, in reference to one who is surrounded with relations, friends, and clients, and one who is destitute of all such support; *condition,* for it makes a great difference whether a man is illustrious or obscure, a magistrate or a private person, a father or a son, a citizen or a foreigner, free or a slave, married or a bachelor, the father of children or childless; *natural disposition,* for avarice, passionateness, sensibility, cruelty, austerity, and other similar affections of the mind, frequently either cause credit to be given to an accusation or to be withheld from it; *manner* of living, for it is often a matter of inquiry whether a person is luxurious, or parsimonious, or mean; *occupations,* for a countryman, a lawyer, a trader, a soldier, a mariner, a physician, act in very different ways. We must consider also *what a person affects,* whether he would wish to appear rich or eloquent, just or powerful. *Previous doings and sayings,* too, are to be taken into account; for the present is commonly estimated from the past. To these some add *commotion of the mind,* which they wish to be understood in the sense of a temporary excitement of the feelings, as anger, or fear; and *designs,* which respect the present, past, and future, but these, though they are accidents of person, should yet be referred, I think, as considered in themselves, to that species of argument which we derive from motives; as also certain *dispositions of mind,* in regard to which it is considered whether a particular person is a *friend* or an *enemy* of another person. [V, 10, 23-9]

. . . . .

I now come to *things,* among which *actions* are most closely connected with persons, and must therefore be first considered. In regard, then, to everything that is done, the question is, either *why,* or *where,* or *when,* or *in what manner,* or *by what means,* it was done. Arguments are consequently derived from the *motives for actions done* or *to be done.* [V, 10, 32-3]

. . . . .

Questions of definition, too, sometimes depend upon motives, as *whether he is a tyrannicide who killed a tyrant by whom he had been caught in adultery;* and *whether he is guilty of sacrilege who took down arms suspended in a temple to drive out enemies of his city.* Arguments are also drawn from *places;* for it often concerns the proof of a fact, *whether the scene of it was mountainous or level, maritime or inland, planted or uncultivated, frequented or lonely, near or distant, suitable or unsuitable for the alleged purpose;* considerations which Cicero treats with very great effect in his defence of Milo. These and similar points most commonly relate to questions of fact, but sometimes also to questions of law, as *whether a place be private or public, sacred or profane, our own or belonging to another....* [V, 10, 36-8]

. . . . .

Place, too, frequently affects the *quality* of an action; for the same act is not allowable or becoming in all places alike; and it is likewise of consequence before what people a question is tried; for every people has its peculiar customs and laws. [V, 10, 40]

. . . . .

Besides it is to be observed that arguments of all kinds are readily drawn either from circumstances that *preceded* the fact in question, or occurred *at the same time* with it, or *happened after* it: From *previous* circumstances, as, *You threatened the deceased with death, you went out at night, you went before him on the road*; and motives for deeds, too, relate to time past: From *contemporaneous* circumstances, which some have distinguished more nicely than was necessary, dividing them into that which is *combined* with an act, as, *A noise was heard,* and that which is *attached* to an act, as, *A cry was raised*: From *subsequent* circumstances, as, *You concealed yourself; you fled; discolorations and swellings appeared on the body.* [V, 10, 45-6]

. . . . .

We must also, especially in questions of fact, regard the *means* of which a party was possessed; for probability inclines us to suppose that a smaller number was killed by a larger, a weaker by a stronger, people asleep by people awake, the unsuspecting by the well-prepared. [V, 10, 49]

. . . . .

Arguments, then, are drawn from *definition,* ... of which there are two modes; for we either inquire simply *whether such a thing is a virtue,* or with a definition previously given, *what virtue is.* [V, 10, 54]

. . . . .

We also define a thing by its nature, ... or by reference to etymology.... [V, 10, 55]

. . . . .

To definitions seem especially to belong *genus, species, difference, property.* [V, 10, 55]

. . . . .

Properties, have reference also to questions dependent on conjecture; for, as it is the property of a good man to act rightly, and of a passionate man to be violent in his language, it is supposed that he who acts rightly is a good man, and that he who is violent in his language is a passionate one.... [V, 10, 64]

* * * * *

Division, in a similar way, serves to prove and to refute. For proof it is sometimes sufficient to establish one half; as in this example: *A man, to be a citizen, must either have been born a citizen, or have been made one*; but in refuting you must overthrow both particulars and show that *he was neither born nor made a citizen.* [V, 10, 65]

* * * * *

As there are three parts of time, so the order of things is comprised in three stages of progress; for everything has a *beginning,* an *increase,* and a *completion;* as first, for instance, there is a quarrel, then one man's blood is shed, then that of several. Here then is an origin for arguments supporting one another; for the *end* may be inferred from the *beginning.* ... [V, 10, 71]

* * * * *

Arguments are also drawn from *similarities*: *If continence be a virtue, abstinence is also a virtue*; *If a guardian ought to give security so likewise should an agent.* [V, 10, 73]

* * * * *

From *dissimilarities*: *If joy is a good, pleasure is not therefore necessarily a good.* ... [V, 10, 73]

* * * * *

From *contrarieties*: *Frugality is a good, for extravagance is an evil.* [V, 10, 73]

* * * * *

From *contradictions*: *He who is wise, is not a fool.* From *consequences* or *adjuncts*: *If justice is a good, we ought to judge with justice; If deceit is an evil, we must not deceive*; and such propositions may be reversed. [V, 10, 74]

* * * * *

Nor are the arguments that follow dissimilar to these; so that they may properly be ranged under the same head, to which, indeed, they naturally belong: *What a man never had he has not lost; A person whom we love we shall not knowingly injure; For a person whom a man has resolved to make his heir, he has had, has, and will have, affection.* But as such arguments are incontrovertible, they partake of the nature of necessary indications. The latter sort, however, I call arguments from what is consequent. . . . [V, 10, 74-5]

. . . . .

There is also a kind of argument from two propositions *relatively consequent,* and which proves the same thing from opposite statements; as, *He who says that the world was produced, says also that it will come to an end; for everything which is produced, comes to an end.* Similar to this is the kind of argument by which that which is done is inferred from that which does, or the contrary; which rhetoricians call an argument *from causes.* Sometimes the consequence *necessarily* happens, sometimes *generally,* though *not necessarily.* Thus *a body,* for example, *casts a shadow in the light, and, wherever there is a shadow, it necessarily proves that there is a body.* [V, 10, 79-80]

. . . . .

Arguments of necessary consequence both from cause and effect are such as these: *If it is wisdom that makes a man good, a good man is necessarily wise.* . . . [V, 10, 82]

. . . . .

Arguments called *apposite* or *comparative* are such as prove the greater from the less, the less from the greater, or equals from equals. A *conjecture* about a fact is supported by arguing from something greater: as, *If a man commits sacrilege, he will also commit an ordinary theft;* from something less, as, *He who readily and boldly tells a lie, will commit perjury.* [V, 10, 86-7]

. . . . .

To sum up the whole in a few words, then, arguments are drawn from *persons, causes, places, time,* . . . *manner, means, definition, genus, species, differences, peculiarities, removal, division, beginning, increase, completion, similarity, dissimilarity, contraries, consequences, causes, effects, issues, connexion, comparison;* each of which is divided into several species. [V, 10, 94]

. . . . .

It seems necessary to be added that arguments are deduced not only from acknowledged facts, but from fictions or suppositions. . . . [V, 10, 95]

. . . . .

But as it is not sufficient to know that *all proofs are to be drawn from persons or from things,* because each of these general heads branches out into an infinity of others, so he who shall have learned that arguments are to be deduced from *preceding* or *coincident* or *subsequent* circumstances, will not necessarily be qualified to judge what arguments proper for any particular cause are to be deduced from such circumstances; especially as most proofs are taken from what is inherent in the nature of a cause, and have nothing in common with any other cause; and these proofs, while they are the strongest, are also the least obvious, because, though we learn from rules what is common to all causes, what is peculiar to any particular cause we have to discover for ourselves. This kind of arguments we may well call arguments from *circumstances,* . . . or from those things which are proper to any individual cause. [V, 10, 100-4]

. . . . .

But no less care ought to be taken as to what you advance, than as to the manner in which what you advance is to be proved. Here the power of invention, if not the greatest, is certainly the first requisite; for as arrows are useless to him who knows not at what he should aim, so arguments are useless to him who has not ascertained to what point they are to be applied. [V, 10, 109]

. . . . .

Let students of eloquence consider also, that every point to which I have called their attention is not to be found in every cause; and that, when a subject for discussion is brought before them, they need not search for every topic of argument, and knock as it were, at its door, to know whether it will answer, and serve to prove what they desire; they need not do this, I say, unless while they are still learners, and destitute of experience. [V, 10, 122]

[*Examples*]

The third sort of proofs, which are introduced into causes *from without,* . . . [let me] translate . . . by *example.* [V, 11, 1]

. . . . .

All arguments, therefore, of this kind, must either be from things *similar,* or *dissimilar,* or *contrary.* Similitudes are sometimes sought, merely for the embellishment of speech; . . . Of all descriptions of proof the more efficacious is that which we properly term *example;* that is, the adducing of some historical fact, or supposed fact, intended to convince the hearer of that which we desire to impress upon him. We must consider, therefore, whether such fact is completely similar to what we wish to illustrate, or only partly so; that we may either adopt the whole of it, or only such portion of it as may serve our purpose. It is a similitude when we say, *Saturninus was justly killed, as were the Gracchi.* A dissimilitude, when we say, *Brutus put his children to death for forming traitorous designs on their country; Manlius punished the valour of his son with death.* A contrariety, when we say, *Marcellus restored the ornaments of their city to the Syracusans, who were our enemies; Verres took away like ornaments from our allies.* [V, 11, 5-7]

. . . . .

Next to example, *comparison* is of the greatest effect, especially that which is made between things nearly equal, without any mixture of metaphor: *As those who have been accustomed to receive money in the Campus Martius, are generally most adverse to those candidates whose money they suppose to be withheld, so judges of a similar disposition came to the tribunal with a hostile feeling towards the defendant.* [V, 11, 22]

. . . . .

Some have separated *analogy* from *similitude*; I consider it comprehended in similitude. For when we say, *As one is to ten, so are ten to a hundred,* there is a similitude, as much as there is when we say, *As is an enemy, so is a bad citizen.* [V, 11, 34]

. . . . .

Hence there have been some that have placed *examples* and *authorities* in the number of *inartificial proofs,* as the orator does not invent them, but merely adopts them. But there is a great difference; for witnesses, and examinations, and like matters, decide on the subject that is before the judges; while arguments *from without,* unless they are made of avail, by the ingenuity of the pleader, to support his allegations, have no force. [V, 11, 43-4]

[*Position of Arguments*]

We must insist on the strongest of our arguments singly; the weaker must be advanced in a body; for the former kind, which are strong in themselves, we must not obscure by surrounding matter, but take care that they may appear exactly as they are; the other sort, which are naturally weak, will support themselves by mutual aid; and, therefore, if they cannot prevail from being strong, they will prevail from being numerous, as the object of all is to establish the same point. [V, 12, 4]

. . . . .

It is also inquired, whether the strongest arguments should be placed in front, that they may take forcible possession of the judge's mind, or in the rear, that they may leave an impression upon it, or partly in front and partly in the rear, so that, according to Homer's arrangement, the weakest may be in the middle; or whether they should be in a progressive order, commencing with the weakest. But the disposition of the arguments must be such as the nature of the cause requires; a rule, as I think, with only one exception, *that our series must not descend from the strongest to the weakest.* [V, 12, 14]

[*Refutation*]

Refutation may be understood in two senses: for the part of the defender consists wholly in refutation; and whatever is said by either party in opposition to the other, requires to be refuted. It is properly in the latter sense that the fourth place is assigned to it in judicial pleadings. But the manner of conducting both is similar; for the principles of argument in refutation can be drawn from no other sources than those used in affirmation. . . . [V, 13, 1]

. . . . .

It is a point of great importance to consider *what* the opposite party has said, and *in what manner*. We must first of all examine, therefore, whether that which we have to answer belongs properly to the cause, or has been introduced into it extrinsically; for if it be inherent in the cause, we must either deny it, or justify it, or prove that the action is illegally brought; besides these there is scarcely any means of defence in any kind of trial. *Deprecation,* at least such as is without appearance of defence, is extremely rare, and before such judges only as are confined to no certain form of decision. . . . [V, 13, 4-5]

. . . . .

Of negation I have specified two forms; that *the matter in question did not happen,* or that *what did happen is not the matter in question.* What cannot be justified, or set aside on a point of law, must necessarily be denied, not only if a definition of it may prove in our favour, but even if nothing but simple denial is left to us. If *witnesses* be produced, we may say much against them; if *writings,* we may descant on the resemblance of hands. Certainly nothing can be worse than confession. When there is no ground either for justification or denial, the last resource for maintaining our cause is *legal exception.* [V, 13, 7-8]

. . . . .

We must consider also whether we ought to attack the charges of an accuser in a body, or overthrow them one by one. We may assail a number at once, if they are either so weak that they may be borne down in a mass, or so annoying that it is not expedient to engage them in detail; for we must then struggle with our whole force, and, if I may be allowed the expression, must fight with the enemy front to front. [V, 13, 11]

. . . . .

The form of our refutation, therefore, must be adapted to the interest of our cause; we may sometimes state the arguments of our adversary separately, and sometimes collect them into a body. . . . [V, 13, 13]

. . . . .

But the defendant must consider *in what manner* that which has been stated by the prosecutor must be refuted. It it be evidently false, it will be sufficient to deny it. . . . [V, 13, 15]

. . . . .

It is the business of a pleader, however, at times, to represent the statements of the adversary in such a way that they may either appear contradictory, or foreign to the question, or incredible, or superfluous, or favourable to our side rather than his own. [V, 13, 17]

. . . . .

As to other charges, the mode of refuting them all is much the same; for they are either to be examined by *conjecture,* whether they are true; or by *definition,* whether they properly concern the cause; or, with regard to their *quality,* whether they are dishonourable, unjust, scandalous, inhuman, cruel, or deserve any other designation that falls under the head of quality. [V, 13, 19]

. . . . .

Common arguments are easily apprehended, but not only because they may be used by either party, but because they are of more service to the defendant than to the prosecutor; for I think it no trouble to repeat what I have often intimated, that he who is the first to employ a common argument, renders it adverse to him; for that is adverse to him which his opponent can use equally well. [V, 13, 29]

. . . . .

But it is the part of a skilful pleader to discover in the case of his adversary particulars that are at variance with one another, or that may be made to appear at variance. . . . [V, 13, 30]

. . . . .

Sometimes an inadvertent remark of our opponent affords us an opportunity of exposing his statements. [V, 13, 31]

. . . . .

Sometimes, for the purpose of effacing an unpleasant impression, what is said severely by one party is eluded with a jest by the other. [V, 13, 40]

. . . . .

It is also a fault in a pleader to be too anxious, and to labour at removing everything that stands in his way; for such solicitude excites distrust in the judge; and very frequently arguments, which, if stated off hand, would have removed all doubt, but which are tardily advanced through excessive precaution, lose credit, because the advocate himself seems to think something additional necessary to support what he alleges. An orator, therefore, should carry confidence in his manner, and speak as if he had the highest assurance of the success of his cause. [V, 13, 51]

. . . . .

As to *order*, there is no part of a cause in which it will give us less trouble; for, if we are the prosecutors, we have first to support our own allegations, and then to refute what is brought against them; if we are defendants, we have to commence with refutation. [V, 13, 53]

[*Syllogisms*]

The *enthymeme* is called by some an oratorical syllogism, by others a part of a syllogism, because the syllogism has always its regular proposition and conclusion, and establishes by means of all its parts that which it has proposed; while the enthymeme is satisfied if merely what is stated in it be understood. [V, 14, 24]

. . . . .

For though I do not think it unlawful to use syllogisms occasionally in a speech, yet I should by no means like it to consist wholly of syllogisms, or to be crowded with a mass of epicheiremata and enthymemes, for it would then resemble the dialogues and disputations of logicians, rather than oratorical pleading; and the two differ widely from one another. [V, 14, 27]

. . . . .

. . . But we orators must compose our speeches to suit the judgment of others, and must frequently speak before people altogether uneducated, or at least ignorant of any other literature than what we teach them, and unless we allure them by gratification, attract them by force, and occasionally excite their feelings, we shall never impress upon them what is just and true. Oratory should be rich and brilliant; but it will have neither of those qualities, if it be pieced out of regular and frequent syllogisms, expressed almost always in the same form, for it will then incur contempt from appearing mean, and aversion from looking servile; if it is copious, it will excite satiety; if it attempts to be swelling, it will meet disdain. Let it hold its course, therefore, not along foot-paths, but through open fields; let it not be like subterranean springs confined in narrow channels, but flow like broad rivers through whole valleys, forcing a way wherever it does not find one. For what is a greater misery to speakers than to be slaves to certain rules. . . . [V, 14, 29-31]

[Peroration]

What was to follow, was the *peroration*, which some have termed the *completion*, and others the *conclusion*. There are two species of it, the one comprising the substance of the speech, and the other adapted to excite the feelings. [VI, 1, 1]

. . . . .

In this part of our speech, what we repeat ought to be repeated as briefly as possible, and we must, as is intimated by the Greek term, run over only the principal heads; for, if we dwell upon them, the result will be, not a recapitulation, but a sort of second speech. [VI, 1, 2]

. . . . .

Both of them also have recourse to the excitement of the feelings; but the defendant more rarely, the prosecutor more frequently and with greater earnestness; for the prosecutor has to rouse the judge, while the defendant's business is to soothe him. [VI, 1, 9]

. . . . .

But the most effective way for the accuser to excite the feelings of the judge, is to make that which he lays to the charge of the accused appear the most *atrocious* act possible, or, if the subject allow, the most *deplorable*. [VI, 1, 15]

. . . . .

The accuser, also, often attempts to excite pity, as when he bewails the sad fate of him whose cause he is pleading, or the destitution of his children or parents. [VI, 1, 18]

. . . . .

Yet our supplications for pity should not be long as it is observed, not without reason, that *nothing dries sooner than tears.* [VI, 1, 27]

. . . . .

We may excite tears, however not only by words, but by acts; and hence it becomes a practice to exhibit persons on their trial in a squalid and pitiful garb, accompanied with their children and parents; hence, too, we see blood-stained swords produced by accusers with fractured bones extracted from wounds, and garments spotted with blood; we behold wounds unbound, and scourged backs exposed to view. [VI, 1, 30]

. . . . .

The student ought above all things to be admonished, also, that an orator should not attempt to excite tears, unless he be endowed with extraordinary genius; for as the effect on the feelings, if he succeeds, is extremely powerful, so, if he is unsuccessful, the result is vapidity; and a middling pleader had better leave the pathos to the quiet meditations of the judges. . . . [VI, 1, 44]

. . . . .

But the business of a peroration is not only to excite feelings of pity, but also to deaden them, either by a set speech, which may recall the judges, when shaken by compassion, to considerations of justice, or by some jocose remark. . . . [VI, 1, 46]

. . . . .

But all these addresses to the feelings, though they are thought by some to have a place only in the exordium and the peroration, in which indeed they are most frequently introduced, are admissible also in other parts, but more sparingly, as it is from them that the decision of the cause must be chiefly evolved; but in the peroration, if anywhere, we may call forth all the resources of eloquence. . . . [VI, 1, 51]

[*Use of Emotional Proof*]

A duty of the orator, accordingly, still remains to be considered, which is of the greatest efficacy in securing his success, and is of far more difficulty than any of those already noticed, I mean that of influencing the minds of the judges, and of moulding and transforming them, as it were, to that disposition which we wish them to assume. [VI, 2, 1]

. . . . .

Throughout the whole of any cause, as I remarked, there is room for addresses to the feelings. [VI, 2, 2]

[*Ethical Proof*]

The [ethos], of which we form a conception, and which we desire to find in speakers, is recommended, above all, by goodness, being not only mild and placid, but for the most part pleasing and polite, and amiable and attractive to the hearers; and the greatest merit in the expression of it, is, that it should seem to flow from the nature of the things and persons with which we are concerned, so that the moral character of the speaker may clearly appear, and be recognized as it were, in his discourse. [VI, 2, 13]

. . . . .

All this species of eloquence, however, requires the speaker to be a man of good character, and of pleasing manners. The virtues which he ought to praise, if possible, in his client, he should possess, or be thought to possess, himself. [VI, 2, 18]

. . . . .

But he who, while he speaks, is thought a bad man, must certainly speak ineffectively; for he will not be thought to speak sincerely; if he did, his [ethos], or character, would appear. [VI, 2, 18]

. . . . .

This kind of eloquence is almost wholly engaged in exciting anger, hatred, fear, envy, or pity; and from what sources its topics are to be drawn is manifest to all, and has been mentioned by me in speaking of the exordium and peroration. [VI, 2, 20]

. . . . .

The chief requisite, then, for moving the feelings of others, is, as far as I can judge, that we ourselves be moved; for the assumption of grief, and anger, and indignation, will be often ridiculous, if we adapt merely our words and looks, and not our minds, to those passions. [VI, 2, 26]

. . . . .

In delivering, therefore, whatever we wish to appear like truth, let us assimilate ourselves to the feelings of those who are truly affected, and let our language proceed from such a temper of mind as we would wish to excite in the judge. [VI, 2, 27]

. . . . .

Though I should wish an orator, moreover, to speak with wit, I should certainly not wish him to seem to affect wit; and he must not therefore speak facetiously as often as he can, but must rather lose a joke occasionally, than lower his dignity. [VI, 3, 30]

[*Division, Partition, Arrangement*]

Let *division*, then, . . . be the distribution of a number of things into its component parts; *partition*, the regular distribution of parts into their members, and a just disposition connecting those that follow with those that precede; and *arrangement* a due distribution of things and their parts in their proper places. But let us remember that arrangement is often altered to suit the interest of a cause, and that the same question is not always discussed first by both parties. . . . [VII, 1, 1-2]

. . . . .

It was my great care, in forensic pleadings, to ascertain, in the first place, all the points that were concerned in any cause. . . . [VII, 1, 4]

. . . . .

First, then, (what is not difficult to be ascertained, but is above all to be regarded,) I settled *what* each party wished to establish, and then *by what means*, in the following way. I considered what the prosecutor would state first; this would either be an *admitted*, or a *contested* point. If it were admitted, the question could not lie in it. I passed therefore to the answer of the defendant, and considered it in the same way. Sometimes, too, what was elicited from thence was admitted. But as soon as there began to be any disagreement, the question arose. [VII, 1, 5-6]

. . . . .

As to what concerns the accuser, I do not altogether dissent from Celsus, who, doubtless following Cicero, persists in maintaining somewhat too positively, on this head, that strong arguments should be advanced in the first place, the strongest of all in the last, and the weaker in the middle; because the judge requires to be moved at the beginning, and pressed forcibly at the end. But on the side of the accused, the strongest argument against him must first be attacked, lest the judge, looking to that point, should regard with too little favour our establishment of other points. Yet this order may occasionally be changed, if the lighter points be evidently false, and the refutation of the heaviest charge extremely difficult; so that, after thus detracting from the credit of the accusers, we may proceed to the last point, when the judge is ready to suppose that *all* the charges may be false. [VII, 1, 10-11]

. . . . .

Hence it is that, after considering some questions, we concede or grant them to the opposite party; for we cannot pass to others unless by dismissing those that come first. This ought to be done in such a manner, that we may not appear to have despaired of them, but to have set them aside, because we can establish our cause without them. [VII, 1, 18-19]

. . . . .

I used also to select those points in which I agreed with my opponent, provided they were to my purpose, and not only to press such matters as he admitted, but to multiply them by division. . . . [VII, 1, 29]

. . . . .

What the accused has done, is sometimes set forth very forcibly in the statement of the case, and, if it takes possession of the mind of the judge, his ears are almost closed against the defence. In general, it is to the advantage of the accuser to amass facts, and of the defendant to separate them. [VII, 1, 31]

. . . . .

All conjecture has reference either to *fact* or *intent*. To each belong three parts of time, the *past,* the *present,* and the *future.* Concerning *fact* there are both *general* and *particular questions*; that is, such as are not limited to the consideration of certain circumstances, and such as are so limited. About *intent* there can be no question, unless where there is a person concerned, and a fact is admitted. [VII, 2, 1-2]

. . . . .

Next to conjecture respecting a fact comes *definition* of it, for he who is unable to prove that he has done nothing, will try, in the next place, to make it appear that he has not done that which is laid to his charge. [VII, 3, 1]

. . . . .

Definition, then, is *an explication of something in question, proper, clear, and concisely expressed.* It consists chiefly, as has been said, in the notification of *genus, species, differences, and peculiarities.* ... [VII, 3, 2-3]

. . . . .

The invariable order in definition is *what a thing is*, and *whether it is this*; and in general there is more difficulty in establishing the definition than in applying it to the matter in hand. [VII, 3, 19]

. . . . .

When it is decided *what a thing is*, the question, *whether it is this*, is almost settled. [VII, 3, 28]

. . . . .

As to *quality*, it is sometimes considered in the most comprehensive sense, and in reference to more points than one; .... [VII, 4, 1]

. . . . .

When the point for decision has respect to punishment, there is offered on the part of him who is accused, either *justification of the charge, or extenuation* of it, or *excuse*, or, as some think, *deprecation.* Of these the most efficient is *justification*, by which we make it appear that the act, which is laid to the charge of the accused, was unobjectionable. [VII, 4, 3-4]

. . . . .

There is another mode of defence, in which we justify an act in itself indefensible by aids drawn *from without.* ... [VII, 4, 7]

. . . . .

In this kind of defence the strongest plea is when we justify the act by the motive of it; such is the plea of Orestes, Horatius, and Milo. It is also called ... "recrimination," because all our defence depends on accusing the person who is indicated by the other party: *He was killed, but he was a robber; he was emasculated, but he was a ravisher.* [VII, 4, 8]

. . . . .

Such are the modes of proceeding in defence of an act; but if a defence can neither be sustained on the motive of the act itself, nor by extrinsic aid, our next course is to *transfer the charge,* if we find it possible, on another party. Hence *translation,* or "exception," has been regarded as forming one of those *states* which have been previously mentioned. [VII, 4, 13]

. . . . .

Should these modes of defence fail us, there remains *excuse,* founded either on *ignorance* or on *necessity.* [VII, 4, 14]

. . . . .

If, again, none of those means which have been mentioned can avail us, we must see whether the charge can be *extenuated.* This is what is by some said to be the *state of quantity.* [VII, 4, 15]

. . . . .

The last method of all is *deprecation;* a mode of address which most rhetoricians do not allow to be admissible into judicial pleadings. . . . [VII, 4, 17]

. . . . .

There remains then only the arrangement of *parts;* and in the parts themselves there must be some one thought first, another second, another third, and so on; and we must take care that these thoughts be not merely placed in a certain order, but that they be also connected one with another, cohering so closely that no joining may appear between them; so that they may form a body, and not a mere collection of members. This object will be attained, if we take care to observe what is suitable for each place, and study to bring together words that will not combat but embrace each other. Thus different things will not seem hurried together from distant parts, all strangers one to another, but will unite themselves, in a sure bond and alliance, with those that precede and those that follow; and our speech will appear not merely a combination of phrases, but all of a piece. [VII, 10, 16-17]

[*Style*]

Let the greatest possible care, then, be bestowed on expression, provided we bear in mind that nothing is to be done for the sake of words, as words themselves were invented for the sake of things, and as those words are the most to be commended which express our thoughts best, and produce the impression which we desire on the minds of the judges. Such words undoubtedly must make a speech both worthy of admiration and productive of pleasure; but not of that kind of *admiration* with which we wonder at monsters; or of that kind of *pleasure* which is attended with unnatural gratification, but such as is compatible with true merit and worth. [VIII, Introd., 32-3]

. . . . .

In reference to words considered singly, we must take care that they be *Latin, intelligible, elegant,* and *appropriate* to that which we wish to express; in regard to words in conjunction, we must see that they be *correct, well arranged,* and *diversified occasionally with figures.* [VIII, 1, 1]

[*Perspicuity*]

With me, however, let the first virtue of composition be *perspicuity*; let there be proper words, and a clear order; let not the conclusion of the sense be too long protracted; and let there be nothing either deficient or superfluous. Thus will our language both deserve the commendation of the learned, and be intelligible to the unlearned.

These observations refer to perspicuity in our words; for how perspicuity in our matter is to be secured, I have shown in my rules concerning the statement of cases. But the case is similar with regard to both; for if we say neither less nor more than we ought, nor anything ill-arranged or indistinct, what we state will be clear, and intelligible even to the moderately attentive hearer. We must bear in mind, indeed, that the attention of the judge is not always so much on the alert as to dispel of itself the obscurity of our language, and to throw the light of his intellect on our darkness, but that he is often distracted by a multiplicity of other thoughts, which will prevent him from understanding us, unless what we say be so clear that its sense will strike his mind as the rays of the sun strike the eyes, even though his attention be not immediately fixed upon it. We must, therefore, take care, not merely that he may understand us, but that he may not be able not to understand us. It is for this reason that we often repeat what we fancy that those who are trying the cause may not have sufficiently comprehended; using such phrases as, *That part of our cause, which, through my fault, has been stated but obscurely,* etc., *on which account I shall have recourse to plainer and more common language;* since, when we pretend, occasionally, that we have not fully succeeded, the admission is sure to be well received from us. [VIII, 2, 22-4]

[*Embellishment*]

I come now to the subject of *embellishment*, in which doubtless, more than in any other department of oratory, the speaker is apt to give play to his fancy. For the praise of such as speak merely with correctness and perspicuity is but small; since they are thought rather to have avoided faults than to have attained any great excellence. [VIII, 3, 1]

. . . . .

But let the embellishment of our style . . . be manly, noble, and chaste; let it not affect effeminate delicacy, or a complexion counterfeited by paint, but let it glow with genuine health and vigour. [VIII, 3, 6]

. . . . .

Recurring to our first division, we may remark that the same kind of embellishment will not be alike suitable for *demonstrative, deliberative,* and *judicial* topics. [VIII, 3, 11]

. . . . .

Though it has been justly said that perspicuity is better promoted by *proper* words, and embellishment by such as are *metaphorical,* we should feel certain, at the same time, that whatever is *improper* cannot *embellish.* [VIII, 3, 15]

. . . . .

Our language indeed is not always to be elevated, but sometimes to be depressed. Humility in our words sometimes gives of itself greater force to what we say. [VIII, 3, 21]

. . . . .

Words are *proper, newly coined,* or *metaphorical.* To proper words antiquity adds dignity; for old words, such as every writer would not think of using, render language more majestic and venerable. [VIII, 3, 24]

[*Making Style Elegant*]

Let us then proceed to consider the nature of *connected discourse,* the embellishment of which requires, above all, attention to two points; *what language we conceive in our minds, and how we express it.* In the first place, we must settle what we would wish to amplify or extenuate; what we would express vehemently or calmly, floridly or austerely, verbosely or concisely, roughly or mildly, grandly or simply, impressively or attractively. We must also consider with what kind of metaphors or other figures, with what thoughts, in what style, and with what arrangement of matter, we may be likely to effect the object which we wish to accomplish.

But in attempting to show by what means a style may be rendered elegant, I shall first touch on the faults which are opposed to elegance; for the beginning of excellence is to be free from error. We must first of all, then, not expect that a style will be elegant which is not appropriate. [VIII, 3, 40-2]

. . . . .

The next fault to unseemliness of expression is that of meanness, ... [VIII, 3, 48]

. . . . .

We must also avoid the fault called . . . , "diminution," when something is wanting to an expression, so that it is not sufficiently full; though this indeed is rather a fault of obscurity than of neglect of ornament in style. [VIII, 3, 50]

. . . . .

A worse fault than this . . . , "sameness of style," which relieves the weariness of the reader with no gratification from variety, but is all of one complexion, by which it is fully proved to be deficient in oratorical art; and, from the tameness of its thoughts and figures of speech, as well as from the monotony of its phraseology, it is most disagreeable not only to the mind but also to the ear. [VIII, 3, 52]

. . . . .

Another fault is . . . , "pleonasm," when a sentence is burdened with superfluous words, as *I saw with my eyes*; for *I saw* is sufficient. [VIII, 3, 53]

. . . . .

There is also a fault called . . . , *superfluous operoseness*, if I may so express myself, differing from judicious care, just as a fidgetty man differs from an industrious one, or as superstition from religion; and, to make an end of my remarks on this point, every word that contributes neither to the sense nor to the embellishment of what we write, may be called vicious. [VIII, 3, 55]

. . . . .

Injudicious affectation, is a fault in every kind of style; for whatever is *tumid*, or *jejune*, or *luscious*, or *redundant*, or *far-fetched*, or *unequal*, may come under this term. . . . [VIII, 3, 56]

. . . . .

Faults in *matter* are, that it is *void of sense*, or *common*, or *contradictory*, or *redundant;* corruption of *style* arises chiefly from the use of words that are *improper, superfluous*, or *obscure in meaning*, or from *feebleness in composition*, or *puerile seeking for similar or equivocal expressions.* [VIII, 3, 57]

. . . . .

The following blemishes also spoil the beauty of composition: *Want of proper arrangement,* . . . *unskilful use of figures,* . . . *inelegant junction of words or phrases.* . . . [VIII, 3, 59]

. . . . .

To throw light upon descriptions *similes* have been very happily invented; some of which, as they strengthen proof, are numbered among arguments; others are adapted to give a lively representation of things. . . . [VIII, 3, 72]

. . . . .

In the use of this kind of illustration we must take the greatest care that what we introduce by way of similitude may not be obscure or unknown; for that which is offered as an illustration of something else, ought to be plainer than that which it is meant to illustrate. [VIII, 3, 73]

. . . . .

It would not become an orator to demonstrate something plain by a reference to something obscure. [VIII, 3, 74]

. . . . .

A beauty akin to the preceding, but of higher merit, is *emphasis*, which intimates a deeper meaning than the words used actually express. [VIII, 3, 83]

. . . . .

And there is a certain pleasing delicacy of style that arises from a nicety of care about the propriety and significancy of words. Of *copiousness* there is one kind that is rich in thought, and another that abounds with flowers. Of *force* there is more than one species; for whatever is complete in its kind, has its proper force. [VIII, 3, 87-8]

. . . . .

I see that amplification, however, is effected chiefly in four ways; by *augmentation*, by *comparison*, by *reasoning*, and by *accumulation*. [VIII, 4, 3]

[Tropes]

A trope is the conversion of a word or phrase, from its proper signification to another, in order to increase its force. [VIII, 6, 1]

. . . . .

I shall speak only of those tropes which are most important and most in use; and in regard to these, too, I shall content myself with observing, that some are adopted for the purpose of adding to *significance*, others for the sake of *ornament;* that some take place in words used *properly*, and others in words used *metaphorically;* and that tropes occur, not only in *single words*, but also in *thoughts*, and in the *structure of composition*. [VIII, 6, 2]

. . . . .

Let us commence, however, with that species of trope, which is both the most common and by far the most beautiful, I mean that which consists in what we call *translatio*. . . .

Metaphor is not only so natural to us, that the illiterate and others often use it unconsciously, but is so pleasing and ornamental, that, in any composition, however brilliant, it will always make itself apparent by its own lustre. If it be but rightly managed, it can never be either vulgar, or mean, or disagreeable. It increases the copiousness of a language, by allowing it to borrow what it does not naturally possess; and, what is its greatest achievement, it prevents an appellation from being wanting for anything whatever. A noun or a verb is accordingly transferred, as it were, from that place in the language to which it properly belongs, to one in which there is either no proper word, or in which the metaphorical word is preferable to the proper. This change we make, either because it is *necessary*, or because it *adds to significance*, or, as I said, because it is more *ornamental*. [VIII, 6, 4-6]

. . . . .

What I say of metaphor may be applied, perhaps with more force, to *synecdoche;* for metaphor has been invented for the purpose of exciting the mind, giving a character to things, and setting them before the eye; synecdoche is adapted to give variety to language, by letting us understand the plural from the singular, the whole from a part, a genus from the species, something following from something preceding. . . . [VIII, 6, 19]

. . . . .

But by far the most ornamental kind of language is that in which the graces of the three figures *comparison, allegory,* and *metaphor* are united. [VIII, 6, 49]

. . . . .

There is, besides, another use of allegory, in enabling us to speak of melancholy things in words of a more cheering nature, or to signify our meaning, for some good purpose, in language at variance with it. . . . [VIII, 6, 57]

. . . . .

Hyperbaton, also, that is, *verbi transgressio,* "transposition of words," as the harmony and beauty of composition often require it, we rank, not improperly, among the excellences of language. For speech would often become rough and harsh, lax and nerveless, if words should be ranged exactly in their original order, and if, as each presents itself, it should be placed side by side of the preceding, though it cannot be fairly attached to it. [VIII, 6, 62]

[*Figures*]

Let the definition of a figure, then, be a *form of speech artfully varied from common usage.* [IX, 1, 14]

. . . . .

It is admitted, then, as far as I know, among most authors, that there are two kinds of figures, those of . . . thought, *mens, sensus,* or *sententiae,* for they are designated by all those terms, and those of . . . words, or diction, or expression, or language, or speech, for they have various names, and it is of no consequence by which name we call them. [IX, 1, 17]

. . . . .

What is more common than *interrogare,* "to ask," or *percontari,* "to question?" for we use both terms indifferently, though one seems to apply properly to mere desire of information, and the other to that of establishing proof. But the thing itself, by whatever name it be distinguished, is susceptible of many varieties of figure. [IX, 2, 6]

. . . . .

But it is an interrogation with a figure, when it is adopted, not for the sake of seeking information, but in order to attack the person

RHETORIC AND PUBLIC SPEAKING

interrogated; for example, *What was your drawn sword doing, Tubero, in the field of Pharsalia?* ... [IX, 2, 7]

. . . . .

A figure is sometimes adopted, too, in a reply; as when a person asks a question about one thing, and a reply is made to him about another more to the respondent's purpose. This may be done, for example, with the view of aggravating a charge; as when a witness against an accused person, being asked, *Whether he had been beaten with a stick by the accused,* replied, *Although I was innocent.* [IX, 2, 12]

. . . . .

Similar to this kind of answer is *dissimulation,* which is used only to excite laughter, and has consequently been noticed in its proper place; for if it be used seriously, it has the effect of a confession. [IX, 2, 14]

. . . . .

The practice also *of questioning and replying to one's self* is generally not unpleasing. ... [IX, 2, 14]

. . . . .

But what has a wonderful effect in pleadings is *anticipation,* ... and by which we prevent objections that may be brought against us. It is used, not sparingly, in other parts of a speech, but is of the greatest effect in the exordium. [IX, 2, 16]

. . . . .

Doubt also may give an air of truth to our statements, as when we feign, for example, to be at a loss where to begin, or where to end, or what to say in preference to something else, or whether we ought to speak at all. [IX, 2, 19]

. . . . .

There is no great difference between doubt and that sort of figure called *communication,* which we use either when we consult, as it were, our opponents, as Domitius Afer in pleading for Cloantilla, *In her agitation, she knows not what is permitted to her as a woman, nor what becomes her as a wife. Perhaps chance has thrown you in the way of the unhappy woman in her anxiety; what advice do you, her brother, and you, the friends of her father, offer?* Or when we pretend to deliberate with the judges, which is a very common artifice, saying, *what do you advise?* [IX, 2, 20-1]

. . . . .

The source of what we call *permission* is almost the same as that of communication. We are said to use this figure, when we leave something to be settled by the judges themselves, or sometimes even by the opposite party. . . . [IX, 2, 25]

. . . . .

As to the figures which are adapted for exciting the feelings, they consist chiefly in *simulation;* for we feign that we are angry, and that we rejoice, or fear, or wonder, or grieve, or feel indignant, or wish, or are moved by other similar affections. [IX, 2, 26]

. . . . .

A figure which is still bolder, and requires, as Cicero thinks, greater force, is the personation of characters, or *prosopopoeia.* This figure gives both variety and animation to eloquence, in a wonderful degree. By means of it, we display the thoughts of our opponents, as they themselves would do in a soliloquy; but our inventions of that sort will meet with credit only so far as we represent people saying what it is not unreasonable to suppose that they may have meditated; and so far as we introduce our own conversations with others, or those of others among themselves, with an air of plausibility, and when we invent persuasions, or reproaches, or complaints, or eulogies, or lamentations, and put them into the mouths of characters likely to utter them. [IX, 2, 29-31]

. . . . .

We also pretend at times, and with good effect, that the images of things and persons are before our eyes, and that their voices sound in our ears, and affect to wonder that the same appearances are not perceptible to our opponents or to the judges. . . . [IX, 2, 33]

. . . . .

This [apostrophe] is done by means of many and various figures; for example, when we feign that we expected something else, or that we feared something more considerable, or that some point may seem of greater importance to the judges, being but imperfectly informed on it, than it really is. [IX, 2, 39]

. . . . .

But as to the figure which, as Cicero says, *sets things before the eyes,* it is used, when a thing is not simply mentioned as having been done, but is mentioned with a representation how it was done, not merely in a general way, but in all its attendant circumstances. This

RHETORIC AND PUBLIC SPEAKING 145

figure I have noticed in the preceding book under *evidentia*, or "illustration." ... [IX, 2, 40]

. . . . .

Thus, as a continued metaphor constitutes an allegory, so a continuation of *ironical tropes* forms the *figure irony.* [IX, 2, 46]

. . . . .

Irony is also used when we assume the air of persons commanding or permitting something. ... [IX, 2, 48]

. . . . .

Or when we allow to our adversaries qualities which we should be unwilling to see recognized in them. ... [IX, 2, 49]

. . . . .

A similar effect is produced, though in a contrary way, when we own as it were to faults from which we are free, and which even touch our opponent. ... [IX, 2, 49]

. . . . .

Not very different from irony are these three modes of speaking, very similar to one another: the first, *Confession,* such as will not hurt the party who makes it; as, *You have, therefore, Tubero, what is most to be desired by an accuser, a confession from the accused;* the second, *Concession,* when we make a show of admitting something unfavourable to us, through confidence in our cause. ... [IX, 2, 51]

. . . . .

... The third, *Acknowledgment,* as Cicero in the same speech, acknowledges that *the judges had been bribed.* [IX, 2, 51]

. . . . .

Sometimes also we exaggerate charges against ourselves, when we might either refute or deny them; a practice which is too frequent to render an example of it necessary. Sometimes, again, by such exaggeration, we render charges against us incredible. [IX, 2, 53]

. . . . .

There is also a kind of *self-interruption,* which is not indeed an aposiopesis, so as to leave a speech unfinished, but a suspension of what we are saying before we come to the natural termination of it, as, *I am too urgent, the young man seems to be moved;* and, *Why should I say more? you have heard the young man himself speak.* [IX, 2, 57]

. . . . .

There are other artifices, too, which are not only pleasing, but are of great service in securing favourable attention to our arguments, as well by the variety which they give, as by their own nature; for, by making our speech appear plain and unstudied, they render us objects of less suspicion to the judge.

One of these is a *repenting,* as it were, of what we have said.... [IX, 2, 59-60]

. . . . .

Of a similar nature, also, are the expressions which we daily use, such as, *Inprudens incidi,* "I have hit upon the matter unawares. [IX, 2, 60]

. . . . .

Or when we pretend to find something suggested to us by the matter of which we are speaking. [IX, 2, 60]

. . . . .

It gives agreeableness to a speech, moreover, to *defer* the discussion of some points, laying them up as it were in the memory of the judge, and afterwards to *reclaim* what we have deposited, to *separate* certain particulars by some figure, (for separation is not itself a figure,) to *bring* others *prominently forward,* and to exhibit the subjects of our speech under various aspects; for eloquence delights in variety; and as the eyes are more attracted by the contemplation of diversified objects, so that is always more gratifying to the mind to which it directs itself with the expectation of novelty. [IX, 2, 63]

. . . . .

Among figures is also to be numbered *emphasis,* which is used when some latent sense is to be elicited from some word or phrase. [IX, 2, 64]

. . . . .

Similar to this figure, or identical with it, is one of which we make great use in the present day; for I must now proceed to treat of a sort of figure which is extremely common, and on which I believe it is earnestly expected that I should make some observations; a figure in which we intimate, by some suspicion that we excite, that something is to be understood which we do not express; not however something contrary to what we express,... but something latent, and to be discovered by the penetration of the hearer. This,... is almost the only mode of expression that is called, among our rhetoricians, *a figure;* and it is from the frequent use of it that certain pleadings have the name of *figurative*. It may be adopted for one of three reasons; first, if it is unsafe to speak plainly; secondly, if it is unbecoming to do so; and, thirdly, if recourse is had to the figure merely for the purpose of ornament, and of giving more pleasure, through novelty and variety, than would be felt if a straightforward narration were offered. [IX, 2, 65-6]

* * * * *

Figures, however, even if they be of the highest possible excellence, ought not to be numerous, for they betray themselves by multiplicity; and, while they are not less objectionable, are less effective. Our forbearance to speak plainly appears then to proceed, not from modesty, but from distrust of our cause; in a word, the judge puts most trust in our figures when he thinks that we are unwilling to express ourselves undisguisedly. [IX, 2, 72]

* * * * *

As to *verbal figures,* they have been perpetually subject to change, and continue to be changed as custom exerts its influence. When, accordingly, we compare the language of our forefathers with our own, we are led to regard almost every phrase that we use as figurative. . . . [IX, 3, 1]

* * * * *

However this may be, verbal figures are of two kinds; one, as they say, lies in the formation of phrases; the other is to be sought chiefly in the collocation of them; and though both kinds equally concern the art of oratory, yet we may call the one rather *grammatical* and the other rhetorical. [IX, 3, 2]

* * * * *

But what we ought chiefly to understand in regard to pleading is, what *places, persons,* and *occasions,* require; for the greater part of figures are intended to please; but when a speaker has to labour to excite emotions of indignation, hatred, or compassion, who would endure to hear him raging, lamenting, or supplicating, in studied antitheses, balanced clauses, and similar cadences? Affected attention to words, in such cases, destroys all trust in his expression of feeling, and, wherever art shows itself, truth is thought to be absent. [IX, 3, 102]

[*Style, continued*]

There are, then, in the first place, two kinds of style; one compact, and of a firm texture; the other of a looser nature, such as is used in common conversation and in familiar letters, except when they treat of something above their ordinary subjects, as questions of philosophy, politics, and the like. [IX, 4, 19]

. . . . .

Composition ... ought to be *elegant, pleasing,* and *varied.* The particulars that require attention in it are three, *order, connexion,* and *rhythm.* The *art* of it lies in adding, retrenching, and altering. The *quality* of it must be suited to the nature of the subjects on which we speak. The *care* required in it is great, but that devoted to thought and delivery should be greater. But all our care must be diligently concealed, in order that our numbers may seem to flow from us spontaneously, and not to be forced or studied. [IX, 4, 146-7]

[*Sources of Skill in Speaking*]

From these authors, and others worthy to be read, a stock of words, a variety of figures, and the art of composition, must be acquired; and our minds must be directed to the imitation of all their excellences; for it cannot be doubted that a great portion of art consists in *imitation,* since, though to invent was first in order of time, and holds the first place in merit, yet it is of advantage to copy what has been invented with success. Indeed the whole conduct of life is based on the desire of doing ourselves that which we approve in others. [X, 2, 1-2]

. . . . .

Such, then, are the means of improvement to be derived from external sources. But of those which we must secure for ourselves, *practice in writing,* which is attended with the most labour, is attended also with the greatest advantage. Nor has Cicero without reason called the pen *the best modeller and teacher of eloquence.* ... [X, 3, 1]

. . . . .

Next follows *correction,* which is by far the most useful part of our studies; for it is believed, and not without reason, that the pen is not least serviceable when it is used to erase. Of correction there are three ways, to *add,* to *take away,* and to *alter.* [X, 4, 1]

. . . . .

[*Extempore Speaking*]

But the richest fruit of all our study, and the most ample recompense for the extent of our labour, is *the faculty of speaking extempore;* and he who has not succeeded in acquiring it, will do well, in my opinion, to renounce the occupations of the forum, and devote his solitary talent of writing to some other employment; for it is scarcely consistent with the character of a man of honour to make a public profession of service to others which may fail in the most pressing emergencies, since it is of no more use than to point out a harbour to a vessel, to which it cannot approach unless it be borne along by the gentlest breezes. There arise indeed innumerable occasions where it is absolutely necessary to speak on the instant, as well before magistrates, as on trials that are brought on before the appointed time; and if any of these shall occur, I do not say to any one of our innocent fellow-citizens, but to any of our own friends or relatives, is an advocate to stand dumb, and, while they are begging for a voice to save them, and are likely to be undone if succour be not instantly afforded them, is he to ask time for retirement and silent study, till his speech be formed and committed to memory, and his voice and lungs be put in tune? [X, 7, 1-2]

. . . . .

Yet if any chance shall give rise to such a sudden necessity for speaking extempore, we shall have need to exert our mind with more than its usual activity; we must fix our whole attention on our matter, and relax, for the time, something of our care about words, if we find it impossible to attend to both. A slower pronunciation, too, and a mode of speaking with suspense and doubt, as it were, gives time for consideration; yet we must manage so that we may seem to deliberate and not to hesitate. [X, 7, 22]

[*Memory*]

I do not think that I need dwell on the consideration *what it is that constitutes memory.* Most, however, are of opinion that certain impressions are stamped on the mind, as the signets of rings are marked on wax. [XI, 2, 4]

. . . . .

If a long speech is to be retained in the memory, it will be of advantage to learn it in parts; for the memory sinks under a vast burden laid on it at once. At the same time, the portions should not be extremely short; for they will then distract and harass the memory. I cannot, however, prescribe any certain length, since this must be suited, as much as possible, to the different divisions of the subject, unless a division, perchance, be of such magnitude that it requires to be subdivided. But certain limits must assuredly be fixed, that frequent meditation may connect the series of words in each, which is attended with great difficulty, and that a repetition of the parts in their order may unite them into a whole. As to those which are least easily remembered, it will be of advantage to associate with them certain marks, the recollection of which may refresh and excite the memory. [XI, 2, 27-8]

. . . . .

If any one ask me, however, what is the only and great art of memory, I shall say that it is *exercise and labour*. To learn much by heart, to meditate much, and, if possible, daily, are the most efficacious of all methods. Nothing is so much strengthened by practice, or weakened by neglect, as memory. [XI, 2, 40]

. . . . .

From this difference in minds a question has arisen, *whether those who are going to deliver a speech should learn it by heart word for word, or whether it be sufficient to master merely the substance and order of particulars.* This is a point on which certainly no general decision can be given; for my own part, if my memory be sufficiently strong, and time be not wanting, I should wish not a single syllable to escape me; else it would be to no purpose to write. Such exactness we should acquire in childhood; and the memory should be brought to such a condition by exercise, that we may never learn to excuse its failures. To be prompted, therefore, and to refer to one's writing, is pernicious, as it grants indulgence to carelessness; nor will a speaker feel that he retains with sufficient security that which he is in no fear of losing. Hence, too, proceed interruptions in the course of our speech, and a mode of delivery halting and irregular, while the speaker, appearing like one who has learned a lesson, destroys the whole grace of what he had written with grace, by making it evident that he did write it. But a good memory gains us credit even for readiness of wit, as we appear, not to have brought what we utter from home, but to have conceived it on the instant; an opinion which is of great service both to the speaker and to his cause; for a judge admires more, and distrusts less, that which he regards as not having been pre-concerted to mislead him. We should therefore consider it as one of the most excellent artifices in pleading to deliver some parts of our speech, which we have extremely well connected, as if they had not been connected at all, and to appear, at times, like persons thinking and doubting, seeking what we have in reality brought with us. [XI, 2, 44-8]

[Delivery]

Delivery is by most writers called *action;* but it appears to derive the one name from the voice, and the other from the gesture; for Cicero calls action sometimes the *language, as it were,* and sometimes the *eloquence of the body.* Yet he makes two constituent parts of action, which are the same as those of delivery, *voice* and *motion.* We, therefore, make use of either term indiscriminately. [XI, 3, 1]

. . . . .

All attempts at exciting the feelings must prove ineffectual, unless they be enlivened by the *voice* of the speaker, by his *look,* and by the *action of almost his whole body.* [XI, 3, 2]

. . . . .

Since delivery in general, ... depends upon two things, *voice* and *gesture,* of which the one affects the eyes and the other the ears, the two senses through which all impressions find their way into the mind, it is natural to speak first of the *voice,* to which, also, the *gesture* is to be adapted.

In regard to it, then, the first thing to be considered is *what sort of voice we have,* and the next, *how we use it.* The natural power of the voice is estimated by its *quantity* and its *quality.* Of these, the *quantity* is the more simple consideration, for it may be said in general that it is either *much* or *little;* but between the extremes of these quantities there are many diversities, and many gradations from the lowest tone to the highest, and from the highest to the lowest. *Quality* is more varied; for the voice is either *clear* or *husky, full* or *weak, smooth* or *rough,* of *smaller* or *larger compass, hard* or *flexible, sharp* or *flat.* The *breath* may also be *longer* or *shorter.* As to the causes whence each of these peculiarities arises, it is not necessary to the design of my work to consider whether the difference lies in those parts of the body in which the breath is generated, or in those through which, as through tubes, it passes; whether it results from the nature of the voice itself, or from the impulse which it receives; or whether strength of lungs, or of the chest, or even of the head, affords it most assistance; for there is need of concurrent aid from all these parts, as well as of a clear formation, not only of the mouth, but also of the nostrils, through which the remainder of the breath is expelled. The general tone of the voice, however, ought to be sweet, not grating.

In the *management of the voice* there are many particulars to be observed; for besides the three main distinctions of *acute, grave,* and *intermediate,* there is need of many other kinds of intonation, as the *forcible* and the *gentle,* the *higher* and the *lower;* and of *slower* or *quicker* time. But between these varieties there are other intermediate varieties; and as the face, though it consists of very few features, is infinitely diversified, so the voice, though it has very few variations that can be named, has yet a peculiar tone in each individual; the voice of a person is as easily distinguished by the ear, as the face by the eye.

But the good qualities of the voice, like those of all our other faculties, are improved by attention and deteriorated by neglect. [XI, 3, 14-19]

. . . . .

As to *rules for delivery,* they are precisely the same as those for language.

For as language ought to be *correct, clear, elegant,* and *to the purpose,* so delivery will be correct, that is, free from fault, if our pronunciation be *easy, clear, agreeable,* and *polished,* that is, of such a kind that nothing of the rustic or the foreign be heard in it. . . . [XI, 3, 30]

. . . . .

If the voice, too, be naturally, so to speak, *sound,* it will have none of those defects to which I just now alluded; and it will, moreover, not be *dull sounding, gross, bawling, hard, stiff, inefficient, thick,* or, on the contrary, *thin, weak, squeaking, small, soft, effeminate;* while the breathing, at the same time, should be neither *short,* nor *unsustained,* nor *difficult to recover.* [XI, 3, 32]

. . . . .

Our pronunciation will be *clear,* if, in the first place, our words are uttered entire; for, by many, part of them is often swallowed, and part never formed, as they fail to pronounce the last syllables of words while they dwell on the sound of the first. But though the full articulation of words is absolutely necessary, yet to count and number, as it were, every letter, is disagreeable and offensive; for vowels very frequently coalesce, and some consonants are elided when a vowel follows. [XI, 3, 33-4]

. . . . .

RHETORIC AND PUBLIC SPEAKING 153

The second requisite to clearness of pronunciation is, *that the phrases be distinct,* that is, that the speaker begin and stop where he ought. He must observe where his words are to be reined in, as it were, and suspended,... and where they are to be altogether brought to a stand. [XI, 3, 35]

. . . . .

That delivery is *elegant,* which is supported by a voice that is *easy, powerful, fine, flexible, firm, sweet, well-sustained, clear, pure, that cuts the air and penetrates the ear;* for there is a kind of voice naturally qualified to make itself heard, not by its strength, but by a peculiar excellence of tone; a voice which is obedient to the will of the speaker, susceptible of every variety of sound and inflexion that can be required, and possessed, as they say, of all *the notes of a musical instrument;* and to maintain it there should be strength of lungs, and breath that can be steadily prolonged, and is not likely to sink under labour. [XI, 3, 40]

. . . . .

The first requisite to be noticed for pronouncing well, is, that an *equality of tone* must be maintained; so that our speech may not proceed by starts, with irregular intervals and tones, confounding long syllables with short, grave sounds with acute, high with low, and halting from disorder in all these particulars, as a person halts in walking from having legs of unequal length. [XI, 3, 43]

. . . . .

The breath, also, must not be drawn too frequently, so as to break our sentences to pieces, nor must it be prolonged until it is spent, for the sound of the voice, when the breath is just lost, is disagreeable; the breathing of the speaker is like that of a man held long under water, and the recovery of the breath is long and unseasonable, as being made, not when we please, but when it is compulsory. When we are about to pronounce a long period, therefore, we must collect our breath, but in such a way as not to take much time about it, or to do it with a noise, or to render it at all observable; in other parts the breath may be freely drawn between the divisions of the matter. But we ought to exercise it, that it may hold out as long as possible. [XI, 3, 53-4]

. . . . .

There are some speakers who do not draw their breath in the ordinary way, but suck it in with a hissing through the interstices of their teeth. Others there are, who, by incessant panting, which can be plainly heard within their mouth, resemble beasts labouring under burdens or in the yoke. [XI, 3, 55]

. . . . .

Others, again, have a tightness of the mouth, and seem to struggle with their words to force them out. To cough, to make frequent expectorations, to hoist up phlegm from the bottom of the chest as it were with a windlass, to sprinkle the by-standers with the moisture from the mouth, and to emit, in speaking, the greater part of the breath through the nostrils, may, though they are not properly faults of the voice, be nevertheless reasonably noticed here, as it is in the use of the voice that they display themselves. [XI, 3, 56]

[Adaptation of Delivery to Subjects]

Hence, in speaking on cheerful subjects, it flows in a *full* and clear tone, and is itself, as it were, *cheerful;* in argument, it rouses itself with its full force, and strains, so to speak, every nerve; in anger, it is *fierce, rough, thick,* and interrupted with frequent respirations, for the breath cannot hold long when it is expelled in extraordinary quantities; in throwing odium on persons or things it is *slower,* because it is in general only those on the weaker side that have recourse to such attempts; but in flattery, confessing, apologizing, supplicating, it is *gentle* and *submissive.* The tone of those who persuade, advise, promise, or console, is *grave.* In expressing fear and shame, the tone is *staid;* in exhortation it is *strong;* in dispute, *voluble;* in expressing pity, *tender* and *mournful,* and purposely somewhat weakened. In oratorical digressions the voice is *flowing,* and of a tranquil clearness; in statements of facts, as well as in familiar conversation, it is of an *even* tone, intermediate between the acute and the grave. In expressing the more vehement feelings it *rises;* in uttering those of a calmer nature, it *falls,* and pitches itself, in either case, higher or lower according to the degree of intensity. [XI, 3, 63-5]

[Delivery, continued]

In action, as in the whole body, the head holds the chief place, as contributing to produce both the gracefulness which I have just mentioned, and expressiveness. What contributes to gracefulness, is, first of all, that the head be held in a proper and natural position; for, by casting down the head, humility is signified; by throwing it back, haughtiness; by leaning it on one side, languor; by keeping it rigid and unmoved, a certain degree of rudeness. It must receive, in the next place, appropriate motions from the nature of the subject on which we speak, that it may agree with the gesture, and act in conformity with the hands and oscillations of the body; for the face must always be turned in the same direction as the gesture, except in speaking of things we disapprove, or are unwilling to allow, or regard with aversion. . . . [XI, 3, 68-70]

. . . . .

But the chief part of the head is the face. With the face we show ourselves suppliant, menacing, soothing, sad, cheerful, proud, humble; on the face men hang as it were, and fix their gaze and entire attention on it, even before we begin to speak, by the face we express love and hate; from the face we understand numbers of things, and its expression is often equivalent to all the words that we could use. [XI, 3, 72]

. . . . .

But what is most expressive in the face is the eye, through which the mind chiefly manifests itself; insomuch that the eyes, even while they remain motionless, can sparkle with joy, or contract a gloomy look under sadness. [XI, 3, 75]

. . . . .

As to the hands, without the aid of which all delivery would be deficient and weak, it can scarcely be told of what a variety of motions they are susceptible, since they almost equal in expression the powers of language itself; for other parts of the body assist the speaker, but these, I may almost say, speak themselves. [XI, 3, 85]

. . . . .

But the masters of the art of gesture will not allow the hand to be raised above the eyes, or to fall lower than the breast; and consequently it must be thought in the highest degree objectionable to lift it to the crown of the head, or to bring it down to the bottom of the belly. It may be advanced as far as the left shoulder, but should never go beyond it. [XI, 3, 112-13]

. . . . .

The left hand never properly performs a gesture alone; but it frequently acts in agreement with the right, either when we enumerate our arguments on our fingers, or when we express detestation by turning our palms toward the left, or presenting them straight before us, or spread them out on either side. [XI, 3, 114]

. . . . .

It is also a general rule, I know, that we should not, as we walk, turn our backs on the judges, but that the inside part of our foot should be constantly presented to the tribunal as we look towards it. This rule cannot always be observed on private trials; but there the space is more confined, and we cannot turn our backs on the judges long. We may at times, however, draw back by degrees. Some speakers even leap back, an act in the highest degree ridiculous. [XI, 3, 127]

. . . . .

It is allowable to walk about while speaking, only when, in public causes, where there are several judges, we wish to impress what we say on each individually. [XI, 3, 130]

. . . . .

As to dress, the orator has no peculiar habit, but what he wears is more observed than that of other men; and it should therefore be, like that of all other persons of note, elegant and manly; for the fashion of the gown, and the shoes, and the hair, is as reprehensible for too much care as for too great negligence. [XI, 3, 137]

. . . . .

Delivery ought to exhibit three qualities; it should *conciliate, persuade,* and *move;* and *to please* will be a quality that naturally combines itself with these. [XI, 3, 154]

. . . . .

As to the attitude, it should be erect, the feet a little apart, in similar positions, or the left a slight degree in advance; the knees straight, but not so as to seem stiff; the shoulders kept down; the countenance grave, not anxious, or stolid, or languid; the arms at a moderate distance from the sides; the left hand in the position which I have before prescribed; and the right, when we are going to commence, a little extended beyond the bosom of the toga, with the most modest possible gesture, as if waiting for the moment to begin. [XI, 3, 159]

[*Orator Must Be Good Man*]

Let the orator, then, whom I propose to form, be such a one as is characterized by the definition of Marcus Cato, *a good man skilled in speaking.* [XII, 1, 1]

. . . . .

It is of importance that an orator should be good, because, should the power of speaking be a support to evil, nothing would be more

RHETORIC AND PUBLIC SPEAKING

pernicious than eloquence alike for public concerns and private, and I myself, who, as far as is in my power, strive to contribute something to the faculty of the orator, should deserve very ill of the world, since I should furnish arms, not for soldiers, but for robbers. [XII, 1, 1]

. . . . .

My judgment carries me still further; for I not only say that he who would answer my idea of an orator, must be a good man, but that no man, unless he be good, can ever be an orator. To an orator discernment and prudence are necessary; but we can certainly not allow discernment to those, who, when the ways of virtue and vice are set before them, prefer to follow that of vice; nor can we allow them prudence, since they subject themselves, by the unforeseen consequences of their actions, often to the heaviest penalty of the law, and always to that of an evil conscience. But if it be not only truly said by the wise, but always justly believed by the vulgar, that no man is vicious who is not also foolish, a fool, assuredly, will never become an orator. [XII, 1, 3-4]

. . . . .

Since an orator, then, is a good man, and a good man cannot be conceived to exist without virtuous inclinations, and virtue, though it receives certain impulses from nature, requires notwithstanding to be brought to maturity by instruction, the orator must above all things study *morality*, and must obtain a thorough knowledge of all that is just and honourable, without which no one can either be a good man or an able speaker. [XII, 2, 1]

. . . . .

I pass on to my second proposition, that no man will ever be thoroughly accomplished in eloquence, who has not gained a deep insight into the impulses of human nature, and formed his moral character on the precepts of others and on his own reflection. [XII, 2, 4]

SUGGESTED READINGS

Baldwin, Charles Sears
  Ancient Rhetoric and Poetic. New York. Macmillan Co. 1924. p62-101
Bennett, Charles E.
  An Ancient Schoolmaster's Message to Present-Day Teachers. *Classical Journal.* 4:149-64 February 1909

Butler, H. E., tr.
   The Institutio Oratoria of Quintilian. New York. G. P. Putnam's Sons. 1921-22. 4v

Carver, P. L.
   Quintilian's Approach to Literature. *University of Toronto Quarterly.* 7:77-94 October 1937

D'Alton, J. F.
   Roman Literary Theory and Criticism; a Study in Tendencies. London and New York. Longmans, Green and Co. 1931. p266-353

Duff, J. Wight
   A Literary History of Rome in the Silver Age. London. T. Fisher Unwin. 1927. p387-421

Harding, Harold F.
   Quintilian's Witnesses. *Speech Monographs.* 1:1-20 September 1934

Ryan, John P.
   Quintilian's Message. *Quarterly Journal of Speech.* 15:171-80 April 1929

Watson, J. S., tr. and ed.
   Institutes of Oratory. London. H. G. Bohn. 1856. 2v

LONGINUS

Although the author of *On the Sublime* was evidently interested in writing about rhetoric, he succeeded more fully in discussing poetry and the critical standards by which it is to be appraised. A work of unquestioned importance in literary criticism, *On the Sublime* contains much on the subject of style, or elevation of expression, which is of value to the student of public speaking. It also sets forth some of the fundamental resemblances and differences between poetry and rhetoric.

Both the authorship and the date of preparation are in doubt. Scholars seem to believe, however, that the work was completed in the first century A. D.

ON THE SUBLIME [1]

[Sources of Sublimity]

There are five sources, if I may so express it, from which the Sublimity of eloquence most copiously flows: pre-supposing as a groundwork common to all these five, a certain power of elocution without which they are nothing. The first and most effectual of these is, a successful boldness in regard to the sentiments. . . . The second is, vehement and enthusiastic passion. These two are, for the most part, natural constituents of Sublimity: the others are chiefly the result of art. The third is, a suitable combination of figures; which are of two kinds; those relating to the sentiment [or metaphors] and those belonging to the language [or tropes]. Next (and in the fourth place,) is majesty of expression, which again may be divided into a judicious selection of words, and a diction sufficiently elaborate, and elevated by Tropes. The fifth constituent of Sublimity, which includes all those that precede it, is a dignified and elevated composition. [VIII]

[Amplification]

[This] . . . occurs when the subject of a treatise, or the argument of a debate admits, in its several divisions, of different commencements and pauses; and the important incidents are brought forward, one after another, rising in gradation to the very summit of grandeur. Now this figure may be introduced either by dignifying some familiar topic, or by aggravating incidents, or by corroborating proofs, or by dividing things done or suffered into their several classes: for the modes of amplification are innumerable. [XI]

[1] From the translation by William T. Spurdens (1836).

[Distinction between Sublimity and Amplification]

Sublimity . . . consists in elevation, and Amplification in quantity: so that the former is frequently found in a single thought, whereas the latter requires enumeration and circumstantiality. Amplification . . . is the completing of a sentence with all its parts and members; which gives a powerful conception of the subject under discussion, by causing the mind to dwell upon it. [XIII]

[Imagery]

Every mental conception communicable by language, whencesoever derived, is known in common discourse by the term *imagery*: but, in a more peculiar sense it is used when, through an enthusiastic feeling, you seem to see what you describe, and to place it before the eyes of your hearers. You must, however, have remarked that there is a difference between the imagery of the orator, and that of the poet: the object of the latter being surprise, and that of the former, elucidation; although they both seek to produce emotion. . . .

The imagery of the poet will allow . . . of an excess of fiction quite surpassing credibility: but that of the orator is always the more beautiful, in proportion to its appearance of feasibility and truth. [XV]

[Use of Figures]

Figures, if immoderately employed, are peculiarly liable to suspicion, and occasion an apprehension of stratagem, trick, deceit. . . . For this reason a figure is always most effective when it is not perceived to be a figure. [XVII]

. . . . .

An accumulation of figures also, usually produces a powerful effect: when two or three, blending, as it were, their united contributions, confer on each other vigour, persuasion, elegance. [XX]

[On Conciseness]

An over-conciseness of phrase is also injurious to sublimity: for every thing great is maimed by excessive constraint. I am not here speaking of such sentences as require brevity, but of such as are curtailed and minced. Conciseness shackles the sense, brevity only gives it a right direction. [XLII]

SUGGESTED READINGS

Baldwin, Charles Sears
Ancient Rhetoric and Poetic. New York. Macmillan Co. 1924. p102-31

Henn, T. R.
Longinus and English Criticism. London. Cambridge University Press. 1934. 161p

Roberts, W. Rhys, ed.
On the Sublime. 2nd ed. London. Cambridge University Press. 1907. x,288p

Spurdens, William T., tr.
Longinus on the Sublime. London. Longman, Rees, Orme, Brown, Green, and Longman. 1836. vi,362p

LEONARD COX

(fl. 1572)

First reasonably complete rhetoric in the English language, Leonard Cox's *Arte or Crafte of Rhethoryke* interests the student today chiefly because it helps to sustain historically the continuity of thinking in the province of oral expression between classical antiquity and the Renaissance. The work is faithful to the older rhetoricians, and particularly to Cicero from whom Cox drew much of his illustrative material.

The *Rhethoryke* deals mainly with invention, indirectly with disposition. Demonstrative and judicial oratory receive the major emphasis. Prepared as it was by a schoolmaster, it may properly be regarded a schoolbook designed to give certain embodiment to literary form, to make felt in England the influence of the Renaissance upsurge in letters. Cox was less the theorist in rhetoric; more the transmitter of older principles designed to improve the expression of his period.

THE ARTE OR CRAFTE OF RHETHORYKE[1]

[Importance of Study of Rhetoric]

And when I hade thus longe prepensyd in my mynde what thynge I myght beste chose out/none offrede it selfe more conuenyent to the profyte of yonge studientes, whiche youre good lordeshyppe hath allwayes tenderly fauored/and also meter to my professyon, then to make some proper worke of the ryght pleasaunt and parsuadyble arte of Rhetoryke/whiche as it is very necessary to all suche as wyll eyther be aduocates and proctoures in the lawe, or els apte to be sente in theyr prynces/Ambassades/or to be techars of goddes worde in suche maner as may be moste sensible and accepte to their audience: And finally to all them that haue any thynge to prepose or to speke afore any companye, what someuer they be. So contraryly I se no scyence that is les taught and declared to scholars/whiche ought chyefly after the knowledge of gramer ones hade to be instructe in thys facultie without the whiche often tymes the rude vtterance of (A iii a) the aduocate greatly hyndrethe and apeyreth his clyentes cause. Lykewyse the vnapte dysposycyon of the precher in orderynge his mater confundyth the memory of hys herers. And bryefly in declaryng of maters, for lake of inuen-

[1] From *The Arte or Crafte of Rhethoryke*, by Leonard Cox. Edited by Frederic Ives Carpenter. Chicago, University of Chicago Press, 1899. By permission of the University of Chicago Press.

cyon and order with due elocucyon, greate tediosnes is engendered to the multytude beynge present/by occasyon where of the speker is many tymes or he haue endyd his tale eyther lefte almost alone to hys no lytle confusyon, or els (whiche is a lyke rebuke to hym) the audyence falleth for werynes of hys ineloquent langage faste on slepe. [41-2]

[Essentials of Art of Rhetoric]

Whosomeuer desyreth to be a good oratour or to dyspute and commune of any maner thynge/hym behoueth to haue foure thynges. The fyrste is called Inuencyon, for he muste fyrste of al imagyne or inuent in his mynde what he shall saye. The .ii. is named iudgement/for he muste haue wyt to discerne and iudge whether tho thinges that he hathe founde in his mynde be conuenient to the purpose or nat/for often tymes yf a man lake thys propriete he may as well tell that that is agaynste hym/as with hym/as experience doth dayly shew. The .iii. is dysposycyon wherby he maye knowe howe to ordre and set euery thynge in his due place. Leste thoughe his inuencyon and iudgement be neuer so goode he maye happen to be counted as the commune prouerbe sayeth To put the carte afore the horse. The .iiii. & is such thynges laste as (sic) he hathe Inuentid and by iudgement knowen apte to his purpose when they ar set in theyr ordre so to speke them that it maye be pleasant and delectable to the audience. [43]

[Invention]

Inuencyon is comprehended in certayn placys/as the Rhetoriciens call them/out of whom he that knoweth the facultye may fetche easyly suche thynges as be mete for the mater that he shal speke of/which mater the Oratour calleth the theme and in oure vulgayre tonge it is callyd improprely the antytheme. [44]

[Kinds of Orations]

The fyrste is callyd Logycall, whiche kynde we call properly disputacion. The secunde is called Demonstratyue. The thyrde Delyberatyue. The .iiii. Judiciall/and these thre laste be properly callid speces or kindes of oracions/whose natures shalbe declarid seperatly here after with the crafte that is required i(n) euery (A v b) of them. [44]

RHETORIC AND PUBLIC SPEAKING

[Instruments of a Theme]

The places or instrumentes of a symple theme ar.
The definicion of the thyng.
The causes.
The partes.
The effectes. [45]

[Sources of Arguments]

The places out of whome are founde argumentes for the prouinge or improuynge of compounde Themes/are these followinge
Diffinicion.
Cause.
Partes.
Lyke.
Contrary. [49]

[Demonstrative Oratory]

The use of an oracyon demonstrative is in prayse or dysprayse/ whiche kynde or maner of oracyon was greatly vsed somtyme in comon accyons/as dothe declare the oracyons of Demosthenes/and also many of Thucidides oracions. And there ben thre maners of oracions demonstratyue. [49]

. . . . .

The fyrst conteyneth the prayse or dysprayse of persones. [49]

. . . .

The secunde kynde (B i b) of an oracyon demonstratyue is: where in is praysed or dispraised/nat the person but the dede. [49]

The thyrde kynde is: wherein is lauded or blamed nother person nor dede/but some other thynge as vertue/vice/iustice/iniurie/ charite/enuie/pacience/wrothe and suche lyke. [49]

[Parts of an Oration]

The partes of an oracion prescribed of Rhetoriciens are these.
The Preamble or exorden.
The Tale or narracion.
The prouinge of the matter or contencion.
The conclusion.

Of the whiche partes mencyon shall be made hereafter in euery kynde of oracions, for they are nat founde generally in euery oracion/but some haue moo partes/and some lesse. [50]

[*Demonstrative Oratory*]

Beneuolence is the place whereby the herer is made willyng to here vs/and it is conteyned in the thynge that we speke of/in them whom we speke to/& in our owne person. The easyest and moste vsed place of beneuolence consysteth in the offyce or duety of the person/whan we shew that it is oure duety to do that we be aboute. [50]

. . . . .

The herers shalbe made attente or dylygente to gyue audyence yf the oratour made promyse that he wyll shewe them newe thynges/ or els necessary or profytable/or yf he saye that it ys an harde mater that he hathe in handelynge or els obscure and nat easy to be vnderstonde excepte they gyue ryght good attendaunce, wherfore it is expedient that yf they wyll haue the percepcyon of it, that they gyue a good eare. [54-55]

. . . . .

(B vi b) Docilite whereby we make the mater playne and easy to be percyued/is nat greatly required in this kinde of oracyon/for it is belonginge properly to derke and obscure causes/in whiche we muste promyse that we wyll nat vse great ambages/or to go (as men saye) rounde about the bussh/but to be short and plaine. [55]

. . . . .

The Narracion or tale wherein persones are praysed/is the declarynge of theyr lyfe and doynges after the fasshyon of an hystorye. The places out of the whiche it is sought are: The persones byrthe. His chyldhode. His adolescencie. His mannes state. His olde age. His dethe and what foloweth after. [55]

. . . . .

The places of confyrmacyon are honesty/perfite lyghtnes or hardines of the dede. For after the proheme of the oracion and the narracyon/then go we to the prouynge of our mater. Fyrst shewing that it was a very honeste dede. And next/that it was nat all onely honesty: but also profitable. Thyrdely as concernynge the easines or difficulti/the praise therof muste be consydered/part in the doer/part in the dede. [63]

. . . . .

RHETORIC AND PUBLIC SPEAKING 167

Confutacion is the soilynge of suche argumentes as maye be induced agaynste our purpose/whiche parte is but lytle vsed in an oracion demonstratiue. [64]

. . . . .

The conclusion is made of a brife enumeracion of suche thynges that we haue spoken of afore in the oracyon and in the mouynge of affections.

In delectable thinges or suche thinges [C vii a] that haue bene well done/we moue our audyence to reioce thereat/and to do lyke.

In sad thynges and heuy/to be sory for them. In yll and peruerse actes/to beware that they folowe nat them to theyr great shame and confusyon. [64]

[Deliberative Oratory]

An oracion deliberatiue is by the whiche we persuade or dissuade any thing/and by the which we aske/or whereby we exorte any man to do a thynge/or els to forsake it/and this kynde of oracion is muche in vse/nat onely in ciuile maters: but also in epistles. [66]

. . . . .

We may begynne our oracion in this kynde/euyn lyke as we dyd in an oracyon demonstratyue/but moste aptly at our offyce or duety/ leste some men wolde thynke that we dyd it more of a priuate affection for our owne commoditie & plesure: than for any other mannes profyte. [66]

. . . . .

In oracyons dylyberatyues we vse very seldome narracyons/but for the more parte in stede of them we make a bryef proposyon conteynynge the summe of our entent. [68]

. . . . .

Nexte foloweth the confirmacion of tho thygnes that we entende to persaude/whiche must be set out of the places of honisty/profyte/ easynes/of difficulty. As if we wyll persuade any thynge to be done/we shall shewe that it is nat onely honest and laudable: but all so profytable and easy ynough to perfourme. Or if we can nat chose but graunte that it is harde/yet we shall shew that it is so honeste a dede/so worthy prayse and besydes so great commodity wyll come thereof/that the hardenes ought in no wyse to fere vs: but rather be as an instigacyon to take the thynge on hande/remembrynge the greke prouerbe. [69-70]

. . . . .

The confutacyon is the foylynge and refellynge of other mennes sayenges that haue or myght be brought agaynste our purpose/wherefore it consysteth in places contrary to the places of confyrmacyon/ as in prouynge the sayenge of the contrary part/neyther to be honeste nor profytable/nor easy to perfourme/or els vtterly impossyble. [71]

. . . . .

The conclusyon standeth in two thinges/that is to saye/a bryefe and compendiouse repetynge of all our reasons that we haue brought for vs afore/and in mouyng of affectyons. [71]

[Judicial Oratory]

Oracyons iudiciall be that longe to controuersies in the lawe and plees/whiche kynde of oracion in old tyme longed onely to Judges and men of lawe/but nowe for the more parte it is neglecte of them/though there be nothynge more necessarye to quicken them in crafty & wyse handeling of theyr maters. [71]

. . . . .

In these oracions the fyrste is to fynde out the state of the cause/ whiche is a short preposicion conteynynge the hole effect of all the controuersies. [71]

. . . . .

Here must be borne away that there be thre maner of states in suche oracyons.
The fyrste is called coniecturall. The second legitime. The thyrde/iudiciall/and euery of these hathe his owne proper places to set out argumentes of them, wherfore they shall be spoken of seuerally. And fyrste we wyll treate of state coniecturall/whiche is vsed whan we be certayne that the dede is done/but we be ignorant who (D v b) dyd it/and yet by certayne coniectures we haue one suspecte/that of very lykelyhode it shulde be he that hathe commytted the cryme. And therfore this state is called coniecturall/bycause we have no manyfeste profe/but all onely great lykelyhodes/or as the Rhetoriciens call them coniectures. [71-2]

. . . . .

The preface is here euyn as it is in other oracions. [72]

. . . . .

The narracion or tale is the shewynge of the dede in maner of an historye/wherin the accuser muste craftly entermengle many suspicyons which shall seme to make his mater prouable. [72]

. . . . .

Out of the narracion must be gaderyd a bryfe sentence/wherein shall stande the hole pithe of the cause/. [73]

. . . . .

Seiunction is whan we shewe wherin our aduersaries and we agre and what it is/wherupon we stryue. [74]

. . . . .

The confyrmacyon of the accuser is fetched out of these places/ wyl/and power. For these two thynges wyll cause the person that is accused to be greatly suspecte that he had wyl to do the thyng that he is accused of/and that he myght well ynoughe brynge it to passe. [75]

. . . . .

The conclusion is as I haue sayd afore in briefe repetynge of the effecte of our reasons/& in mouynge the Judges to our (E iv b) purpose. [79]

. . . . .

As state coniecturall cometh out of this questyon (who dyd the dede) so whan there is no dout but that the dede is done/and who dyd it/many tymes controuersy is had/whether it hathe bene done laufully or nat. And this state is negociall or iuridiciall/whiche conteyneth the ryght or wronge of the dede. [79-80]

. . . . .

The preamble and narracion as afore. [80]

. . . . .

The confirmacion hath certayn places appropred thereto/but here muste be marked that state negocyall is double/absolute/and assumptyue. [80]

. . . . .

State negociall absolute is whan the thynge that is in controuersy is absolutely defended to be laufully done. [80]

. . . . .

The places of confirmacyon in state absolute are these/nature/lawe/custome/equity or reason/iugement/necessity/bargayne or couenant. [80]

. . . . .

State assumptyue is whan the defence is feble of it selfe/but yet it may be holpen by some other thynge added to it. And the places longynge to this state are grauntynge of the faute/remouyng of the faute/or (as we say in our tongue) layeng it from vs to an other/& translatynge of the faute. [80]

. . . . .

The conclusions in these oracyons are lyke to the conclusions of other. [82]

. . . . .

State legitime is whan the controuersy standeth in definicyon or contrary lawes/or doutful wrytynges/or racyocynacyon/or translacyon/. [82]

. . . . .

Definicion (as Tully wryteth) is whan in any wrytynge is some worde put/the significacion wherof requireth exposicion. [83]

. . . . .

Contrary lawes are where the tone semeth euidently to contrarye the other. [84]

. . . . .

Doubtful wrytynge is where either the mynde of the author semeth to be contrary to that that is wryten/which som call wrytynge & sentence/or els it is whan the wordes may be expounded dyuers wayes. [84]

. . . . .

Raciocinacion is whan the mater is in controuersy/wherupon no law is decreed/but yet the iugement therof may be founde out by lawes made vpon maters somdele resemblynge thereunto. [86]

. . . . .

Translacion is whiche the lawyers cal excepcion/as yf a person accused pleade that it is nat lawfull for the tother to accuse hym/or that the Juge can be no iuge in that cause. &c. [87]

SUGGESTED READINGS

Carpenter, Frederic I.
   Leonard Cox and the First English Rhetoric. *Modern Language Notes.* 13:292-4. 1898

   (ed.) *The Arte or Crafte of Rhethoryke* (of Cox). Chicago. University of Chicago Press. 1899. 117p

THOMAS WILSON
(1525?-1581)

Thomas Wilson's *Arte of Rhetorike* is the first comprehensive treatment of rhetoric in the English language, containing much of the best material from the classical writers together with original interpretations and analyses. Book I sets up the preliminary definitions and classifications, and then covers invention rather fully; Book II discusses disposition; and Book III deals with elocution, memory, and delivery.

The *Rhetorike* urges the cultivation of a simple style characterized by plainness, aptness, good composition, and, finally, exornation or embellishment.

THE ARTE OF RHETORIKE [1]

[Definition of Rhetoric]

Rhetorique is an Arte to set forthe by vtteraunce of woordes, matter at large, or (as Cicero doeth saie) it is learned, or rather an artificiall declaration of the minde, in the handelying of any cause, called in contention, that maie through reason largely be discussed. [1]

[Province of Rhetoric]

An Orator must bee able to speake fullie of all those questions, whiche by lawe and mannes ordinance are enacted, and appointed for the vse and profite of man, such as are thought apt for the tongue to set forward. [1]

[Ends of Oratory]

Three thynges are required of an Orator.
    To teache.
    To delight.
    And to perswade. [2]

* * * * *

First therefore, an Orator must labour to tell his tale, that the hearers maie well know what he meaneth, and vnderstande hym wholie, the whiche he shall with ease doe, if he vtter his mynde in

---

[1] From the 1567 edition. London, Jhon Kyngston, 1580. Both the spelling and pagination are irregular in certain parts of the text. The only change which the compiler has made in the text, however, is the inclusion of the letter "n" following certain marked vowels.

plaine woordes, such are vsuallie receiued, and tell it orderly, without goyng about the busshe. [2]

. . . .

The next part that he hath to plaie, is to chere his geastes, and to make them take pleasure, with hearyng of thinges wittely deuised, and pleasauntly set forthe. [3]

. . . .

Thirdlie, suche quicknesse of witte must be shewed, and suche pleasaunt sawes so well applied, that the eares maie finde muche delite, whereof I will speake largelie, when I shall intreate of mouyng laughter. [3]

[*Means of Attaining Eloquence*]

First nedefull it is that he, which desireth to excell in this gift of Oratorie, and longeth to proue an eloquent man, must naturally haue a witte, and an aptnesse thereunto; then must he to his booke, and learne to be wel stored with knowledge, that he maie be able to minister matter for all causes necessary. The which when he hath got plentifully, he must vse muche exercise, bothe in writyng, and also in speakyng. For though he haue a wit and learnyng together, yet shall thei bothe little auaile without muche practise. [4]

[*Parts of Rhetoric*]

Any one that will largely handle any matter, must fasten his mynde firste of all, vpon these fiue especiall pointes that followe, and learne them euery one.

    i. Inuention of matter.
    ii. Disposition of the same.
    iii. Elocution.
    iiii. Memorie.
    v. Utteraunce. [5-6]

[*Invention*]

The findyng out of apt matter, called otherwise Inuention, is a searchyng out of thynges true, or thynges likely, the whiche maie reasonable set forthe a matter, and make it appere probable. [6]

[*Disposition*]

Therefore, in the second place is mentioned, the setlyng or orderyng of thynges inuented for this purpose, called in Latine

Dispositio, the whiche is nothing els but an apt bestowyng, and orderly placyng of thinges, declaryng where euery argument shalbe sette, and in what maner euery reason shalbe applied for confirmation of the purpose. [6]

[*Style, Memory, and Delivery*]

But yet what helpeth it though wee can finde good reasons, and knowe how to place them, if wee haue not apt woordes and picked Sentences, to commende the whole matter. Therefore, this pointe must needes followe to beautifie the cause, the whiche beyng called Elocution, is an appliyng of apte woordes and sentences to the matter, founde out to confirme the cause. When all these are had together it auaileth little, if man haue no Memorie to containe them. The Memorie therfore must be cherished, the whiche is a faste holdyng bothe of matter and wordes couched together, to confirme any cause.

Be it now that one haue al these fower, yet if he want the fift all the other doe little profite. For though a manne can finde out good matter and good woordes, though hee can handsomely sette them together, and cary them verie well awaie in his mynde, yet it is to no purpose if he haue no vtterance, when he should speake his mynde, and shewe men what he hath to saie. Vtterance therefore, is a framyng of the voyce, countenaunce, and gesture after a comely maner. [6]

[*Parts of a Speech*]

There are seuen partes in euery Oration.
    i. The Enterance or beginnyng.
    ii. The Narration.
    iii. The Proposition.
    iiii. The Deuision or seuerall partyng of thinges.
    v. The Confirmation.
    vi. The Confutation.
    vii. The Conclusion. [7]

. . . . .

The Entraunce or beginnyng is the former parte of the Oration, whereby the will of the standers by, or of the Judge is fought for, and required to heare the matter.

The Narration is a plain and manifest pointyng of the matter, and an euident settyng forthe of all thynges that belong vnto the same, with a breef rehersall grounded vpon some reason.

The Proposition is a pithie sentence comprehended in a smal roome, the somme of the whole matter.

The Deuision is an openyng of thynges, wherein wee agree and reste vpon, and wherin we sticke and stande in trauers, shewyng what we haue to saie in our owne behalfe.

The Confirmation is a declaration of our owne reasons, with assured and constant proofes.

The Confutation is a dissoluyng, wipyng awaie of all suche reasons as make against vs.

The Conclusion is a clarkely gatheryng of the matter spoken before, and a lappyng vp of it altogether. [7]

[Kinds of Speeches]

Nothyng can be handled by this art, but the same is conteined within one of these three causes. Either the matter consisteth in praise, or dispraise of a thing or els in consultyng, whether the cause bee profitable, or vnprofitable: or lastly, whether the matter be right or wrong. [11]

[Demonstrative Oratory]

The Oration demonstratiue standeth either in praise, or dispraise of some one man, or of some one thing, or of some one deede doen. [11]

. . . .

There are diuers thynges whiche are praised and dispraised, as men, countries, citees, places, beastes, hilles, riuers, houses, castelles, deedes doen by worthy men, and pollicies inuented by greate warriers, but moste commonly men are praised for diuers respectes, before any of the other thynges are taken in hande. [11]

. . . .

The partes of an Oration, made in praise of a man. } The Enteraunce.
The Narration.
Sometymes the confutacion.
The Conclusion. [9]

[Deliberative Oratory]

An Oration deliberatiue, is a meane, wherby we doe perswade, or disswade, entreate, or rebuke, exhorte, or dehort, commende, or comforte any man. In this kinde of Oracion, wee doe not purpose

RHETORIC AND PUBLIC SPEAKING

wholy to praise any bodie, nor yet to determine any matter in controuersie, but the whole compasse of this cause is, either to aduise our neighbour to that thing, which wee thinke most nedefull for him, or els to call hym backe from that follie, whiche hindereth much his estimacion. [21]

. . . . .

And the reasons, whiche are commonly vsed to enlarge suche matters, are these that followe.

{ The thing is honeste.
    Profitable.
    Pleasaunt.

{ Saufe.
    Easie.
    Harde.

{ Lawfull and meete.
    Praise worthie.
    Necessarie. [30]

. . . . .

The places of exhortyng, and dehortyng are the same whiche wee vse in perswadyng, and disswadyng, sauyng that he whiche vseth perswasion, seketh by argumentes to compasse his deuise: he that labors to exhort, doeth stirre affection.

Erasmus sheweth these to be moste especiall places, that doe pertaine vnto exhortations.

{ Praise or commendation.
    Expectation of all men.
    Hope of victorie.
    Hope of renowne.
    Feare of shame.
    Greatness of reward.
    Rehearsall of examples in all ages, and especially
        of thynges lately doen. [64]

[Judicial Oratory]

Oration Judiciall, is an earneste debatyng in open assemblie, of some weightie matter before a Judge, where the complainaunte commenseth his action, and the defendaunt thereupon aunswereth at his perill, to all suche thynges as are laied to his charge. [87]

. . . . .

Not onely it is needefull in causes of iudgement, to consider the scope whereunto we must leauell our reasons, and direct our inuention: but also we ought in euery cause to haue a respect vnto some one especiall pointe and cheef article: that the rather the whole drift of our doynges, maie seme to agree with our first deuised purpose. For by this meanes our iudgement shalbe framed to speake with discretion, and the ignoraunte shall learne to perceiue with profite, whatsoeuer is said for his instruction. [88]

. . . . .

A state therefore generally, is the cheef grounde of a matter, and the principall pointe whereunto bothe he that speaketh should referre his whole wit, and thei that heare should cheefly marke. [89]

. . . . .

A state thereof in matters of Judgemente, is that thyng whiche doeth arise vpon the first demaunde, and deniall made betwixt men, whereof the one part is the accuser, and the other part the persone, or persones accused. It is called a State, because we doe stande and rest vpon some one pointe, the whiche must wholie and onely be proued of the one side, and denied of the other. I cannot better terme it in Englishe, then by the name of an issue, the whiche not onely ariseth vpon muche debatyng, and long trauers vsed, wherupon all matters are saied to come to an issue: but also else where an issue is saied to be then, and so often as bothe partes stande vpon one pointe, the whiche doeth as well happen at the first beginnyng, before any probations are vsed, as it doeth at the latter endyng, after the matter hath at large bene discussed. [90]

. . . . .

Now that wee knowe what an Issue is, it is nexte most nedefull, to shewe how many there are in nomber. The wisest and beste learned haue agreed uppon three onely and no lesse, the whiche are these followyng.

The State. { i. Coniecturall.
              ii. Legall.
              iii. Juridiciall.

And for the more plaine vnderstandyng of these darcke woordes, these three questions followyng, expounde their meanyng altogether.

{ i. Whether the thing be, or no.
  ii. What it is.
  iii. What maner of thyng it is. [90]

. . . . .

And to make these matters more plaine, I will adde an example for euery state seuerally.

Of the State Coniecturall.

The Assertion.
Thou hast killed this man.
The Answere.
I haue not killed hym.
The State or Issue.
Whether he hath killed this man, or no. Thus we see vppon the auouchyng and deniall, the matter standeth vpon an Issue.

Of the State Legall.

The Assertion.
Thou hast committed treason in this facte.
The Answere.
I deny it to be Treason.
The State or Issue.
Whether his offence doen maie be called treason, or no. Here is denied that any suche thing is in the deede doen, as is by worde reported, and saied to be.

Of the State Iuridicial.

The Assertion.
Thou hast kill this man.
Answere.
I graunt it, but I haue doen it lawfully, because I killed him in myne owne defence.
The Issue.
Whether a man maie kill one in his owne defence, or no, and whether this man did so, or no. [91-2]

[*Parts of an Oration: Especially Those Used in Judgment*]

The firste is called a plaine beginnyng, when the hearer is made apte to giue good eare out of hande, to that whiche shall followe.

The seconde is a priuie twinyng, or close crepyng in, to win fauour with muche circumstaunce, called insinuation. [101]

. . . . .

And because the winning of victorie resteth in three poincts: First, in apt teaching the hearers what the matter is, next in gettyng them to giue good eare, and thirdly in winnyng their fauor: We shall make them vunderstande the latter easely, if first of all we begin to expounde it plainly and in briefe wordes, settyng out the meanyng, make them harken to their saiynges. And by no meanes better shall the standers by knowe what we saie, and cary awaie that whiche thei heare, then if at the first we couch together, the whole course of our tale in as small roume as wee can, either by definyng the nature and substaunce of our matter, or els by diuidyng it in an apt order, so that neither the hearers bee troubled, with confoundyng of matter, and heapyng one thing in an others necke, nor yet their memory dulled with ouerthwart rehearsall, and disorderly telling of our tale. Wee shall make the people attentiue, and glad to heare vs, if we will promise them to speake of weightie matters, of wholsome doctrine, such as thei haue heretofore wanted: yea, if we promise to tell them thinges concernyng either their owne profit, or the aduancement of their countrie, no doubt we shall haue them diligent hearers. Or els if thei like not to heare weightie affaires, we maie promise them straunge newes, and perswade them we will make them laugh, and thinke you not that thei will rather heare a foolishe tale, than a wise & wholsome counsail. . . . [102-3]

* * * * *

Wee shall get fauour for our owne sakes, if we shall modestly set foorth our bounden dueties, and declare our seruice doen, without al suspition of vauntyng, either to the common weale, as in seruyng either in the warres abroade, or els in bearing some office at home, concerning the tranquillitie of our countrie: or in helping our frendes, kinsfolkes, and poore neighbours, to declare our goodnesse doen heretofore towardes theim: and lastly, if wee shewe without all ostentation, as well our good willes towardes the Judges there, as also pleasures doen for them in tymes paste to the outermoste of our power. And if any thyng seme to let our cause by any misreporte, or euill behauiour of our partes heretofore: best it were in moste humble wise to seke fauour, and sleightly to aduoide al such offences laied to our charge. [103-4]

* * * * *

A priuie beginnyng, or crepyng in otherwise called Insinuation, must then, and not els be vsed, when the Judge is greaued with vs, and our cause hated of the hearers. [105]

* * * * *

After the preface and first Enteraunce, the matter must be opened, and euery thyng liuely tolde, that the hearers may fully perceiue what we goe aboute, now in reportynge an acte doen, or vtteryng the state of a controuersie, wee must vse these lessons, whereof the first is to bee shorte, the next to be plaine, and the thirde is to speake likely, and with reason, that the hearers maie remember, vnderstande, and beleue the rather suche thinges as shalbe saied. [108]

. . . . .

After our tale is tolde, and the hearers haue well learned what we meane, the next is to reporte wherein the aduersarie and we can not agree, and what it is, wherein wee doe agree. And then to parte out such principall poinctes, whereof we purpose fully to debate, and laie them out to bee knowen: that the hearers maie plainly see, what wee will saie, and perceiue at a worde the substaunce of our meanyng. Now, *Tullie* would not haue a diuision to bee made, of, or aboue three partes at the moste, nor yet lesse then three neither, if neede so require. For if we haue three chiefe groundes, wherevpon to rest, appliyng all our arguments therevnto, we shall both haue matter inough to speake of, the hearers shall with ease vnderstande our meanyng, and the whole Oration shall sone bee at an ende. Notwithstandyng, this lesson must not so curiously be kepte, as though it were sinne to make the diuision of fower, or fiue partes: but it was spoken for this end, that the diuision should be made of as fewe as maie be possible, that men maie the better cary it awie, and the reporter with more ease, maie remember what he hath to saie. [111]

. . . . .

Quintilian willeth, that straight and immediatly after the Narration, ther should also bee vsed suche sentences as might be full of pithe, and containe in them the substaunce of muche matter, the rather that the hearers may be stirred vpon the onely report of some sentencious saiyng, or weightie text in the Lawe. As in speakyng largely against extortion, one might after his reasons applied to the purpose, bring in a pithie and sentencious proposition. . . . [113]

. . . . .

When we haue declared the cheef pointes, whereunto we purpose to referre all our reasons, wee muste heape matter, and finde our argumentes to confirme the same to the vttermoste of our power, makyng firste the strongest reasons that wee can, and nexte after, gatheryng all the probable causes together, that beyng in one heape, thei maie seme strong and of greate waight. And whatsoeuer the aduersarie hath saied against vs, to answere therevnto as tyme and place maie beste serue. That if his reasons bee light, and more good maie bee doen in confutyng his, then in confirmyng our owne: it were beste of all to sette vpon hym, and put awie by Arte, all that he hath fondly saied without wit. For prouyng the matter, and searchyng out the substaunce or nature of the cause, the places of *Logique* must helpe to sette it forward. But when the persone shall bee touched, and not the matter, we must seeke els where, and gather these places together. [114]

. . . . .

A Conclusion, is the handesomely lappyng vp together, and breef heapyng of all that whiche was said before, stirryng the hearers by large vtterance, and plentifull gatheryng of good matter, either the one waie or the other. [116]

. . . . .

The other part of a conclusion, resteth either in augmentyng and vehemently enlargyng that, whiche before was in fewe wordes spoken to sett the Judge or hearers in a heate: or els to mittigate, and assage displeasure conceived with muche lamentyng of the matter, and mouyng them thereby the rather to shewe mercie. [116]

[*Amplification*]

Amplification is a figure in *Rhetorique*, whiche consisteth moste in augmentyng, and diminishyng of any matter, and that diuers waies.

The Deuision of Amplification.

Amplification and diminishyng, either is taken out of the substances in thynges, or els of wordes. Out of the substances and matter affections are deriued: out of woordes suche kindes of amplifications as I will now shewe, and partly haue shewed before, when I spake of the conclusion, or lappyng vp of any matter.

The first kinde of amplification is, when by changyng a worde, in augmentyng we vse a greater, but in diminishyng, we vse a less. [123]

. . . . .

Now in all these kindes, where woordes are amplified thei seeme muche greater, if by correction the sentence be vtterde, and greater wordes compared with them, for whom thei are vtterde. In the which kinde of speeche, we shall seeme as though we went vp by staiers, not onely to the toppe of a thyng, but also aboue the toppe. [123]

. . . . .

There is an other kinde of Amplification, when vnto the hiest there is added somethyng higher then it is. As thus, There is no better Preacher emong them all, except *Hugh Latimer,* the Father of al Preachers. [125]

. . . . .

Sometyme we amplifie by comparyng, and take our ground vpon the weakest and leaste, the whiche if thei seeme greate, then must that needes appeare greate, which we would amplifie and increase. [125]

. . . . .

By contraries sette together, thynges oftentymes appeare greater. [127]

. . . . .

There is also a notable kinde of amplification, when we would extenuate and make lesse greate faultes, whiche before wee did largely increase: to the ende that other faultes might seeme the greatest aboue all other. [128]

. . . . .

There is a kinde of amplifying, whiche in speaking of twoo that fought together, we praise hym muche that hadde the worse, because we would the other to haue more praise. [129]

. . . . .

From the straightnesse of a thyng. Eloquence must nedes be a wonderfull thyng, when so fewe haue attained it.
Likewise, notable aduentures doen by a fewe, are more praise worthie, then such as haue been doen by a greate nomber. [130]

. . . . .

Vehemincie of wordes, full often helpe the matter forwards when more is gathered by cogitation, then if the thyng had bene spoken in plaine woordes. [130]

. . . . .

We encrease our cause, by heapyng of woordes and sentences together, couchyng many reasons into one corner, whiche before were scatterde abroade, to the intent that our talke might appere more vehement. [130]

. . . . .

It is an excellent kinde of amplifiyng, when thinges encreased, and thynges diminished, are bothe sette together, that the one maie the rather beautifie the other. [131]

. . . . .

Likewise, contraries beyng rehearsed, and euill immediately vttered after the good, make muche for encrease. [132]

. . . . .

Because the beauty of amplifiyng, standeth moste in apte mouyng of affections: It is nedefull to speake somewhat in this behalfe, that the better it maie be knowen what thei are, and howe it maie bee vsed. Affections therefore (called Passions) are none other thyng, but a stirryng or forcyng of the mynde, either to desire, or els to deteste and lothe any thyng, more vehemently then by nature we are commonly wont to doe. We desire those thynges, we loue theim, and like theim earnestly, that appere in our iudgement to be Godly: we hate and abhorre those thynges that seme naught, vngodly, or harmefull vnto vs. Neither onely are we moued with those thinges, whiche we thinke either hurtfull, or profitable for our selues, but also wee reioyce, wee sorie, or wee pittie an other mannes happe. [132]

[*Disposition*]

Disposition as *Tullie* doth define it: is a certaine bestowing of things, an and apt declaring what is meete for euery part, as time and place doe best require.

. . . . .

There are two kindes of disposyng, and placyng of matter. The one is, when we followe the appointed rule of *Rhetorique*, the whiche Nature doeth almoste teache vs: The other is wholie fashioned by the discretion of hym that makes the Oration.

Rhetorique doeth teache vs, and Nature also leadeth vs thereunto, firste to speake some what before we open our matter, after that to tell the cause of our entente, settyng foorthe the matter plainly that all maie vnderstande it, then to proue our owne cause by good reason, and to confute all suche thynges, as contrary to our purpose: laste of all, to gather the whole in a somme, concludyng the matter breefly, and so to make an ende. Now to place those reasons, which should bothe serue to confirme, and to confute; and to tell in what parte of the Oration, it were beste to vse this reason and that reason, that the rather we might proue, teach and perswade: a right wiseman had neede to take this matter in hande. For euen as tyme, the place, the iudge, and the matter it self shall giue cause: so muste a wise bodie take his aduauntage. Sometymes it shall bee expediente to vse no preface at all, or els when the matter is well knowne, it will bee good to leaue the matter vntolde, and straight to seeke the confirmation, vsyng some strong reason for the same purpose. Yea, sometymes it maie doe good, to neglect the naturall order, and beginne first to proue the cause, and afterward to tell it better then it was tolde before.

If the Judge or the hearers, shalbe wearied with other reportes before, it is best to go to the matter, and proue it out of hande, with as breef reasons and as strong as can bee gathered possible. And in prouyng of our matters we had neede euermore, rather to weye our reasons, then to number them, and thinke not that then we shall doe beste when we haue the strongest. And first of all the strongest should be vsed, and the other placed in the middest of the oration, the whiche beyng heaped together will make a good mustar. And yet this also would be learned, wheras we vsed the best reasons at the firste, wee should also reserue some that were like good for the latter ende: that the hearers might haue them freshe in their remembrance, when thei should giue iudgement. The slender reasons that can do lesse good, and yet not at all (for some may better be omitted) would be placed in the middest (as I saied) that both thei might be lesse marked, or beyng heaped there together thei might dooe more good, especially when bothe weightie reasons went before, weightie reasons also followed after. Now a wiseman that hath good experience in these affaires, and is able to make hymself a *Rhetorique* for euery matter, will not be bound to any precise rules, nor keepe any one order, but suche onely as by reason he shall thinke best to vse, beyng maister ouer arte, rather then arte should be maister ouer hym, rather makyng arte by witt, then confoundyng witte by art. And vndoubtedly euen in so dooyng he shall doe right well, and content the hearers accordyngly. [160-1]

[*Use of Rules*]

Rules were therfore giuen, and by muche obseruation gathered together, that those whiche could not see Arte hid in an other mannes dooynges, shold yet see the rules open all in an order set together: and thereby iudge the rather of their doynges, and by earnest imitation, seeke to resemble suche their inuention. [162]

. . . . .

And I knowe that rules were made first by wisemen, and not wisemen made by rules. [162]

[*Elocution*]

Fower partes belonging to Elocution.

{ i. Plainnesse.
ii. Aptnesse.
iii. Composition.
iiii. Exornation. [164]

. . . . .

Among all other lessons this should first be learned, that we neuer affect any straunge ynkehorne termes, but to speake as is commonly receiued: neither seking to be ouer fine, nor yet liuyng ouercarelesse, vsing our speeche as moste men doe, and ordering our wittes as the fewest haue doen. [164]

. . . . .

Such are thought apt wordes, that properly agree vnto that thyng whiche thei signifie, and plainly expresse the Nature of the same. [168]

. . . . .

Composition therefore is an apte iouynyng together of woordes in suche order, that neither the eare shall espie any gerre, nor yet any man shalbe dulled with ouerlong drawyng out of a sentence, nor yet muche confounded with minglyng of clauses suche as are needelesse, beyng heaped together without reason, and vsed without number. [169]

. . . . .

Exornation, is a gorgious beautifiyng of the tongue with borrowed wordes, and change of sentence or speeche with muche varieties. [172]

. . . . .

There are three kindes of figures, the one is, whem the nature of wordes is chaunged from one signification to an other, called a *Trope* of the Grecians: The other serueth for wordes when thei are not chaunged by nature, but only altered by speaking, called of the Grecians a *Scheme*. The third is, when by diuersitie of inuention, a sentence is many waies spoken, and also matters are amplified by heapyng examples, by dilatyng arguments, by comparyng of thynges together, by similitudes, by contraries, and by diuers other like, called by *Tullie* Exornation of sentences or colours of *Rhetorike*.

By all whiche figures euery Oration maie be muche beautified, and without the same, not one can attaine to be coumpted an Oratour, though his learnyng otherwise be neuer so greate. [173]

[*Memory*]

Memorie is the power retentiue of mynde, to keepe those thynges, which by mannes witt are conceiued, or thus. Memory is the power of the minde that conteineth thinges receiued, that calleth to mynde thynges past, and renueth of freshe, thinges forgotten. [213]

[*Delivery*]

Pronunciation is an apt ordering, both of the voice, countenaunce, and all the whole bodie accordyng to the worthines of such wordes and matter, as by speache are declared. [212]

. . . . .

Pronunciation standeth partly in fashionyng the tongue, and partly in framyng the gesture.

The tongue or voice is praise worthie, if the vtteraunce be audible, strong, and easie, and apte to order as wee liste. Therefore, they that minde to get praise in tellyng their minde in open audience, must at the first beginnyng, speake some what softlie, vse meete pausing, and beyng somewhat heated, rise with their voice, as tyme and cause shall beste require. They that haue no good voices by nature, or cannot vtter their wordes, must seeke for helpe elswhere. Exercise of the bodie, fastyng, moderation in meate and drinke, gapyng wide, or singyng plaine song, and counterfeictyng those that doe speake distinctly, helpe muche to haue a good deliueraunce. [222]

. . . . .

Gesture is a certain comely moderation of the countenance, and all other parts of mans bodie, aptly agreeyng to those thynges whiche are spoken. That if we shall speake in a pleasunt matter, it is meete that the looke also should bee cherefull, and all the gestures stirryng thereafter. The hedde to bee holden vpright, the forehedde without frounying, the browes without bendying, the nose without blowing, the eyes quicke and pleasaunt, the lippes not laied out, the teeth without grennyng, the armes not muche caste abroade, but comely sette out, as time and cause shall best require: the handes sometymes opened, and sometymes holden together, the fingers poinctyng, the breaste laied out, and the whole bodie stirryng altogether, with a semely moderation. By the whiche behauiour of our bodie after suche a sorte, we shall not onely delite men with the fight, but perswade theim the rather the truthe of our cause. [224-5]

SUGGESTED READINGS

Mair, G. H., ed.
    (Wilson's) *Arte of Rhetorique*. Oxford. Clarendon Press. 1909. xxxiv,236p

Wagner, Russell H.
    The Text and Editions of Wilson's Arte of Rhetorique. *Modern Language Notes*. 44:421-8 November 1929

    Thomas Wilson's Arte of Rhetorique. *Quarterly Journal of Speech*. 15:423-5 June 1929

    Thomas Wilson's Contributions to Rhetoric. In *Papers in Rhetoric*. Ed. by Donald C. Bryant. St. Louis, Mo. Private subscription. 1940. p1-7

    Wilson and His Sources. *Quarterly Journal of Speech*. 15:525-37 November 1929

JOHN BULWER
(fl. 1644-1654)

Bulwer's work deals exclusively with bodily action in delivery. It is a highly systematized classification of the many gestures which a speaker may use to convey various shades of meaning. More than that, it is also a sort of rationale of the whole subject of gesture, containing notes on its historical antecedents in literature and on the use to which action can be put generally.

Chirologia contains 64 descriptive analyses of the gestures of the hand, and, under the sub-division of *Dactylogia*, 25 additional analyses of the gestures of the fingers. *Chironomia*, which is subjoined to *Chirologia*, contains 49 canons of the gestures of the hand; under the sub-head of *Indigitatio*, appear 30 additional canons of the gestures of the fingers.

Because of the inaccessibility of this work, all of the descriptions and canons are reproduced—without elaborative detail, of course—in the following section.

CHIROLOGIA [1]

[Descriptions of the Gestures of the Hand]

Supplico. Gestus I. *The Stretching Out of The Hands* is a naturall expression of gesture, wherein wee are significantly *importunate, intreat, request, sue, solicite, beseech,* and ask *mercy* and *grace* at the Hands of others. [11]

Oro. Gestus II. *To Raise The Hand Conioyned or Spread out Towards Heaven* is the habit of *Devotion,* and a naturall and universall forme of *Prayer,* practised by those who are in *adversity,* and in *bitter anguish of Minde;* and by those who *give publique thanks and praise to the most High.* [14]

Ploro. Gest. III. *To Wring The Hands* is a naturall expression of excessive griefe, used by those who *condole, bewaile,* and *lament.* [28]

Admiror. Gest. IV. *To Throw Up The Hands To Heaven* is an expression of *admiration, amazement,* and *astonishment,* used also by those who flatter and *wonderfully praise;* and *have others in high regard,* or *extoll* anothers speech or action. [29]

[1] London, T. Harper, 1644.

Applaudo. Gest. V. *To Clap The Raised Hands One Against Another*, is an expression proper to them who *applaud, congratulate, rejoice, assent, approve,* and *are well pleased,* used by all Nations. [30]

Indignor. Gest. VI. *To Smite Suddenly on The Left Hand With The Right,* is a declaration of some *mistake, dolour, anger,* or *indignation....* [32]

Explodo. Gest. VII. *To Clap the Right Fist Often On The Left Palme,* is a naturall expression used by those who *mocke, chide, brawle,* and *insult, reproach, rebuke,* and *explode,* or *drive out with noise,* commonly us'd by the vulgar in their bickerings, as being the Scolds taunting dialect, and the loud naturall Rhetorique of those who declame.... [34]

Despero. Gest. VIII. *To appeare with Fainting and Dejected Hands,* is a posture of *feare, abasement of minde,* and *abject* and *vanquished courage,* and of utter *despaire.* [35]

Otio indulgeo. Gest. IX. *To Fold The Hands,* is a gesture of *idlenesse,* an expression often seene in the *Hands* of lazy Lubbers amus'd with *sloath,* who keepe their dull *Hands* so knit together, to maintain a drowsie league with sleepe.... [35-6]

Tristem animi recessum indico. Gest X. *To Hold The Fingers Inserted Between Each Other Acrosse,* is their *sluggish* expression who are fallen into a *melancholy muse.* [38]

Innocentiam Ostendo. Gest. XI. *To Imitate The Posture of Washing The Hands By Rubbing The Back of One In The Hollow of The Other With A Kind Of Detersive Motion,* is a gesture sometimes used by those who would *professe their innocency,* and declare they have no Hand in that soule businesse, not so much as by their manuall assent; as it were assuring by that gesture, that *they will keepe their Hands undefiled, and would wash their Hands of it: not have any thing to doe therein.* [40]

Lucri apprehensionem plaudo. Gest. XII. *To Rub the Palmes of the Hands Together, with a Kind of Applause, Much After The Manner as Some Are Wont To Do Who Take Paines To Heat Their Hands,* is an itching note of *greedy haste,* many times used by such who *applaud some pleading thought of deceit,* that they have in their heads. [40-1]

RHETORIC AND PUBLIC SPEAKING

Libertate resigno. Gest. XIII. *To Hold Forth The Hands Together*, is their naturall expression who *yeeld, submit*, and *resigne up themselves with supplication* into the power of another. [41]

Protego. Gest. XIV. *To Extend Out The Right Hand By The Arme Foreright*, is the naturall habit wherein we sometimes *allure, invite, speak to, cry after, call, or warne to come, bring into, exhort, give warning, admonish, protect, pacifie, rebuke, command, justifie, avow, enquire, direct, instruct, order, shew a generous confidence, hardinésse, and authority; give free liberty of speech, manifest a readinesse to answer, and make an apology for our selves, and appeare to undertake a business*. [42]

Triumpho. Gest. XV. *To Put Out The Raised Hand, And To Shake It As It Were Into A Shout*, is their naturall expression who *exalt, brag, boast, triumph,* and by *exultant* gesture express the *raptures of their joy*; they also who would declare their *high applause*, or would *congratulate*; and they who have *drunke*, doe commonly use the same gesture. [46]

Silentium Postulo. Gest. XVI. *The Becking With The Raised Hand* hath beene ever with all Nations accounted a signe of *craving audience*, and *intreating a favourable silence*. [47]

Juro. Gestus XVII. *To Lift Up The Right Hand To Heaven*, is the naturall forme and ceremony of an *oath*, used by those who *call God to witnesse*, and would *adjure, confirme*, or *assure by the obligation of an oath*. [50]

Asseveratione Deu Attestor. Gestus XVIII. *To Extend And Raise Up Both The Hands To Heaven*, is an expression of *establishment*, and a most strong kinde of *asseveration*, implying as it were *a double oath*. [51]

Suffragor. Gest. XIX. *To Hold Up The Hand* is a naturall token of *approbation, consent, election*, and of giving *suffrage*. [52]

Respuo. Gestus XX. *The Flirting Out Of The Back Part of The Hand, Or Put-By Of The Turning Palme*, is their naturall expression who would *refute, deny, prohibit, repudiate, impute*, or *to lay to ones charge, reject* or *pretend to lay for an excuse*, or would *twit and hit one in the teeth with a thing*, and signifie *disdaine*. [54]

Invito. Gestus XXI. *To Shew Forth The Hand, And So Forthwith To Call Backe As It Were And Bring It Againe Unto Us With A Waving Motion*, is a naturall Gesture, and a vulgar *compellation*, which we significantly in *calling* for men whom we *bid to come neare and approach unto us.* . . . [55]

Dimitto. Gestus XXII. *To Wag and Wave the Hand From us,* is an expression by gesture significant to *prohibit, bid one be gone, keepe off, forbid, dismisse,* and *bid farewell and adieu.* . . . [56]

Minor. Gestus XXIII. *To Shew And Shake The Bended Fist At One,* is their habit, who are *angry, threaten,* would *strike terrour, menace, revenge, shew enmity, despite, contemn, humble, chalenge, defie, expresse hate,* and *offer injury,* tell one what he must looke for at their Hands. [57]

Mendico. Gestus XXIV. *To Hold Out The Hand Hollow In Manner Of A Dish,* is their habit who *crave, beg, covet,* and *shew a greedy readinesse to receive;* and there is a certaine forme or semblance of the thing implied, in this unusuall capacity of the *Hand.* [59]

Munero. Gestus XXV. *To Put Forth The Right Hand Spread,* is the habit of *bounty, liberality,* and a *free* heart. . . . [61]

Auxilium fero. Gestus XXVI. *To Extend And Offer Out The Right Hand Unto Any,* is an expression of *pity,* and of an intention to *afford comfort* and *reliefe:* used also as a token of *assurance, peace, security,* and *promised safety,* and *salvation.* [65-6]

Commisereor. Gestus XXVII. *To Let Down The Hand with intent to reare some languishing creature from off the ground,* is a greater expression of *pity* and *commiseration,* then to afford a STRETCHED OUT HAND to one who riseth of his owne accord. . . . [67]

Irascor. Gestus XXVIII. *To Strike A Table Or Some Such Like Thing With The Hand,* is the gesture of one *angry,* or *grieved in minde,* and *very impatient.* [67]

Cohorto. Gestus XXIX. *To Hold Up The Hand Hollow Above The Shoulder Points, And To Shake It In Orbe By The Turne And Returne Of The Wrest,* is their naturall expression who *encourage, embolden,* and *exhort one to be of good cheere.* [69]

Praeclara Aggredior. Gestus XXX. *To Exalt Or Lift Up The Stretch'd Out Hand,* is the habit of one attempting to *doe and take some famous exploit in Hand*: and is a naturall posture of an *exalted* and *victorious power.* [69-70]

Profero. Gestus XXXI. *To Present The Hand,* is their expression who *profer* or *deliver a thing as their act and deed.* [71]

RHETORIC AND PUBLIC SPEAKING

Effoeminate festino. Gestus XXXII. *To Wag The Hand In A Swinging Gesture,* is their naturall expression who would *endeavour to hasten and assist themselves in progressive motion,* and withall denotes a kinde of *wantonnesse* and *effeminacy.* [72]

Demostro non habere. Gestus XXXIII. *To Shake Out The Hand,* is their naturall expression who would shew that *they have not, nor desire to have a thing.* [74]

Castigo. Gestus XXXIV. *To Shake Or Hold The Stretched And Raised Hand Over Any,* is their expression who *offer to chastise* and *shew a willingnes to strike or take revenge.* [74]

Pugno. Gestus XXXV. *To Strike One With The Fist,* is their Gesture who would be *avenged* of those that have offended them, and would *right themselves* by this wilde vindictive justice of their *Hands.* [75]

Reprehendo. Gestus XXXVI. *To Box Or Smite One With The Palm Of The Hand,* is their expression who would *rebuke* or *correct* another for some saucie speech or action. [76]

Apprehendo. Gestus XXXVII. *To Lay Hand Upon One* is their expression who with *authority apprehend* and lay hold of one as a delinquent to *secure their person.* [76]

Manumitto. Gestus XXXVIII. *To Let Go Ones Hold And Take Off The Hand From Any One,* is their gesture who would signifie a *willingnesse to release one that was before in their possession and power,* as having some *reason to grant them their liberty.* [77]

Incito. Gestus XXXIX. *To Clap One On The Back Or Shoulder With The Hand,* is their expression who would *hearten* and *encourage* others; a gesture obvious in the *Hand* that takes part with those that are in sight, and desires to set men or beasts together by the ears. [78]

Foveo. Gestus XL. *We Use To Stroke Them Gently With Our Hand* whom we *make much of, cherish, humour,* or *affectionately love,* an expression very obvious among the actions of common life.... [78]

Admoneo. Gest. XLI. *To Take Hold Gently Of Anothers Hand,* is a gesture used by those who *admonish* and *perswade,* which hee that shall set himselfe to observe the actions of men, may upon such occasions finde used to the same intents and purposes. [78-9]

Confido. Gestus XLII. *To Lean Upon Anothers Hand,* is their gesture who make a confiding use of the staffe of their age or affection, an expression importing that they much rely upon their faith and friendship.... [80]

Impedio. Gestus XLIII. *To Hold Fast Anothers Hand* in the signification of *hindrance* and *restraint,* is a gesture so obvious in the cholericke perturbations of humane life, that it needs no illustration by example, since we may every day meet with satisfaction in the publique streets.... [81]

Recordo. Gestus XLIV. *To Iog One The Elbow,* is the usuall intimation of those who *put others in minde,* and take upon them the part of a Remembrancer.... [81]

Recommendo. Gestus XLV. *To Take One By The Hand* in courtesie, to *recommend* them unto another by way of presentation, is an usuall expression in the *Hands* of men, a gesture significant and remarkable.... [81-2]

Officiose duco. Gestus XLVI. *To Lead One By The Hand,* is their expression who *take care of the weaknesse and inability of others in matters of progressive motion,* used most commonly to young children whom *wee would teach and assist to goe with more ease and safety.*... [83]

Impatientia prodo. Gestus XLVII. *To Apply The Hand Passionately Unto The Head,* is a signe of *anguish, sorrow, griefe, impatiencie,* and *lamentation,* used also by those who *accuse* or *justifie* themselves. [84]

Sollicite Cogito. Gestus XLVIII. *To Rub Or Scratch The Head With The Hand,* is their naturall gesture who are in *anguish* or *trouble of minde;* for commonly when we are in *doubt,* and *uncertaine what to doe,* we musing SCRATCH OUR HEAD. [85]

Pudeo. Gestus XLIX. *The Recourse Of The Hand To The Face* in *shame,* is a naturall expression.... [86]

Adoro. Gest. L. *To Kisse The Hand,* is their *obsequious* expression who would *adore & give respect* by the courtly solemnity of a *salutation* or *valediction.* [87]

Distante Amicum revereor. Gest. LI. *To Bring The Hand To Our Mouth, And Having Kissed It, To Throw It From Us,* is their expression who would *present their service, love, and respect to any that are distant from them.* [88]

Conscienter affirmo. Gest. LII. *To Lay The Hand Open To Our Heart,* using a kinde of bowing gesture, is a garb wherein we *affirm a thing, swear* or *call God to witnesse a truth.* . . . [88]

Poenitentia ostendo. Gest. LIII. *To Beat And Knock The Hand Upon The Breast,* is a naturall expression of the *Hand,* used in *sorrow, contrition, repentance, shame,* and in *reprehending our selves.* . . . [89]

Dolorem noto. Gestus LIV. *To Hold The Hands Upon The Loins, Sides Or Hip,* is their expression who *feel some paine in those regions of the body.* . . . [91]

Indignatione timeo. Gest. LV. *The Smiting Of The Hand Upon The Thigh,* in the practise and conversation of common life, was ever frequent, and is so deeply imprinted in the Maners of men, that you shall in vaine perswade a man *angry* and *inraged.with griefe,* to contain his *Hand* from this passion. [91]

Data fide promitto. Gest. LVI. *To Strike Anothers Palm,* is the habit and expression of those who *plight their troth, give a pledge of faith and fidelity, promise, offer truce, confirme a league, buy, sell, grant, covenant, bargaine, give or take handsell, engage themselves in suretiship, refer their controverseries to an arbiter, put to comprimise or chuse an umpier, engage themselves to be true and trusty, warrant and assure.* [93]

Reconcilio. Gestus LVII. *To Shake The Given Hand* is an expression usuall in *friendship, peacefull love, benevolence, salutation, entertainment,* and *bidding welcome; reconciliation, congratulation, giving thanks, valediction,* and *wel-wishing.* [109]

Injurias remitto. Gestus LVIII. *To Presse Hard And Wring Anothers Hand,* is a naturall *insinuation of love, duty, reverence, supplication, peace, and of forgivenesse of all injuries.* [116]

Suspicionem & Odium noto. Gest. LIX. *To Draw Backe The Unwilling Hand Instead Of Reaching It Out To Imbrace The Hand Of Another,* is a sign of *enmity* likely to prove inveterate, used by those who *flatly refuse to agree, & reject* that proffered amity which they have in suspition. [120]

Chare diligo. Gest. LX. *We Put Forth Both Our Hands To Embrace* those we love, as if we would bring them home into our heart and bosome, as some *dear* and *pretious* thing, as *Aristotle* gives the reason of the gesture. [122]

Honoro. Gestus LXI. *To Apprehend And Kisse The Backe Of Anothers Hand*, is their naturall expression who would give a token of their *serviceable love, faith, loyalty, honourable respect, thankfull humility, reverence, supplication, and subjection.* [122]

Reservatione Saluto. Gestus LXII. *To Offer The Backe Of The Right Hand To Be Kissed* by others, which *Plinie* calls a religious ceremony used by all Nations, is an expression of *state* used by *proud* and *scornfull* persons, who affect the garbe of great ones, and are willing to afford a *sleight respect* to one they thinke unworthy of a higher touch. [130]

Furacitatem noto. Gestus LXIII. *To Put Forth The Left Hand As It Were By Stealth*, is their significant endeavour who have *an intent unseene to purloine and convey away something.* [133]

Benedico. Gestus LXIV. *The Imposition of The Hand*, is a naturall gesture significantly used in *condemnation, absolution, pardon* and *forgivenesse, benediction, adoption, initiation, confirmation, consecration, ordination, sanation,* and *in gracing our meales.* [137]

CHIROLOGIA: DACTYLOGIA

[Descriptions of the Gestures of the Fingers]

Inventione laboro. Gestus I. *The Finger In The Mouth Gnawn And Suckt,* is a gesture of *serious and deep meditation, repentance, envy, anger,* and *threatened revenge.* [158]

Fleo. Gest. II. *To Put Finger In The Eye,* is their expression who *crie,* and would by that endeavour of nature *ease themselves* and *give vent to their conceived heavinesse.* [160]

Approbo. Gest. III. *To Hold Up The Thumbe,* is the gesture of one *giving his voice or suffrage,* of one that *helpeth with his word at the time of election,* and of one shewing his *assent* or *approbation....* [161]

Extollo. Gest. IV. *To Hold Up Both the Thumbs,* is an expression importing a transcendency of praise. [161]

Collateraliter Monstro. Gestus V. *To Point With The Turned Out Thumbe* is a note of demonstration.... [162]

Indico. Gest. VI. *The Fore-Finger Put Forth, The Rest Contracted To A Fist*, is an expresse of *command* and *direction*; a gesture of the *Hand* most *demonstrative*. [162]

Terrorem incutio. Gest. VII. *The Holding Up Of The Fore-Finger*, is a gesture of *threatening* and *upbraiding*. [166]

Veneratione saluto. Gestus VIII. *The Fore-Finger Kissed* in the naturall greetings of the *Hand*, hath been ever tooke for a *complementall salutation*, and is used by those who *adore, worship, give honor, thanks,* or a *faire respect*. [167]

Silentium indico. Gest. IX. *The Laying of the Fore-Finger Upon The Mouth*, is their habit who would express their *silence, conviction, shame, ignorance, reverence, servile feare, modesty, a revolving meditation, admiration and amazement*. [168]

Redarguo. Gestus X. *The Bowing Downe Of The Fore-Finger For a checke of silence,* and to *redargue*, is an action often found in the *Hands* of men. [170]

Compello. Gest. XI. *The Lifting Up and Bowing Of The Index Towards The Face*, is a usuall gesture of *invitation* as naturally significant to that intent, as the inward waving of the whole *Hand*. . . . [170]

Veto. Gestus XII. *The Raising Up And Bowing The Fore-Finger From Us*, is a gesture naturall to those who *becken a retreat* or *forbid*. . . . [171]

Diffidentiam noto. Gestus XIII. *To Feel With The Fingers Ends*, is their scepticall expression who *endeavour to satisfie themselves by information of the Fact, in the qualities of a thing*. [171]

Mollicie prodo. Gestus XIV. *To Scratch The Head With One Finger*, is a kinde of *nice* and *effeminate* gesture, bewraying a *close inclination to vice*. . . . [172]

Convicium facio. Gest. XV. *The Putting Forth Of The Middle-Finger, The Rest Drawn Into A Fist* on each side, . . . is a naturall expression of *scorne* and *contempt*. [173]

Contemno. Gestus XVI. *To Compresse The Middle-Finger With The Thumbe By Their Complexion Producing A Sound And So Casting Out Our Hand*, is a gesture we use to signifie our *contempt of unprofitable things,* & to shew by gesture how we *sleight, contemne, insult,* and *undervalue* any thing. [176]

Ironiam infligio. Gestus XVII. *To Bend The Middle-Finger While It Stifly Resteth Upon The Thumb, And So In Iesting-wise To Let It Off*, is a triviall expression whereby we with a *Fillip inflict a trifling punishment, or a scoffe*. [177]

Contemptuose provoco. Gestus XVIII. *To Becken With Eare-Finger*, is their usuall concise expression, who are advanced by confidence to relie upon the strength of their ability, and would by a provoking signall dare, *chalenge, defie*, and *bid one prepare for an encounter*, implying a *strong presumption* of the *victory*, as if they esteemed him as nothing in their *Hand*. [179]

Avaritiam prodo. Gestus XIX. *To Gripe The Left Hand The Thumbe Clutched In Withall*, is the hold-fast gesture of *tenacious avarice*, and significant to discover the *miserable* and *penurious* condition of a close-fisted niggard, a parcell of the character of an old pinch-penny. [179]

Offensiun culam resentio. Gest. XX. *To Give One A Rap With The Fingers Half Bent, Or Knuckles*, is their expression who would vent their *sleight anger* or *dislike* upon others; or would softly and *modestly* knocke at some doore. [180]

Iram importentem prodo. Gestus XXI. *To Put The Fingers Into A Gripe Or Claw-Like Aspect, And to Scratch or Claw* another therewith, is the *impotent* expression of a *curst heart that eagerly desires to set a marke of its displeasure upon those that have provoked it to a splenitique use of its pounres*. [181]

Stultitiae notam infigo. Gestus XXII. *To Present The Index And Eare-Finger Wagging, With The Thumb Aplied Unto The Temples*, is their expression who would scornfully reprove any for failing in any exercise of wit, or for some absurd stumble of a tripping and inconsiderate lip, or for some errour in manners and behaviour: For, this most ridiculous affront implies such *men to be Asses*. [181-2]

Improbitatem objicio. Gestus XXIII. *To Locke The Thumbe Betweene The Next Two Fingers*, is an *ironicall* vulgarisme of the *Hand*. . . . [183]

Parce do. Gest. XXIV. *To Give With Two Fingers*, is a *parcimonious* expression of the *Hand* often seen in *clutch-fists niggards*, and *pinch-pennies*. . . . [184]

Numero. Gestus XXV. *To Begin With The First Finger Of The Left Hand, And To Tell On To The Last Finger Of The Right*, is the naturall and simple way of *numbring & computation*. . . . [184]

CHIRONOMIA [2]

[Canons Relating to Management of Hands]

Canon I. The *Hand* lightly opened, timorously displayed before the breast, and let fall by short turnes under the heaving shoulders, is an *humble* and neat action, becomming those who *daunted dismaid*, begin to speak as if their tongue were *afraid* to encounter with the publicke eare; and such who shunning a profuse excesse of words, would *sparingly* expresse their mindes, or *asswage* and *mitigate* the censorious expectation of their auditours, by an ingenious insinuation of a *diminutive* action. [27-8]

Canon II. The stretching forth of the *Hand* is the forme of pleading, and hath a secret *helpe* and *preparative* to ready speaking, and commendeth an *Apology* or any set speech to the Auditours. [28-9]

Canon III. The indulgent putting forth of the *Hand* towards the Auditours, signifying a kinde of *Humanity*, and *good will*, is a *benevolent* action, fit for those who *praise* or *congratulate*. . . . [30]

Canon IV. The gentle and wel-ordered *Hand*, throwne forth by a moderate projection, the *Fingers* unfolding themselves in the motion, and the shoulders a little slackned, affords a familiar force to any *plaine continued speech* or *uniforme discourse*. . . . [30-1]

Canon V. The *Hand* directed towards the Auditours, with a kinde of *impetuous agitation of the Arme*, maintaining its gravity with a swift recourse, is an action *intense* and *full* of *vehemencie*, fit to *threaten, denounce, reprehend,* and *assevere,* and by its extension, implies *power,* and a *prevalent authority.* [31-2]

Canon VI. The *Hand* restrained and kept in, is an argument of *modesty,* and *frugall pronunciation,* a *still* and *quiet* action, suitable to a milde and *remisse* declamation. [32]

Canon VII. The *Hand* put forth and raised aloft, is an action of *congratulatory exclamation and amplification of joy.* [35]

Canon VIII. The *Hand* collected, the *Fingers* looking downewards, then turned and resolved, is a set form accommodated to their intention who would openly *produce their reasons.* [35]

[2] *Chirologia. . . Whereunto Is Added Chironomia,* London, T. Harper, 1644. The two parts contained in the one volume are separately paginated.

Canon IX. The hollow *Hand* raised above the shoulder with some kinde of grave motion of the wrest, doth *cheere, exhort embolden* and *encourage*. [35-6]

Canon X. The palme (the Fingers all joyned together) turn'd up, and by the return of the wrest, in one motion, spread and turned about with the *Hand,* is an action convenient for *admiration*. [36]

Canon XI. The *Hand* (the Fingers all joyned at their tops) referred to the vocall passage of the minde, doth *lightly admire;* and fits their occasion who in the interim are moved with *sudden indignation,* and in the end fall to *deprecate, amazed with fear*. [36]

Canon XII. The turned up *Hand,* (the Thumbe bent in, and the other Fingers remisse) transferred to the Northern side of our body, and then prone to our South side, so, lightly waved to and fro, doth very aptly *distinguish contraries,* and may *shew the variety of numbers*. [37]

Canon XIII. The *hand* after one sort is not still disposed to *aske* a *question*; yet commonly when wee *demand,* however it be composed, we use to change or turne our *hand* raising it a little upwards. [37]

Canon XIV. The *hand* erected, and then so moved, that the inside is turned out, is a sensible Action that apparently presents *the least disparity* or *difference*. [37-8]

Canon XV. The *Hand* that by alternate motions contracts and unfolds itselfe, doth aid them in their pronunciation who are very *instant to urge a thing*. [38]

Canon XVI. The turning of the *Hand* may serve to signifie an *easie dexterity of performance*. [38]

Canon XVII. The *Hand* brought to the stomacke, and spread gently thereon, is a gesture of Rhetoricall *asseveration*. [39]

Canon XVIII. The shewing forth of the *Hand,* or beckning with the same, are Rhetorically significant to *speake* to, *call after, invite, bring in,* and *warne to come*. [40]

Canon XIX. The *Hand* rais'd & stretched out with the arme, or the *Hand* waved towards the auditors, are advãtageous actions for them who would imply a *generous confidence,* and their *authoritie* and *abilitie to effect a thing:* it serves also to *call for,* and *demand silence,* and for the *prologue* to an act of *pacification*. [41]

Canon XX. The *Hand* propellent to the left-ward, the left shoulder brought forward, the Head inclined to the Southward of the Body, is an action accommodated to *aversation, execration,* and *negation.* [43]

Canon XXI. To shake the *Hand,* with bended browes, doth *abhorre, deny, dislike, refuse,* and *disallow.* [43]

Canon XXII. The *hand* resilient or leapeing back to the Northward of the Body, whence it did descend, makes an action fit to *abominate,* and to accompany words of *refusall* or *dislike,* and may serve also in point of *admiration.* [43]

Canon XXIII. The *Hand* with a general percussion, now greater, now lesse; now flat, now sharpe, according to the diversitie of the affections, is fitted to *distinguish the Comma's & breathing parts of a sentence.* [44]

Canon XXIV. By his *Hand* referr'd unto him, an Oratour may *shew himselfe,* when he speakes anything concerning himselfe. [44]

Canon XXV. The *Hand* bent into a fist, and the Pulpit or Barre strooke therewith, is an action of Rhetoricall heate, and very artificially accompanies *Anger,* and a more *vehement contention.* [44-5]

Canon XXVI. The *palm* strook upon a book, (held usually in the left hand of an Orator) doth serve to *excite* and *rowze up the Auditours.* [45]

Canon XXVII. To clap the *hand* suddenly upon the breast, is an acti-of *increpation,* proper in their hands, who would *arrest their speech, and non-suit it by silence.* ... [45]

Canon XXVIII. The *Hand* brought unto the stomack, & in a remisse garb spread thereon, doth *conscienciously assevere,* & becomes them who *affirme any thing of themselves.* [46]

Canon XXIX. The Breast stricken with the *Hand,* is an action of *Griefe, sorrow, repentance,* and *indignation.* [46]

Canon XXX. The Forehead stricken with the *Hand,* is an action of *dolour, shame,* and *admiration.* [47]

Canon XXXI. The Thigh smitten with the *Hand,* was the gesture of one *pleading more vehemently,* of one *grieved* and *fuming* with *indignation,* of one *taking notice of an others errour,* or *confessing himselfe deceived.* [51]

Canon XXXII. The left hand thrust forth with the Palme turned backward, the left shoulder raised, so that it may aptly consent with the head bearing to the *Right Hand,* agrees with their intention who *refuse, abhor, detest,* or *abominate* some execrable thing, against which their mindes are bent as a distastefull object, which they would seem to *chafe away,* and *repell.* [52-3]

Canon XXXIII. The left hand explained into a Palme, obtaines a forme of *perspicuity.* [53]

Canon XXXIV. Both the turned out Palmes bent to the left side, is a more passionate forme of *destestation,* as being a redoubled action. [54]

Canon XXXV. Both *Hands* objected with the Palmes adverse, is a fore-right adjunct of pronunciation, fit to helpe the utterance of words comming out in *destestation, despite* and *exprobration.* [54]

Canon XXXVI. Both *Hands* extended forth, the Palmes driving out to both sides, doubles the Action to all the same intents and purposes of *aversenesse.* [54]

Canon XXXVII. Both *Hands* clasped and wrung together, is an Action convenient to manifest *griefe* and *sorrow.* [55]

Canon XXXVIII. Both Hands dejected, make *supplication* more Canonicall. [55]

Canon XXXIX. Both *Hands* a little or farre dis-joyned, shew the *manner* and *abundance.* [55]

Canon XL. Both *Hands* extended out forward together, is an Action Commodious for them who *submit, invoke, doubt, speak to, accuse,* or *call by name, implore* or *attest.* [55]

Canon XLI. Both *Hands* lightly smitten together, is convenient enough to express a certaine *anxious* and *turbulent heat of cogitation* of an Oratour, that cannot sufficiently explaine his minde, or doe as he would. [56]

Canon XLII. The *Hands* gently set together by a sweet approach, causing a low sound by their light encounter or complosion, make an opportune cadence of Action, to attend the *close* or *period of a sentence.* [56-7]

Canon XLIII. Both *Hands* smitten together with a certaine kinde of gravity, doth *affirme* with Rhetoricall *asseveration.* [57]

Canon XLIV. Both the Palmes held respective to the body, declare *benevolence*. [57]

Canon XLV. Both Palms held averse before the Breast, denote *Commiseration*. [57]

Canon XLVI. The *Hands* address to both sides, are well disposed to *satisfie* or to *request*. [58]

Canon XLVII. If both *Hands* by turnes behave themselves with equall Art, they fitly move to set off any matter that goes by way of *Antithesis* or *opposition*. [58]

Canon XLVIII. We may use likewise the advantage of both *Hands,* when wee would present by some ample gesture the *immensity of things; some spaces far and wide extent, a great number, almost infinite, large affections,* or when the voyce is reiterate by *conduplication.* [58-9]

Canon XLIX. Both *Hands* modestly extended and erected unto the shoulder points, is a proper forme of *publicke benediction.* for the *Hands* of an Ecclesiasticall Oratour when hee would dismisse his Auditours. [59]

INDIGITATIO

[*Canons Relating to Management of Fingers*]

Canon I. The two inferior *Fingers* shut in, and the other three presented in an eminent posture in the extended *Hand*, is a *speaking* Action, significant to *demand silence,* and *procure audience.* [67]

Canon II. The Thumbe erect, the other Fingers gently bent in, is a convenient composition of the *Hand* for an *exordium*, and to lead to the forming of the other actions of the Hand. . . . [70]

Canon III. If any thing be to be *shewed*, the Thumb must be bent in, the other foure *Fingers* remisse. [71]

Canon IV. The *Index* joyned to the Thumbe, the other *Fingers* remisse, is another forme of the *Hand*, fit for an *exordium.* [71]

Canon V. The middle *Finger* applied unto the Thumbe, the other three let loose, is a fashion of the *Hand*, most of all commodious for a *Proem.* [71]

Canon VI. The two middle *Fingers* brought under the *thumb,* is an Action more *instant* and *importunate,* and doth *urge* more then is convenient for an Exordium or Narration. [72-3]

Canon VII. The top of the *Fore-finger* moved to joyne with the naile of the *Thumbe* that's next unto it, the other fingers in remitter, is opportune for those who *relate, distinguish,* or *approve.* 'Tis also fit for them that *mildly councell* and becomes the phrases of *pompous Elocution,* with which *Rhetoricians* polish and enrich their Orations. 'Tis seasonable also for *Narrations* and *Panegyriques,* where a soft & pellucid Oration flowes with the copious streames of Eloquence, and it availes in any *painted kinde of speech,* and agrees with an *Epidixis.* [73-4]

Canon VIII. The two last *Fingers* drawn to the bottome of Cytherea's brawny hill, or the pulpe of the *Thumb*; the *Thumb* apprest unto the middle joynt of the two next: if the Dexter *Hand* so form'd, doe smite with a light percussion on the sinister *Palme,* it doth conspicuously *distribute & digest* the numbers, arguments, and members of an Oration. [74]

Canon IX. The top of the *Thumb* joyn'd to the middle of the naile of the Right Index, the other Fingers remisse; is fit to *distinguish contraries.* [75]

Canon X. The left *Thumb* prest downe by the *Index* of the Right Hand, doth *urge* and *instantly enforce* an argument. [75]

Canon XI. The top or grape of the left *Index* gently apprehended, puts the *Hand* into a Rhetorical shape for *disputation.* [75]

Canon XII. The middle joynt of the left *Index* apprehended, intends more *earnestness,* and sublimates the sense of words unto a point of greater *vehemencie.* [75]

Canon XIII. The upper joynt of the *Index* apprehended, the two next *Fingers* a little bowed, the *eare-finger* in the meane time scarce bent at all; hath a Rhetoricall force in *Disputations.* [76]

Canon XIV. The *Mid-finger* prest to the *Palm,* and the others at their own behest, makes the *Hand* competently apt for to *upbraid.* [76]

Canon XV. The two *Middle-fingers* bent inward, and their Extremes presented in a fork, doth object a *scoffe,* and doth *contumeliously reproach.* [76]

Canon XVI. The *Vice-hand,* or *Thumb,* extended out with the *Eare-Finger,* the other *Fingers* drawn in; doth denote *amplitude.* [76-7]

Canon XVII. The *Thumbe* that presents itselfe upright, out of a Right-hand bent into a Fist; is a *grave masculine* action, fit to advance the sense of *Magnanimitie.* [77]

Canon XVIII. The *Thumbe* turn'd out, by a received custome, is made an act of *Demonstration.* [77]

Canon XIX. The three last *Fingers* contracted close to the *Palme,* and compres'd by the *Champion* of the *Hand,* and the *Index* display'd in full length; *upbraides*: is a point of *indigitation,* most *demonstrative.* [77]

Canon XX. The *Index* erected from a Fist, doth *Crave and expect attention*; and, if mov'd, it doth *threaten* and *denounce.* [78]

Canon XXI. The *Index* advanced from a *fist,* and inclin'd respective to the shoulder; hath a great facultie to *confirme, collect* and *refute.* [78]

Canon XXII. The *Index* (the rest compos'd into a Fist) turn'd down perpendicular; doth *urge, inculcate* and drive the point into the heads of the Auditours. [79]

Canon XXIII. Both the *Indexes* joyn'd, and pyramidically advanc'd; doe *exalt the Force that flowes from more splendid and glorious Elocution.* [79]

Canon XXIV. Both the *Indexes,* with acountenance averse, directed to one side, doe point out an *ironicall intention.* [79-80]

Canon XXV. The *Middle Finger* put forth, and brandish'd in extent, is an action fit to *brand* and *upbraide men with sloth, effeminacie, and notorious vices.* [80]

Canon XXVI. The middle *Finger* strongly comprest by the *Thumbe,* and their collision producing a flurting sound, and the *Hand* so cast out, is an Action convenient to *slight* and *undervalue,* and to express the vanity of things. . . . [81]

Canon XXVII. If the Ring *Finger* by a single Action goe out of the open *Hand,* as it were to serve the Tact, it may much advance their utterance, who in discourse touch and handle a matter lightly. [82]

Canon XXVIII. The Fare *Finger* appearing erect out of a bended Fist, doth by that action obtain a force to explaine more subtill things. [83]

Canon XXIX. The Right *Index*, if it marshal-like goe from *Finger* to *Finger*, to note them out with a light touch, it doth fit their purpose who would *number their arguments*, and by a visible distinction set them all on a row upon their *Fingers*. [83]

Canon XXX. To lift up, or put forth some of the *Fingers*, is a plaine way of Rhetoricall Arithmeticke fit to signifie a small number, a simple action serving well enough their occasions who would inculcate two or three chiefe points to an ignorant multitude. [85]

SUGGESTED READINGS

Bulwer, John
Chirologia: or the naturall language of the hand. Composed of the speaking motions, and discoursing gestures thereof. Whereunto is added Chironomia: or the art of manuall rhetoricke. Consisting of the naturall expressions, digested by art in the hand, as the chiefest instrument of eloquence, by historicall manifesto's, exemplified out of the authentique registers of common life, and civill conversation. With types, or chyrograms: a long-wish'd for illustration of this argument. London. T. Harper. 1644. 2v in 1

FRANÇOIS DE FÉNELON
(1651-1715)

Fénelon, the Archbishop of Cambray, resolves the rules of speaking to three essentials, namely, proving, painting, and moving the passions. Although the *Dialogues* are not to be listed among the great works in the literature of rhetoric, they merit attention as a reasonable plea for a more simple and natural manner in pulpit oratory.

DIALOGUES CONCERNING ELOQUENCE [1]

[*Rhetoric As a Kind of Painting*]

A. I will give you one then, which perhaps will satisfy you. We have seen that eloquence consists not only in giving clear, convincing proofs; but likewise in the art of moving the passions. Now in order to move them, we must be able to paint them well; with their various objects and effects. So that I think the whole art of oratory may be reduced to proving, painting, and raising the passions. Now all those pretty, sparkling, quaint thoughts that do not tend to one of these ends, are only witty conceits.

C. What do you mean by painting? I never heard that term applied to rhetoric.

A. To paint, is not only to describe things; but to represent the circumstances of them, in such a lively, sensible manner, that the hearer shall fancy he almost sees them with his eyes. For instance: if a dry historian were to give an account of Dido's death, he would only say, she was overwhelmed with sorrow after the departure of Aeneas; and that she grew weary of her life, so went up to the top of her palace, and, lying down on her funeral pile, she stabbed herself. Now these words would inform you of the fact; but you do not see it. When you read the story in Virgil, he sets it before your eyes. When he represents all the circumstances of Dido's despair; describes her wild rage; and death already staring in her aspect; when he makes her speak at the sight of the picture and sword that Aeneas left, your imagination transports you to Carthage; where you see the Trojan fleet leaving the shore, and the queen quite inconsolable. You

[1] From the translation by William Stevenson. *Dialogues Concerning Eloquence*, by François de Salignac de la Mothe Fénelon. 1st American ed., Boston, Farrand, Mallory and Company, 1810.

enter into all her passions, and into the sentiments of the supposed spectators. It is not Virgil you then hear: you are too attentive to the last words of unhappy Dido, to think of him. The poet disappears: and we see only what he describes; and hear those only whom he makes to speak. Such is the force of a natural imitation, and of painting in language. Hence it comes that the painters and the poets are so nearly related; the one paints for the eyes; and the other for the ears: but both of them ought to convey the liveliest pictures to people's imagination. I have taken an example from a poet to give you a livelier image of what I mean by painting in eloquence: for poets paint in a stronger manner than orators. Indeed the main thing in which poetry differs from eloquence is, that the poet paints with enthusiasm, and gives bolder touches than the orator. But prose allows of painting in a moderate degree: for, without lively descriptions it is impossible to warm the hearer's fancy, or to stir his passions. A plain narrative does not move people: we must not only inform them of facts; but strike their senses, by a lively, moving representation of the manner and circumstances of the facts we relate. [69-72]

SUGGESTED READINGS

Stevenson, William, tr.
Dialogues of M. De Fénelon. 1st. American ed. Boston. Farrand, Mallory and Co. 1810. v,174p

JOHN LAWSON
(1712-1759)

Lawson delivered the substance of these *Lectures* in Trinity College, Dublin, and published them in 1752. The following passages will give the reader some impression of the character and style of the work. Although not distinguished for originality of treatment, the *Lectures* present a reasonably complete account of the art of rhetoric, with heavy reliance upon the classical authors.

LECTURES CONCERNING ORATORY [1]

[On the Usefulness of Imitation]

The Arguments by which we prove the Usefulness of Imitation are drawn from two Sources, Experience and Reason. Let us briefly unfold some of each.

Look back on former Ages: What hath been the Practice of Mankind? How have they who excelled in any Science or Art proceeded? Did they set out upon their own single Stock, or did they borrow from the Fund of others? The Point is easily decided. It is a Fact not to be controverted, that the most eminent Persons in all Kinds of Literature owe their first Materials to the Discovery of others; nay, and derive from Example a great Part of their Skill in the Management of those Materials. [109-10]

. . . . .

Thus Experience is on the Side of Imitation. The second Source of Arguments on this Head is *Reason*. Let us next consult her: She bids us first apply ourselves to human Nature. Are Men so formed, that a single Person is able, by the Power of his own Genius, to carry an Art from its first Rudiments to Perfection? Do we not see how gradual Improvement hath been in every Nation? That Arts and Sciences have always had their Infancy and Manhood, as it were, no less than the human Race; weak and rude at their first Dawning, they received Strength and Growth by Degrees, and at last arose to Maturity. Doth not this Observation evince, beyond Controversy, the Usefulness of Imitation? Men assist each other. Some lucky Hit, or happy inventive Genius, opens the right Source; others, following his Steps, collect and guide the Waters in proper Channels. For such

[1] 3rd ed., Dublin, printed by G. Faulkner, 1760.

are the Weakness and Indolence of Man, so limited are his Talents, so many the Accidents to which he is liable, and his Life at the utmost shut up within so narrow Bounds, that it is scarcely possible for the same Person to light upon the right Vein, to pursue it steadily, and trace it to its farthest Limit: No, this must be the work of many Hands, imitating and improving each upon the other, for the most Part of Generations, labouring in Succession. Whoever pursueth the History of Knowledge will find this to have been the Fact almost without Exception. The Temple of Arts, if we may so speak, cannot be raised by one Person, seldom in one Age; Generation after Generation worketh upon it, each mounting upon the Labours of the foregoing. Nor is it so perfect at this Day, but that it may admit of Addition: somewhat is still wanting in Extent and Ornament. [112-13]

. . . . .

Imitation is indeed necessary and sufficient, while you are a Learner, to instruct and put you into a right Method: If you would set up for yourself, you must have beside some Stock of your own. Hitherto you have subsisted by the Help and Bounty of others; You are now fledged, should leave the Support and Track of the Parent-Birds, if I may so speak, trust to your own Wings, and soar alone.

Indeed the Perfection of Imitation consisteth herein; not in borrowing the Designs and Words of the Antients, which, if done with Discretion, is not only allowable, by generally pleasing; but in acquiring their Air and Manner, in a Resemblance of their Purity, Life, and Elevation; let the Materials be as much as you can your own; but endeavour to possess yourself of their Skill in putting them together, and in finishing; so that your Work may in Evenness, Solidity, and Lustre, resemble the Master-pieces which they have left behind them.

He who takes the Whole is rather a Plagiary than an Imitator: But he who, rich in a Fund of his own, adds to it by discreetly borrowing from the Antients, transferring into his Performance their Skill and Spirit, and making one regular uniform Work, is truly an Imitator, and may be allowed to have the Praise of an Original. [123-4]

[*Persuasion and Conviction*]

The Answer is not difficult. As the End of Eloquence is Persuasion, and, strictly speaking, all Persuasion ought to be founded in Conviction alone, it must be acknowledged, that all Address to the Passions is grounded in the Imperfection of Mankind; it is faulty if not necessary. If our Hearers were always serious, attentive, knowing, and unprejudiced, we should have nothing to do but to lay Truth before them in its own genuine Shape: But as Men actually are, we find it necessary, not only to shew them what is right, but to make Use of all the Skill we have, to induce them stedfastly to behold it. In every publick Assembly some are ignorant, many wandering in their Thoughts, or otherwise intent, not few biassed, and all indolent and quickly fatigued, Impediments which every Speaker must study to remove, or the Goodness of his Cause will but little avail: Truth hath Enemies within, who would bar up every Avenue against her; you must raise up friends there, if you seek to have Admission granted to her.

Now this being not the Frailty of particular Persons, but the State and Frame of human Nature, the Orator who would attempt to persuade upon Principles of severe Reason must be for the most Part unsuccessful. His Fate would be much the same with that of the Politician who should deal with Men as if they were perfectly just, and ground all his Schemes upon a Supposition of universal Probity.
[165]

[Cautions Regarding Attempts to Move Passions]

It remains to finish my Design, that I should point out some Cautions, very useful to be observed in Attempts to move the Passions.

First, "CONSIDER well whether the Point you are to discourse upon requires or may admit of the Pathetick." It is obvious, that there are many Subjects which do not; the Value of one, it's Circumstances, Nature may render that Treatment improper. For certainly nothing can be more disgusting to an Audience than to observe a Speaker torturing himself and them, in order to affect them mightly on a Subject of small Importance. As again it must be an unpleasing Disappointment to be paid with Exclamations and Vehemence of Sound, where they expect solid Argument. The Rule is, reflect thus within yourself before you begin: "If another were to speak on this Point, how would I wish him to treat of it? Should I desire to be instructed or moved, pleased or convinced? Act thou accordingly."

Another material Observation not always adverted to is, that "The principal Regard should ever be paid to Reason. To persuade you should convince." Conviction indeed need not, nay cannot always be brought about by a Chain of strict Argument, which few can perfectly comprehend, and yet fewer are disposed to listen to: But in all Cases the Ground-work must be Reason. This should be the Basis; upon which you may raise whatsoever you think conducive to your Purpose, of Ornament or Pathetick; but this it is, which must give

Strength and Consistence to your Discourse. Without this the most magnificent Oration is but like those Fabricks which appear sometimes in the Clouds, that the first Blast of Wind disperseth into shapeless Air. [178-9]

. . . . .

Hence follows a third Rule. "Let your Address to the Passions be as short as it conveniently may, for two Reasons," both upon the last mentioned Account, that you may bestow more Time and Care upon the rational Part: And likewise, because Nothing more quickly tires and disgusts than Addresses of this Sort. The Passions, as we have seen, were given to rouse us from Indolence, to make us active and enterprizing. Hence they are quick, lively, powerful, but soon subside. And this was graciously ordained, that, having answered their End, they might become weak, and easily manageable by Reason. Wherefore, "follow Nature. Seek not to keep long in Motion a Spring formed for quick, but short Action." [180]

. . . . .

A Former Observation leads to a fourth Rule; "In speaking to all Passions, as much as possible conceal your doing so." It should be perceived only by the Effects, otherwise it appears like a Design to deceive, and puts your Hearer on his Guard. To this Purpose a Greek Critick[k] recommends the Use of the Sublime, as hiding the other in it's superior Brightness. [183]

. . . . .

And in this Respect; *Lastly,* There is one Fault very common, against which we can never be too well prepared; that is, "The persisting in a pathetick Strain before an Audience entirely unmoved." In which Case a Speaker not only disgusts and tires, but never fails to become ridiculous. If one speak off-hand, or from Memory, he may easily perceive how the audience is affected by visible Marks in their Countenance and Behaviour: If he finds them listless and unconcerned, he may lower his Tone, he may shift his Sails, and change his Course: But where you rely on a studied Discourse, this is impracticable; You have engaged in a Career which you must finish, however disgraceful. For this Reason an [m] eminent Writer our own hath laid it down as a Kind of general Rule, not to attempt moving the Passions in a premeditated Discourse, because the Odds are that you fail. [185]

SUGGESTED READINGS

Lawson, John
    Lectures concerning Oratory. Delivered in Trinity College, Dublin. 3rd ed. Dublin. Printed by G. Faulkner. 1760. xvii,xii,457p

JOHN WARD
(1679?-1758)

Like John Quincy Adams' two-volume set of *Lectures,* Ward's *System of Oratory* is an unusually complete restatement of classical doctrines. Its interest and value rest in the exhaustiveness of the treatment and in the clarity of exposition of the ancient principles.

A SYSTEM OF ORATORY [1]

[*Essential Qualities of Discourse*]

Now there are four qualities, more especially suited to the character of an orator, which should always appear in his discourses, in order to render what he sais acceptable to his hearers; and these are, *Wisdom, Integrity, Benevolence,* and *Modesty.* [I, 142]

[*Definition of Oratory*]

Oratory is the art of speaking well upon any subject, in order to persuade. [I, 19]

[*Purpose of Oratory*]

The principal *end* and design of oratory is *to persuade.* For which reason it is frequently called *the art of persuasion.* Indeed the orator has often other subordinate views: as when he endeavours either to delight his hearers, with what is pleasant and agreeable; or to conciliate their good opinion, by a smooth and artful address: but still both these are in order to persuade and excite them to action. [I, 27]

[*Definition of a State*]

By the *State of a Controversy* then we are to understand, the principal point in dispute between contending parties, upon the proof of which the whole cause or controversy depends. [I, 77]

[*How Orator Is Formed*]

There are three things necessary to form a good orator; *nature, art,* and *practice.* Nature begins the work, art conducts it, and practice completes it. [II, 393]

. . . . .

[1] London, J. Ward, 1759. 2v.

It seems plain therefore, that nature and art must both concur, in order to form an orator.

But there are other helps conducive to this end, besides a system of rules. . . . And these are *hearing, reading, writing,* and *imitation.* . . . [II, 396]

[*Adaptation of Style to Circumstances*]

But the chief distinction of stile arises from the different subjects, or matter of discourse. The same way of speaking no more suits all subjects, than the same garment would all persons. A prince and a peasant ought not to have the same dress, and another different from both becomes those of a middle station in life. The stile therefore should always be adapted to the nature of the subject, which rhetoricians have reduced to three ranks or degrees; the *low* or *plain* stile, the *middle* or *temperate,* and the *lofty* or *sublime.* [II, 126]

[*Definition of Invention*]

For invention, considered in general, is the discovery of such things, as are proper to persuade. And in order to attain this end, the orator proposes to himself three things; to prove or illustrate the subject upon which he treats, to conciliate the minds of his hearers, and to ingage their passions in his favor. [I, 44]

SUGGESTED READINGS

Ward, John
   A System of Oratory, Delivered in a Course of Lectures, Publicly Read at Gresham College, London. London. J. Ward. 1759. 2v

THOMAS SHERIDAN
(1719-1788)

Sheridan is remembered principally for his advocacy of the natural manner in delivery. He was opposed to all devices and techniques which interfered in any way with the spontaneous, conversational expression of the speaker. In his *Lectures on Elocution* he deplores the general deficiency of skill in reading and speaking, offering as a clue to the condition the following suggestion: "'. . . there are few persons, who, in private company, do not deliver their sentiments with propriety and force in their manner, whenever they speak in earnest.' Consequently here is a sure standard fixed for propriety and force in public speaking; which is, only to make use of the same manner in the one, as in the other. And this, men certainly would do, if left to themselves, and if early pains were not taken, to substitute an artificial method, in the room of that which is natural."

LECTURES ON ELOCUTION [1]

[On Necessity of Employing a Natural Delivery]

When we reflect that the end of public speaking is persuasion (for the view of every one who harangues in public is to bring his hearers into his way of thinking); and that in order to persuade others to the belief of any point, it must first appear, that the person who attempts it is firmly persuaded of the truth of it himself; how can we suppose it possible that he should effect this, unless he delivers himself in the manner which is always used by persons who speak in earnest? How shall his words pass for the words of truth, when they bear not its stamp? [6]

[Definition of a Just Delivery]

A just delivery consists in a distinct articulation of words, pronounced in proper tones, suitably varied to the sense, and the emotions of the mind; with due observation of accent; of emphasis, in its several gradations; of rests or pauses of the voice, in proper places and well-measured degrees of time; and the whole accompanied with expressive looks, and significant gesture. [12]

[Affectation in Delivery]

In such a situation of things, the rule by which all public speakers are to guide themselves is obvious and easy. Let each, in the first

[1] London, printed for J. Dodsley, 1781.

place, avoid all imitation of others; let him give up all pretensions to art, for it is certain that it is better to have none, than not enough; and no man has enough, who has not arrived at such a perfection of art, as wholly to conceal his art; a thing not to be compassed but by the united endeavours, of the best instruction, perfect patterns, and constant practice. Let him forget that he ever learned to read; at least, let him wholly forget his reading tones. Let him speak entirely from his feelings; and they will find much truer signs to manifest themselves by, than he could find for them. Let him always have in view, what the chief end of speaking is; and he will see the necessity of the means proposed to answer the end. The chief end of all public speakers is to persuade; and in order to persuade, it is above all things necessary, that the speaker, should at least appear himself to believe, what he utters; but this can never be the case, where there are any evident marks of affectation or art. On the contrary, when a man delivers himself in his usual manner, and with the same tones and gesture, that he is accustomed to use, when he speaks from his heart; however aukward that manner may be, however ill-regulated the tones, he will still have the advantage of being thought sincere; which of all others, is the most necessary article, towards securing attention and belief; as affectation of any kind, is the surest way to destroy both. [148-9]

[*Persuasion and Conviction*]

Upon the whole, there are two kinds of language, necessary to all who would wish to answer the end of public speaking. The one is, the language of ideas; by which the thoughts which pass in a man's mind, are manifested to others; and this language is composed chiefly of words properly ranged, and divided into sentences. The other, is the language of emotions; by which the effects that those thoughts have upon the mind of the speaker, in exciting the passions, affections, and all manner of feelings, are not only made known, but communicated to others; and this language is composed of tones, looks, and gesture. The office of a public speaker is, to instruct, to please, and to move. If he does not instruct, his discourse is impertinent; and if he does not please, he will not have it in his power to instruct, for he will not gain attention; and if he does not move, he will not please, for where there is no emotion, there can be no pleasure. To move therefore, should be the first great object of every public speaker; and for this purpose, he must use the language of emotions, not that of ideas alone, which of itself has no power of moving. [164-5]

SUGGESTED READINGS

Sheridan, Thomas

British Education, or the Source of the Disorders of Great Britain. Being an essay towards proving, that the immorality, ignorance, and false taste, which so generally prevail, are the natural and necessary consequences of the present defective system of education—with an attempt to show, that a revival of the art of speaking, and the study of our own language, might contribute, in a great measure, to the cure of those evils. London. P. and J. Dodsley. . . . 1756. 536p

A Course of Lectures on Elocution: together with two dissertations on language; and some other tracts relative to those subjects. new ed. London. Printed for J. Dodsley. 1781. xxiii,320p

Lectures on the Art of Reading. In 2 parts. London. Printed for J. Mawman. 1805. 297p

THOMAS GIBBONS
(1720-1785)

Gibbons' work is a good example of the stylistic approach to rhetoric. It is devoted exclusively, with proper admonitions for the avoidance of their excessive use, to tropes and figures. In the introduction to the book, Gibbons acknowledges reliance upon classical writers, naming particularly, among the ancients, Aristotle, Cicero, Dionysius of Halicarnassus, Horace, Seneca, Quintilian, Longinus, Hermogenes, and Tiberius Rhetor. The book contains numerous quotations from the ancients and the moderns to illustrate the stylistic embellishments.

Gibbons' book is of interest in that it presents a systematic classification of the tropes and figures which are often scattered in less orderly manner in other rhetorics devoting some attention to this phase of the subject.

RHETORIC[1]

[Definition of a Trope]

A Trope is the changing a word or sentence with advantage, from its proper signification to another meaning. Thus, for example, God is a Rock. [1]

[Distinction between Trope and Figure]

The true distinction between *Tropes* and *Figures* may be easily conceived. A Trope is a change of a word or sentence from one sense into another, which its very etymology imports; whereas it is the nature of a Figure not to change the sense of words, but to illustrate, enliven, ennoble, or in some manner or another embellish our discourses: and so far, and so far only, as the words are changed into a different meaning from that which they originally signify, the Orator is obliged to the Tropes, and not to the Figures of *Rhetoric*. [3]

[Use of Tropes]

As Tropes infuse a dignity into our language, and shed a lustre over our expressions, when they are well-chosen and applied; so, on the other hand, when they are mean in themselves, when they are thrown out without judgment, or are in any other respect defective

[1] London, J. and W. Oliver, 1767.

and faulty, they render our discourses mean and contemptible, or in some way or another miserably sink their value. [3-4]

. . . . .

Tropes may be sown too thick, or disgust by being injudiciously and profusely clustered. [4]

. . . . .

I might add, that an injudicious multitude of Tropes, instead of enlightening and enlivening, in which consists their great service, cloud and obscure, and it may be sometimes even what I might call *strangle* our meaning, and therefore they ought to be discreetly used, and rather sparingly sprinkled, than superfluously lavished upon our discourses. [6-7]

. . . . .

Tropes may be blameable for being too extravagant, and beyond the just allowances of nature and reason, and even of the indulgence that may be granted to the most bold and fiery genius. [7]

. . . . .

Tropes may become faulty by being too mean and low. As Tropes should not swell into a vain and wild extravagance, so neither should they shrivel into a minute and contemptible littleness. [12]

. . . . .

We should guard against all far-fetched and obscure Tropes. Let the materials out of which our Tropes are formed lie within the reach of every person's understanding, if possible, and not cost the learned pains to investigate their propriety, and leave the unlearned only a company of hard unintelligible words on which to ruminate, when they should gain from our discourses clear and profitable ideas. [13]

. . . . .

Another fault of Tropes consists in their being harsh and unsuitable to what they would represent. There ought to be care taken that there be an agreement or analogy between the Trope and the proper word for which it stands; for when there is not this relation, our expressions will be uncouth and unpleasant, if not absolutely ridiculous. [14]

. . . . .

We should guard against every Trope that may appear in the least degree finical and fantastical. Our Tropes should be bold and manly, free and natural, without being stiffened by affectation, or subtilised by a perile and trifling fancy. [15]

. . . . .

Let us avoid all filthy and impure Tropes. We should take heed that no Tropes we make use of, either as to sound or sense, convey any idea that will not be agreeable to a chaste mind, or make any trespass upon delicacy. [17]

[*Classification of Tropes*]

A *Metaphor* is a *Trope*, by which a word is removed from its proper signification into another meaning upon account of Comparison. [22]

Instances of Metaphors from Scripture might be produced in vast variety. Thus our blessed Lord is called *a vine, a lamb, a lion*, &c. [24]

Two things ought to be especially regarded as to Metaphors, that they are not in the least degree inconsistent, and that they are not pursued too far. [28]

. . . . .

An *Allegory* is a change or continuation of Tropes, and more generally of Metaphors; and differs from a single Trope in the same manner as a cluster on the vine does from only one or two grapes. [54-5]

Some examples of the Allegory may be very proper to be produced. Not to be tedious in the citations of them, let the following instances suffice:

> Did I but purpose to embark with thee
> On the smooth surface of a summer's sea,
> While gentle zephyrs play in prosp'rous gales,
> And fortune's favour fills the swelling sails;
> But would forsake the ship, and make the shore,
> When the winds whistle, and the tempests roar, &c. [55]

. . . . .

A *Metonymy* is a Trope, in which one name is put for another, for which it may be allowed to stand by reason of some relation or coherence between them. [66]

This change of name is principally used these four ways: (1) When the cause is put for the effect. Thus Mars among the Heathens is used for *war*, Ceres for *corn*, and Bacchus for *wine*. [66]

Another kind of *Metonymy* is, when the effect is put for the cause. Death is called pale, because it makes the countenance pale. [67]

Another kind of *Metonymy* is, when the subject is put for the adjunct, that is, for some circumstance or appendage belonging to or depending upon the subject. "He has a good heart," that is, he has courage, which is supposed to reside in the heart. [67]

Another kind of *Metonymy* is, when the adjunct is put for the subject. "*Gen.* xxxi. 53. Jacob sware by the fear of his father Isaac, that is, by the God whom Isaac feared." [68]

. . . . .

A *Synecdoche* is a Trope, which puts the name of the whole for a part, or the name of a part for the whole; a general name for a particular under that general, or a particular for the general. [71]

The *Synecdoche* puts the whole for a part. . . . In like manner, *man* shall sometimes mean the soul of a man, as Lazarus, *Luke* xvi. 23. is said to be in Abraham's bosom. . . . [72]

A *Synecdoche* puts a part for the whole. . . . We have instances of this kind in Scripture; *Isa.* vii. 2. the tribe of Ephraim is put for the whole people of *Israel.* . . . [72]

The *Synecdoche* uses the general name for a particular of the same kind. Put up your *weapon,* that is, your sword. [72]

The *Synecdoche* puts a particular name for a general. Thus the *Cretan* sea signifies in Horace the sea in general. . . . [73]

In *Psal.* xlvi. 9. The Almighty is said to break the bow, and cut the spear in sunder, and to burn the chariot in the fire; that is, God destroys all the weapons of war, and blesses the world with peace. [73-4]

. . . . .

Under the Synecdoche we may also range the *Antonomasia,* which is a Trope by which we put a proper for a common name, or a common name for a proper. [74]

An *Antonomasia* puts a proper for a common name. Thus, that man is an *Hercules,* that is, an uncommonly strong man. [75]

An *Antonomasia* puts a common for a proper name. Thus, he is gone to the City, or he is come from the City, meaning *London.* [75]

. . . . .

An *Irony* is a Trope, in which one contrary is signified by another; or, in which we speak one thing, and design another, in order to give the greater force and vehemence to our meaning.

RHETORIC AND PUBLIC SPEAKING

The way of distinguishing an *Irony* from the real sentiments of the speaker or writer, are by the accent, the air, the extravagance of the praise, the character of the person, the nature of the thing, or the vein of the discourse: for if in any of these respects there is any disagreement from the common sense of the words, it plainly appears that one thing is spoken, and another is designed. [77-8]

In the sacred Writings we have frequent instances of the *Irony*. Thus the Prophet ELIJAH, I *Kings* xviii. 27. speaks in Irony to the Priests of *Baal*, Cry aloud, for he is a GOD; either he is talking, or he is pursuing, or he is on a journey, or peradventure he sleeps, and must be awaked. [78]

. . . . .

Under the *Irony* we may include the *Sarcasm*, which may be defined to be an *Irony* in its superlative keenness and asperity. [80]

. . . . .

An *Hyperbole* is a Trope, that in its representation of things either magnifies or diminishes beyond or below the line of strict truth, or to a degree which is disproportioned to the real nature of the subject.

This Trope is branched into two kinds. (1) That kind of *Hyperbole* which increases beyond the truth. Such are the expressions, *whiter than snow, blacker than a raven, swifter than the wind*, and the like. [84-5]

(2) The other sort of *Hyperbole* falls below the truth. Thus we speak of *moving slower than a snail*, of *being as deaf as a rock*, as *blind as a mole*, and of *being wasted to a skeleton*. [85]

. . . . .

A *Catachresis* is the most licentious as to language of all the Tropes, as it borrows the name of one thing to express another, which has either no proper name of its own; or if it has, the borrowed name is used either for surprising by novelty, or for the sake of a bold and daring energy. [98]

A *Catachresis* borrows the name of one thing to express another, which has no proper name of its own. Thus QUINTILIAN allows us to say, that we *dart* a ball or a stake, though darting belongs only to a javelin. [98]

A *Catachresis* borrows the name of one thing to express another; which thing, though it has a name of its own, yet under a borrowed name surprises us with novelty, or infuses into our discourses a bold and daring energy. Thus VIRGIL says,

> The goat himself, man of the flock, had stray'd.

by man, evidently intending the father and leader of the flock. [99]

[General Nature of Figures]

A Figure is the fashioning or Dress of a Composition, or an emphatical manner of speaking different from what is plain and common. A Figure essentially differs from a Trope, as in a Figure there is no translation of a word from its proper into an improper sense; and it is distinguishable from ordinary language, as it casts a new form upon speech, and by that mean ennobles and adorns our discourses.

Figures are divided into two kinds. *Figures of language,* and *Figures of sentiment.* *Figures of language* are such sort of Figures as only regard our words which are repeated in some new and uncommon order, or with eloquence and beauty fall into an harmony of sound. *Figures of sentiment* are such as consist not only in words, but ideas; and by these means infuse a strength and vigour into our discourses. The real difference between *Figures of language* and *Figures of sentiment* plainly appears from hence, that if in Figures of language you alter the order of the words, or make a change in them, the Figures vanish; but let never so much alteration be made as to the words in Figures of sentiment, the Figures will still continue, for as the Figures rest upon the ideas, it is impossible that they should be destroyed by a mutation of language. The first class of Figures is only the body, the last is the very soul of our compositions. [119-21]

[Use of Figures]

Let our discourses be founded upon reason, and let us establish everything we advance with solid and convincing arguments. We are first to labour to enlighten the understanding, and inform the judgment, and then introduce our *Figures* to affect and engage the passions, and thereby secure a complete triumph over our audience. [122]

. . . . .

Let us be sparing in the use of *Figures*. We should not needlessly multiply them, and seem in our discourses over-wrought, and, as I might say, encumbered with *Figures*. . . . [123]

. . . . .

Let not our *Figures* be too much adorned and refined into too nice an exactness. The less art the better. [124]

[Classification of Figures]

An *Ecphonesis* is a Figure, that by an exclamation shews some strong and vehement passion. It is expressed by such interjections, as, *O! Oh! Ah! Alas!* and the like, which may be called the signs of this Figure. [128]

* * * * *

Aporia, or *doubting,* is a Figure whereby we express an hesitation where to begin our discourse, or a difficulty what to do in some arduous affair, or what to resolve upon in some critical emergency. [134]

We have an instance of this Figure preserved by Cicero from a speech by Gracchus: "Miserable man that I am! whither shall I turn myself? where can I go? To the capitol? but it swims with my brother's blood. To my home? what to see a mother wretched, bewailing herself, and overwhelmed with sorrow!" [135]

* * * * *

The *Epanorthosis* is a Figure whereby we retract or recall what we have spoken or resolved. [141]

Archbishop Tillotson employs this Figure, when he says, "What is it then can give men the heart and courage; but I recal that word, because it is not true courage, but fool-hardiness, to outbrave the judgments of God?" [142]

* * * * *

Aposiopesis is a Figure whereby a person, often through the power of some passion, as anger, sorrow, fear, &c. breaks off his speech without finishing the sense. [149]

* * * * *

Apophasis, or *denial,* is a Figure by which an Orator pretends to conceal or omit what he really and in fact declares. [157]

The use of this Figure in my opinion may be various.

(1) By the aid of the *Apophasis,* the speaker **introduces, without any difficulty, and without any suspicion of being ill-natured or ungenerous,** some criminal charges against a person, which may be foreign indeed from the matter under immediate consideration, and therefore may require art to mention them, but yet may be of such a nature as may considerably assist his general argument and cause.

(2) By this Figure we may crowd abundance of sentiment into a small compass, and arm our discourses as with an invincible strength, by collecting and compacting our ideas; and how much is such a method to be preferred to a tedious and minute detail of circumstances, which grows languid upon the hearer by a weak and subtil diffusion?

(3) The *Apophasis* may be a grateful surprise to our audience, and powerfully operate upon their minds. While they hear us saying, *We omit such and such things,* or *we shall not touch upon them,* or *we shall not mention them,* we appear to them as if we thought the things which we pretend to wave were light and inconsiderable; when, to their astonishment (and astonishment will always be attended with a strong impression) they are evidently very weighty and momentous. Arguments delivered in this unexpected manner, fall like accidental fire from heaven, which strikes much more powerfully than the regular expanded lustres of the day. [161-2]

. . . . .

Anacoenosis is a Figure by which the speaker applies to his hearers or opponents for their opinion upon the point in debate; or when a person excuses his conduct, gives reasons for it, and appeals to those about him whether they are not satisfactory. [163]

The use of this Figure seems to lie, (1) In its familiarity. It has something of the air of conversation; and though discourses ought not to be turned into mere conversation, yet a proper and decent mixture of such a sort of freedom entertains our hearers, both on account of its variety, and its apparent condescension and good-nature.

(2) This Figure pays a compliment to our audience, in that there is an appeal made to their judgment, their equity, and good disposition. [166]

(3) In the *Anacoenosis* there appear a great regard to truth, and an assurance of the goodness of our cause. [166]

(4) This Figure, when addressed to an adversary, carries powerful conviction into his conscience, and makes him as it were condemn himself. [167]

Anastrophe or inversion, is a Figure by which we suspend our sense, and the hearer's expectation; or a Figure by which we place last, and perhaps at a great remove from the beginning of the sentence, what, according to common order, should have been mentioned first. [168]

. . . . .

Erotesis is a Figure by which we express the emotion of our minds, and infuse an ardor and energy into our discourses, by proposing questions. [176]

. . . . .

Prolepsis is a Figure by which a speaker suggests an objection against what he is advancing, and returns an answer to it: or it is a Figure by which a speaker, more especially at the entrance upon his discourse, removes any sort of obstruction that he foresees may be likely to prevent the success of his cause. [191]

The use of this Figure is very considerable.

(1) By it attention is relieved, since the speaker, by the help of the *Prolepsis,* prevents a tedious uniformity in his address; and the hearer may be much entertained by finding, that the orator departs for a while from the usual order and form of discourse, to indulge a kind of familiar dialogue.

(2) By this Figure the speaker gains the reputation of foresight and care. The *Prolepsis* shews that the orator is master of his subject, and that he has a full view of its connexions and consequences, in that he sees what may be objected against, as well as what may be alledged for his cause.

(3) This Figure manifests the assurance of the speaker, that truth and justice are on his side: he fears not an objection; he starts it himself, he dares to meet and encounter it, and will shew his audience how effectually he can disarm and dissolve it. [198-9]

(4) When the speaker appears desirous to represent matters fairly, and not to conceal any objection that may be made against his discourse, such a conduct may tend to secure the favour of his auditory, as it carries with it the face of a commendable impartiality. And,

(5) and Lastly, By this Figure some advantage is gained over an adversary. He is prevented in his exceptions, and either confounded and silenced, or obliged to a repetition, which is not likely to be so striking and forcible as the mention of a thing fresh and untouched before. [199-200]

. . . . .

Epanaphora is a Figure, in which the same word is gracefully and emphatically repeated; or in which distinct sentences, or the several members of the same sentence, are begun with the same word. [207-8]

. . . . .

Apostrophe is a Figure in which we interrupt the current of our discourse, and turn to another person, or to some other object, different from that to which our address was first directed. [213]

. . . . .

Periphrasis is a Figure in which we use more words than what are absolutely necessary, and sometimes less plain words, either to avoid some inconvenience and ill-effect which might proceed from expressing ourselves in fewer or clearer words, or in order to give a variety and eloquence to our discourses, and multiply the graces of our composition. [224]

. . . . .

Synchoresis is a Figure whereby we grant or yield up something, in order to gain a point, which we could not so well secure without it. [200]

. . . . .

Asyndeton is a Figure, occasioned by the omission of conjunctive particles, which are dropped either to express vehemence or speed; or sometimes it may be from a noble negligence of nice accuracy, arising from an attention to our ideas.

SALLUST furnishes us with an example of this sort in his description of the *Moors*: "There was then, says he, an horrible spectacle in the open plains, pursuit, flight, slaughter, captivity." [233-4]

. . . . .

The very opposite to this Figure is the *Polysyndeton*; for as the *Asyndeton* drops, so the *Polysyndeton* on the contrary abounds with conjunctive particles. [236]

. . . . .

Oxymoron is a Figure, in which the parts of a period or sentence disagree in sound, but perfectly accord with one another in meaning; or, if I may so call it, it is sense in the masquerade of folly.

We may find instances of this kind in the common language of mankind, or that may appear very easy and natural in familiar conversation. *A coward dies often, a brave man but once.* [240]

. . . . .

Enantiosis is a Figure, by which things very different or contrary are compared or placed together, and by which they mutually set off and enhance each other. [248]

One more instance of the *Enantiosis* shall close the examples from Scripture: *2 Cor.* vi. 4, 8-10. "But in all things approving ourselves as the ministers of GOD—By honour and dishonour, by evil report and good report; as deceivers, and yet true; as unknown, and yet well-known; as dying, and behold we live; as chastened, and not killed; as sorrowful, yet always rejoicing; as poor, yet making many rich; as having nothing, and yet possessing all things." [260-1]

. . . . .

Climax, according to Mr. Blackwall's definition, is, "when the word or expression, which ends the first member of a period, begins the second, and so on; so that every member will make a distinct sentence, taking its rise from the next foregoing, till the argument and period be beautifully finished: or, in the terms of the schools, it is when the word or expression, which was predicate in the first member of a period, is subject in the second, and so on, till the argument and period be brought to a noble conclusion." [265]

. . . . .

The *Hypotyposis* is a Figure, by which we give such a distinct and lively representation of what we have occasion to describe, as furnishes our hearers with a particular, satisfactory, and complete knowledge of our subject. [276]

It may not be unserviceable to give some directions concerning the *Hypotyposis.* As,

(1) Let our descriptions be exact and faithful copies from nature. [320]

(2) Let us know when we have said enough, and avoid tautology. [320]

(3) In our descriptions, let us not be minute and particular in gathering up every circumstance, especially if our subject be great and solemn. [323]

(4) Let the words of our description, as nearly as possible, answer our ideas. Let harsh ideas be conveyed in harsh words, magnificent ideas in sonorous language, gentle ideas in a smooth stile, swiftness in short and quick, and slowness in heavy and long-extended periods. [324]

. . . . .

The *Prosopopeia* is a Figure which consists in describing good and bad qualities of the mind, or the passions or appetites of human nature as real and distinct persons; in clothing with corporeal forms, or endowing with speech and action imaginary beings, or general notions and abstracted ideas; in introducing persons silent as speaking, or persons deceased as living; and in making rocks, woods, rivers, temples, and other inanimate beings, assume the powers and properties, and express the emotions of living, and even reasonable creatures. [330]

. . . . .

Parabole is a Figure that compares one thing with another, to which it bears a resemblance. [399]

Paraboles may be serviceable for illustration. [400]

We shall next shew that the *Parabole* conduces to sublimity. [416]

Paraboles may greatly entertain the mind, and by raising images different from the subject upon which we are treating, relieve and delight our audience or our readers. [421]

. . . . .

An *Epiphonema* is a pertinent and instructive remark at the end of a discourse or narration. [462]

We shall find instances of this Figure in some of the finest Writers. "Hence we may learn, says CICERO, that there is no duty so sacred and solemn, which it is not usual with avarice to injure and violate." [462-3]

SUGGESTED READINGS

Gibbons, Thomas
Rhetoric; or a View of the Principal Tropes and Figures in Their Origin and Powers; with a Variety of Rules to Escape Errors and Blemishes, and Attain Propriety and Elegance in Composition. London. Printed by J. and W. Oliver, for J. Buckland and J. Payne. 1767. 478p

GEORGE CAMPBELL
(1719-1796)

Campbell's *Philosophy of Rhetoric* may very well be the most important contribution to rhetoric since Quintilian. Surely its influence upon pedagogical technique in contemporary speech composition is more pervasive than that of any other work since the *Institutes*.

Campbell's claim to distinction rests upon three sound contributions. (1) He sets forth clearly and incisively a treatment of style which still serves the student of written composition and oral discourse as a guide to practice and critical appraisal. (2) He develops in some detail and with discerning insight a body of material on emotional proof, far more useful than that of any similar analysis in the other rhetorics of the eighteenth and nineteenth centuries. The hearers "as men in general" and as "men in particular" are analyzed with respect to their faculties and the circumstances instrumental in operating upon them. A short section is also devoted to the consideration which the speaker ought to have of himself. (3) He considers the ends of speaking in terms of audience response, thus helping to establish a classification of purposes to which all present day writers adhere.

THE PHILOSOPHY OF RHETORIC[1]

[*The General Nature of Eloquence*]

In speaking, there is always some end proposed, or some effect which the speaker intends to produce in the hearer. The word *eloquence*, in its greatest latitude, denotes "that art or talent by which the discourse is adapted to its end."

All the ends of speaking are reducible to four: every speech being intended to enlighten the understanding, to please the imagination, to move the passions, or to influence the will.

Any one discourse admits only one of these ends as the principal. Nevertheless, in discoursing on a subject, many things may be introduced which are more immediately and apparently directed to some of the other ends of speaking, and not to that which is the chief intent of the whole. But then these other and immediate ends are in effect but means, and must be rendered conducive to that which is the primary intention. Accordingly, the propriety or the impropriety of the introduction of such secondary ends will always be inferred from their subserviency or want of subserviency to that end which is,

[1] New ed., New York, Harper and Brothers, 1851.

in respect of them, the ultimate. For example, a discourse addressed to the understanding, and calculated to illustrate or evince some point purely speculative, may borrow aid from the imagination, and admit metaphor and comparison, but not the bolder and more striking figures, as that called vision or fiction, prosopopoeia, and the like, which are not so much intended to elucidate a subject as to excite admiration. Still less will it admit an address to the passions, which, as it never fails to disturb the operation of the intellectual faculty, must be regarded by every intelligent hearer as foreign at least, if not insidious. It is obvious that either of these, far from being subservient to the main design, would distract the attention from it.

There is, indeed, one kind of address to the understanding, and only one, which, it may not be improper to observe, disdains all assistance whatever from the fancy. The address I mean is mathematical demonstration. As this doth not, like moral reasoning, admit degrees of evidence, its perfection in point of eloquence, if so uncommon an application of the term may be allowed, consists in perspicuity. Perspicuity here results entirely from propriety and simplicity of diction, and from accuracy of method, where the mind is regularly, step by step, conducted forward in the same track, the attention no way diverted, nothing left to be supplied, no one unnecessary word or idea introduced. On the contrary, an harangue framed for affecting the hearts or influencing the resolves of an assembly, needs greatly the assistance both of intellect and of imagination.

In general, it may be asserted that each preceding species, in the order above exhibited, is preparatory to the subsequent; that each subsequent species is founded on the preceding; and that thus they ascend in a regular progression. Knowledge, the object of the intellect, furnisheth materials for the fancy; the fancy culls, compounds, and, by her mimic art, disposes these materials so as to affect the passions; the passions are the natural spurs to volition or action, and so need only to be rightly directed. This connexion and dependancy will better appear from the following observations.

When a speaker addresses himself to the understanding, he proposes the *instruction* of his hearers, and that, either by explaining some doctrine unknown, or not distinctly comprehended by them, or by proving some position disbelieved or doubted by them. In other words, he proposes either to dispel ignorance or to vanquish error. In the one, his aim is their *information*; in the other, their *conviction*. Accordingly, the predominant quality of the former is *perspicuity*; of the latter, *argument*. By that we are made to know, by this to believe.

The imagination is addressed by exhibiting to it a lively and beautiful representation of a suitable object. As in this exhibition the task of the orator may, in some sort, be said, like that of the painter, to consist in imitation, the merit of the work results entirely from these two sources: dignity, as well in the subject or thing imitated as in the manner of imitation, and resemblance in the portrait or performance. Now the principal scope for this class being in narration and description, poetry, which is one mode of oratory, especially epic poetry, must be ranked under it. The effect of the dramatic, at least of tragedy, being upon the passions, the drama falls under another species, to be explained afterward. But that kind of address of which I am now treating attains the summit of perfection in the *sublime*, or those great and noble images which, when in suitable colouring presented to the mind, do, as it were, distend the imagination with some vast conception, and quite ravish the soul.

The sublime, it may be urged, as it raiseth admiration, should be considered as one species of address to the passions. But this objection, when examined, will appear superficial. There are few words in any language (particularly such as relate to the operations and feelings of the mind) which are strictly univocal. Thus, admiration, when persons are the object, is commonly used for a high degree of esteem; but, when otherwise applied, it denotes solely an internal taste. It is that pleasurable sensation which instantly arises on the perception of magnitude, or of whatever is great and stupendous in its kind; for there is a greatness in the degrees of quality in spiritual subjects analogous to that which subsists in the degrees of quantity in material things. Accordingly, in all tongues, perhaps without exception, the ordinary terms which are considered as literally expressive of the latter, are also used promiscuously to denote the former. Now admiration, when thus applied, doth not require to its production, as the passions generally do, any reflex view of motives or tendencies, or of any relation either to private interest or to the good of others; and ought, therefore, to be numbered among those original feelings of the mind, which are denominated by some the reflex senses, being of the same class with a taste of beauty, an ear for music, or our moral sentiments. Now the immediate view of whatever is directed to the imagination (whether the subject be things inanimate or animal forms, whether characters, actions, incidents, or manners) terminates in the gratification of some internal taste; as a taste for the wonderful, the fair, the good; for elegance, for novelty, or for grandeur.

But it is evident that this creative faculty, the fancy, frequently lends her aid in promoting still nobler ends. From her exuberant stores most of those tropes and figures are extracted which, when properly employed, have such a marvellous efficacy in rousing the passions, and by some secret, sudden, and inexplicable association, awakening all the tenderest emotions of the heart. In this case, the address of the orator is not ultimately intended to astonish by the loftiness of his images, or to delight by the beauteous resemblance which his painting bears to nature; nay, it will nor permit the hearers even a moment's leisure for making the comparison, but, as it were, by some magical spell, hurries them, ere they are aware, into love, pity, grief, terror, desire, aversion, fury, or hatred. It therefore assumes the denomination of *pathetic,* which is the characteristic of the third species of discourse, that addressed to the passions.

Finally, as that kind, the most complex of all, which is calculated to influence the will, and persuade to a certain conduct, is in reality an artful mixture of that which proposes to convince the judgment, and that which interests the passions, its distinguishing excellence results from these two, the argumentative and the pathetic incorporated together. These, acting with united force, and, if I may so express myself, in concert, constitute that passionate eviction, that *vehemence* of contention, which is admirably fitted for persuasion, and hath always been regarded as the supreme qualification in an orator. It is this which bears down every obstacle, and procures the speaker an irresistible power over the thoughts and purposes of his audience. It is this which hath been so justly celebrated as giving one man an ascendant over others, superior even to what despotism itself can bestow; since by the latter the more ignoble parts only, the body and its members, are enslaved; whereas from the dominion of the former nothing is exempted, neither judgment nor affection, not even the inmost recesses, the most latent movements of the soul. What opposition is he not prepared to conquer on whose arms reason hath conferred solidity and weight, and passion such a sharpness as enables them, in defiance of every obstruction, to open a speedy passage to the heart?

It is not, however, every kind of pathos which will give the orator so great an ascendency over the minds of his hearers. All passions are not alike capable of producing this effect. Some are naturally inert and torpid; they deject the mind, and indispose it for enterprise. Of this kind are sorrow, fear, shame, humility. Others, on the contrary, elevate the soul, and stimulate to action. Such are hope, patriotism, ambition, emulation, anger. These, with the greatest facility, are made to concur in direction with arguments exciting to resolution and activity; and are, consequently, the fittest for producing what, for want of a better term in our language, I shall henceforth denominate the *vehement*. There is, besides, an intermediate kind of passions, which do not so congenially and directly either restrain us from acting or incite us to act; but, by the art of the speaker, can, in an oblique manner, be made conducive to either. Such are joy, love, esteem, compassion. Nevertheless, all these kinds may find a place in suasory discourses, or such as are intended to operate on the will. The first is properest for dissuading; the second, as hath been already hinted, for persuading; the third is equally accommodated to both. [23-7]

[*Relation of Logic to Eloquence*]

The sole and ultimate end of logic is the eviction of truth; one important end of eloquence, though, as appears from the first chapter, neither the sole, nor always the ultimate, is the conviction of the hearers. Pure logic regards only the subject, which is examined solely for the sake of information. Truth, as such, is the proper aim of the examiner. Eloquence not only considers the subject, but also the speaker and the hearers, and both the subject and the speaker for the sake of the hearers, or, rather, for the sake of the effect intended to be produced in them. [54-5]

[*Necessity of Understanding the Nature of Hearers*]

Rhetoric, as was observed already, not only considers the subject, but also the hearers and the speaker. The hearers must be considered in a twofold view, as men in general, and as such men in particular. As men in general, it must be allowed there are certain principles in our nature which, when properly addressed and managed, give no inconsiderable aid to reason in promoting belief. Nor is it just to conclude from this concession, as some have hastily done, that oratory may be defined "The art of deception." The use of such helps will be found, on a stricter examination, to be in most cases quite legitimate, and even necessary, if we would give reason herself that influence which is certainly her due. In order to evince the truth considered by itself, conclusive arguments alone are requisite; but in order to convince me by these arguments, it is moreover requisite that they be understood, that they be attended to, that they be remembered by me; and, in order to persuade me by them to any particular action or conduct, it is farther requisite that, by interesting me in the subject, they may, as it were, be felt. It is not, therefore, the understanding alone that is here concerned. If the orator would prove successful, it is necessary that he engage in his service all these different powers of the mind, the imagination, the memory, and the passions. These are not the supplanters of reason, or even rivals in her sway; they are her handmaids, by whose ministry she is enabled to usher truth into the heart, and procure it there a favourable reception. As handmaids, they are liable to be seduced by sophistry in the garb of reason, and sometimes are made ignorantly to lend their aid in the introduction of falsehood. But their service is not on this account to be dispensed with; there is even a necessity of employing it founded in our nature. [93-4]

. . . . .

But to descend to particulars: the first thing to be studied by the speaker is, that his arguments may be understood. If they be unintelligible, the cause must be either in the sense or in the expression. It lies in the sense if the mediums of proof be such as the hearers are unacquainted with; that is, if the ideas introduced be either without the sphere of their knowledge, or too abstract for their apprehension and habits of thinking. It lies in the sense likewise, if the train of reasoning (though no unusual ideas should be introduced) be longer, or more complex, or more intricate, than they are accustomed to. But as the fitness of the arguments in these respects depends on the capacity, education, and attainments of the hearers, which in different orders of men are different, this properly belongs to the consideration which the speaker ought to have of his audience, not as men in general, but as such men in particular. The obscurity which ariseth from the expression will come in course to be considered in the sequel. [95]

. . . . .

The second thing requisite is that his reasoning be attended to; for this purpose the imagination must be engaged. Attention is prerequisite to every effect of speaking, and without some gratification in hearing, there will be no attention, at least, of any continuance. Those qualities in ideas which principally gratify the fancy are vivacity, beauty, sublimity, novelty. Nothing contributes more to vivacity than striking resemblances in the imagery, which convey, besides, an additional pleasure of their own.

But there is still a farther end to be served by pleasing the imagination than that of awakening and preserving the attention, however important this purpose alone ought to be accounted. [95]

. . . . .

Where, then, lies the difference between addressing the judgment and addressing the fancy? and what hath given rise to the distinction between ratiocination and imagery? The following observations will serve for an answer to this query. It is evident that, though the mind receives a considerable pleasure from the discovery of resemblance, no pleasure is received when the resemblance is of such a nature as is familiar to everybody. Such are those resemblances which result from the specific and generic qualities of ordinary objects. What gives the principal delight to the imagination is the exhibition of a strong likeness, which escapes the notice of the generality of people. The similitude of man to man, eagle to eagle, sea to sea, or, in brief, of one individual to another individual of the same species, affects not the fancy in the least. What poet would ever think of comparing a combat between two of his heroes to a combat between other two? Yet nowhere else will he find so strong a resemblance. Indeed, to the faculty of imagination this resemblance appears rather under the notion of identity, although it be the foundation of the strongest reasoning from experience. [96]

. . . . .

Farther, vivid ideas are not only more powerful than languid ideas in commanding and preserving attention, they are not only more efficacious in producing conviction, but they are also more easily retained. Those several powers, understanding, imagination, memory, and passion, are mutually subservient. [97]

. . . . .

Now, as nothing can operate on the mind which is not in some respect present to it, care must be taken by the orator that, in introducing new topics, the vestiges left by the former on the minds of the hearers may not be effaced. [98]

. . . . .

The speaker's attention to this subserviency of memory is always so much the more requisite, the greater the difficulty of remembrance is, and the more important the being remembered is to the attainment of the ultimate end. [98]

. . . . .

As to order in time, which in composition is properly styled Method, it consisteth principally in connecting the parts in such a manner as to give vicinity to things in the discourse which have an affinity; that is, resemblance, causality, or other relation in nature; and thus making their customary association and resemblance, as in the former case, co-operate with their contiguity in duration, or immediate succession in the delivery. [99]

. . . . .

To conclude: when persuasion is the end, passion also must be engaged. If it is fancy which bestows brilliancy on our ideas, if it is memory which gives them stability, passion doth more: it animates them. Hence they derive spirit and energy. To say that it is possible to persuade without speaking to the passions, is but, at best, a kind of specious nonsense. The coolest reasoner always, in persuading, addresseth himself to the passions some way or other. This he cannot avoid doing if he speak to the purpose. To make me believe, it is enough to show me that things are so; to make me act, it is necessary to show me that the action will answer some end. [99]

. . . . .

But if so much depend on passion, where is the scope for argument? Before I answer this question, let it be observed, that, in order to persuade, there are two things which must be carefully studied by the orator. The first is, to excite some desire or passion in the hearers; the second is, to satisfy their judgment that there is a connexion between the action to which he would persuade them, and the gratification of the desire or passion which he excites. This is the analysis of persuasion. The former is effected by communicating lively and glowing ideas of the object; the latter, unless so evident of itself as to supersede the necessity, by presenting the best and most forcible arguments which the nature of the subject admits. In the one lies the pathetic, in the other the argumentative. [100]

. . . . .

When the first end alone is attained, the pathetic without the rational, the passions are indeed roused from a disagreeable langour by the help of the imagination, and the mind is thrown into a state which, though accompanied with some painful emotions, rarely fails, upon the whole, to affect it with pleasure. But if the hearers are judicious, no practical effect is produced. [100]

. . . . .

On the contrary, when the other end alone is attained, the rational without the pathetic, the speaker is as far from his purpose as before. You have proved beyond contradiction that acting thus is the sure way to procure such an object. I perceive that your reasoning is conclusive, but I am not affected by it. Why? I have no passion for the object. I am indifferent whether I procure it or not. You have demonstrated that such a step will mortify my enemy. I believe it: but I have no resentment, and will not trouble myself to give pain to another. Your arguments evince that it would gratify my vanity.

But I prefer my ease. Thus passion is the mover to action, reason is the guide. Good is the object of the will, truth is the object of the understanding. [100-101]

[*Circumstances Operating On the Passions*]

These are perhaps all reducible to the seven following: probability, plausibility, importance, proximity of time, connexion of place, relation of the actors or sufferers to the hearers or speaker in the consequences. [103-104]

. . . . .

The first is *probability,* which is now considered only as an expedient for enlivening passion. Here again there is commonly scope for argument. Probability results from evidence, and begets belief. Belief invigorates our ideas. Belief raised to the highest becomes certainty. [104]

. . . . .

The second circumstance is *plausibility,* a thing totally distinct from the former, as having an effect upon the mind quite independent of faith or probability. It ariseth chiefly from the consistency of the narration, from its being what is commonly called natural and feasible. [104]

. . . . .

The third circumstance I took notice of was *importance,* the appearance of which always tends, by fixing attention more closely, to add brightness and strength to the ideas. [108]

. . . . .

An action may derive importance from its own nature, from those concerned in it as acting or suffering, or from its consequences. It derives importance from its own nature if it be stupendous in its kind, if the result of what is uncommonly great, whether good or bad, passion or invention, virtue or vice, or what in respect of generosity is godlike, what in respect of atrocity is diabolical; it derives importance from those concerned in it when the actors or the sufferers are considerable, on account either of their dignity or of their number, or of both; it derives importance from its consequences when these are remarkable in regard to their greatness, their multitude, their extent, and that either as to the many and distant places affected by them, or as to the future and remote periods to which they may reach, or as to both. [108-109]

. . . . .

First, as to *proximity of time,* every one knows that any melancholy incident is the more affecting that it is recent. Hence it is become common with story-tellers, that they may make a deeper impression on their hearers, to introduce remarks like these: that the tale which they relate is not old, that it happened but lately, or in their own time, or that they are yet living who had a part in it or were witnesses of it. Proximity of time regards not only the past, but the future. An event that will probably soon happen hath greater influence upon us than what will probably happen a long time hence. [109]

. . . . .

Local *connexion,* the fifth in the above enumeration, hath a more powerful effect than proximity of time. [110]

. . . . .

Who is not more curious to know the notable transactions which have happened in his own country from the earliest antiquity, than to be acquainted with those which have happened in the remotest regions of the globe, during the century wherein he lives? It must be owned, however, that the former circumstance is more frequently aided by that of personal relation than the latter. Connexion of place not only includes vicinage, but every other local relation, such as being in a province under the same government with us, in a state that is in alliance with us, in a country well known to us, and the like. [111]

. . . . .

Still greater is the power of *relation* to the persons concerned, which was the sixth circumstance mentioned, as this tie is more direct than that which attacheth us to the scene of action. It is the persons, not the place, that are the immediate objects of the passions love or hatred, pity or anger, envy or contempt. [111]

. . . . .

Some have generally greater influence than others; some, again, have greater influence with one person, others with another. They are consanguinity, affinity, friendship, acquaintance, being fellow-citizens, countrymen, of the same surname, language, religion, occupation, and innumerable others. [111]

. . . . .

But of all the connexive circumstances, the most powerful is *interest,* which is the last. [111]

. . . . .

The reason is, a person present with us, whom we see and hear, and who, by words, and looks, and gestures, gives the liveliest signs of his feelings, has the surest and most immediate claim upon our sympathy. We become infected with his passions. We are hurried along by them, and not allowed leisure to distinguish between his relation and our relation, his interest and our interest. [112]

[Calming Unfavorable Passions]

I come now to the second question on the subject of passion. How is an unfavourable passion or disposition to be calmed? The answer is, either, first, by annihilating, or at least diminishing, the object which raised it; or, secondly, by exciting some other passion which may counterwork it. [115]

. . . . .

By proving the falsity of the narration, or the utter incredibility of the future event, on the supposed truth of which the passion was founded, the object is annihilated. It is diminished by all such circumstances as are contrary to those by which it is increased. These are, improbability, implausibility, insignificance, distance of time, remoteness of place, the persons concerned such as we have no connexion with, the consequences such as we have no interest in. [115]

. . . . .

The second way of silencing an unfavourable passion or disposition is by conjuring up some other passion or disposition which may overcome it. [116]

[Ethical Proof]

Sympathy in the hearers to the speaker may be lessened several ways, chiefly by these two: by a low opinion of his intellectual abilities, and by a bad opinion of his morals. The latter is the more prejudicial of the two. [119]

. . . . .

As to personal prejudices in general, I shall conclude with two remarks. The first is, the more gross the hearers are so much the more susceptible they are of such prejudices. Nothing exposes the mind more to all their baneful influences than ignorance and rudeness; the rabble chiefly consider who speaks, men of sense and education what is spoken. [120]

. . . . .

The second remark is, that when the opinion of the audience is unfavourable, the speaker hath need to be much more cautious in every step he takes, to show more modesty, and greater deference to the judgment of his hearers; perhaps, in order to win them, he may find it necessary to make some concessions in relation to his former principles or conduct, and to entreat their attention from pure regard to the subject, that, like men of judgment and candour, they would impartially consider what is said, and give a welcome reception to truth, from what quarter soever it proceed. Thus he must attempt, if possible, to mollify them, gradually to insinuate himself into their favour, and thereby imperceptibly to transfuse his sentiments and passions into their minds. [120]

[Analysis of the Passions]

My first observation shall be, that almost all the simple passions of which the mind is susceptible may be divided into two classes, the *pleasant* and the *painful*. It is, at the same time, acknowledged that the pleasures and the pains created by the different passions differ considerably from one another both in kind and degree. [151]

. . . . .

The second observation is, that there is an attraction or association among the passions, as well as among the ideas of the mind. [152]

. . . . .

My third observation is, that pain of every kind generally makes a deeper impression on the imagination than pleasure does, and is longer retained by the memory. It is a common remark of every people and of every age, and consequently hath some foundation in human nature, that benefits are sooner forgotten than injuries, and favours than affronts. [153]

. . . . .

The fourth observation is, that from a group of passions (if I may so express myself) associated together, and having the same object, some of which are of the pleasant, others of the painful kind—if the pleasant predominate, there ariseth often a greater and a more durable pleasure to the mind than would result from these if alone and unmixed. [153]

. . . . .

The fifth observation is, that under the name *pity* may be included all the emotions excited by tragedy. In common speech, all, indeed, are included under this name that are excited by that species of eloquence which is denominated the pathetic. The passions moved by tragedy have been commonly said to be *pity* and *terror*. [154]

. . . . .

My sixth and last observation on this head is, that pity is not a simple passion, but a group of passions strictly united by association, and, as it were, blended by centring in the same object. [155]

[*Language*]

Eloquence hath always been considered, and very justly, as having a particular connexion with language. It is the intention of eloquence to convey our sentiments into the minds of others, in order to produce a certain effect upon them. Language is the only vehicle by which this conveyance can be made. The art of speaking, then, is not less necessary to the orator than the art of thinking. Without the latter, the former could not have existed; without the former, the latter would be ineffective. [162]

. . . . .

It will be so; and this very acknowledgment shows that many terms and idioms may be common, which, nevertheless, have not the general sanction, no, nor even the suffrage of those that use them. The use here spoken of implies not only *currency*, but *vogue*. It is, properly, *reputable custom*. [164]

. . . . .

Agreeably, then, to this first qualification of the term, we must understand to be comprehended under general use *whatever modes of speech are authorized as good by the writings of a great number, if not the majority, of celebrated authors.* [168]

. . . . .

Another qualification of the term *use* which deserves our attention is, that it must be *national*. This I consider in a twofold view, as it stands opposed both to *provincial* and *foreign*. [168]

. . . . .

Words, therefore, are by no means to be accounted the worse for being old, if they are not obsolete; neither is any word the better for being new. On the contrary, some time is absolutely necessary to constitute that custom or use on which the establishment of words depends. [173]

[*Canons of Usage*]

The first canon, then, shall be, When use is divided as to any particular word or phrase, and the expression used by one part hath been preoccupied, or is in any instance susceptible of a different signification, and the expression employed by the other part never admits a different sense, both perspicuity and variety require that the form of expression which is in every instance strictly univocal be preferred. [177]

. . . . .

The second canon is, In doubtful cases regard ought to be had in our decisions to the analogy of the language. [179]

. . . . .

The third canon is, When the terms of expressions are in other respects equal, that ought to be preferred which is most agreeable to the ear. [181]

. . . . .

The fourth canon is, In cases wherein none of the foregoing rules gives either side a ground of preference, a regard to simplicity (in which I include etymology when manifest) ought to determine our choice. [181]

. . . . .

The fifth and only other canon that occurs to me on the subject of divided use is, In the few cases wherein neither perspicuity nor analogy, neither sound nor simplicity, assists us in fixing our choice, it is safest to prefer that manner which is most conformable to ancient usage. [182]

[*Further Criteria of Good Usage*]

I shall therefore subjoin a few remarks under the form of canons, in relation to those words or expressions which may be thought to merit degradation from the rank they have hitherto maintained, submitting these remarks entirely, as everything of the kind must be submitted, to the final determination of the impartial public. [184]

. . . . .

The first canon on this subject is, All words and phrases which are remarkably harsh, and unharmonious, and not absolutely necessary, may justly be judged worthy of this fate. [184-5]

. . . . .

The second canon on this subject is, When etymology plainly points to a signification different from that which the word commonly bears, propriety and simplicity both require its dismission. [187]

. . . . .

The third canon is, When any words become obsolete, or, at least, are never used, except as constituting part of particular phrases, it is better to dispense with their service entirely, and give up the phrases. [188]

. . . . .

The fourth and last canon I propose is, All those phrases which, when analyzed grammatically, include a solecism, and all those to which use hath affixed a particular sense, but which, when explained by the general and established rules of the language, are susceptible either of a different sense or of no sense, ought to be discarded altogether. [189]

[Purity of Language]

Purity, it was said, implies three things. Accordingly, in three different ways it may be injured. First, the words used may not be English. This fault hath received from grammarians the denomination of *barbarism*. Secondly, the construction of the sentence may not be in the English idiom. This hath gotten the name of *solecism*. Thirdly, the words and phrases may not be employed to express the precise meaning which custom hath affixed to them. This is termed *impropriety*. [193]

[Perspicuity]

Of all the qualities above mentioned, the first and most essential is *perspicuity*. [239]

. . . . .

But whatever be the ultimate intention of the orator, to inform, to convince, to please, to move, or to persuade, still he must speak so as to be understood, or he speaks to no purpose. [239]

[Causes of Obscurity]

This is the first offence against perspicuity, and may arise from several causes. First, from some defect in the expression. There are in all languages certain elliptical expressions, which use hath established, and which, therefore, very rarely occasion darkness. When they do occasion it, they ought always to be avoided. [240]

. . . . .

Often, indeed, the affectation of conciseness, often the rapidity of thought natural to some writers, will give rise to still more material defects in the expression. [241]

. . . . .

Another source of obscurity is a bad arrangement of the words. In this case the construction is not sufficiently clear. One often, on first hearing the sentence, imagines, from the turn of it, that it ought to be construed one way, and, on reflection, finds that he must construe it another way. [242]

. . . . .

A discourse, then, excels in perspicuity when the subject engrosses the attention of the hearer, and the diction is so little minded by him that he can scarcely be said to be conscious that it is through this medium he sees into the speaker's thoughts. On the contrary, the least obscurity, ambiguity, or confusion in the style, instantly removes the attention from the sentiment to the expression, and the hearer endeavours, by the aid of reflection, to correct the imperfections of the speaker's language. [244]

. . . . .

Another source of obscurity is when the same word is in the same sentence used in different senses. This error is exemplified in the following quotation: "That he should be in earnest it is hard to conceive; since any reasons of doubt which he might have in this case would have been reasons of doubt in the case of other men, who may give *more*, but cannot give *more evident*, signs of thought than their fellow creatures." This errs alike against perspicuity and elegance; the word *more* is first an adjective, the comparative of *many*; in an instant it is an adverb, and the sign of the comparative degree. [245]

. . . . .

A cause of obscurity also arising from the use of pronouns and relatives is when it doth not appear at first to what they refer. [246]

. . . . .

Another cause of obscurity is when the structure of the sentence is too much complicated or too artificial, or when the sense is too long suspended by parentheses. [247]

. . . . .

Another source of darkness in composing is the injudicious introduction of technical words and phrases. . . . [247]

. . . . .

The last cause of obscurity I shall take notice of is very long sentences. This rarely fails to be conjoined with some of the other faults before mentioned. [248]

[Double Meanings]

It was observed that perspicuity might be violated not only by obscurity, but also by double meaning. The fault in this case is, not that the sentence conveys darkly or imperfectly the author's meaning, but that it conveys also some other meaning which is not the author's. His words are susceptible of more than one interpretation. When this happens, it is always occasioned either by using some expression which is equivocal—that is, hath more meanings than one affixed to it, or by ranging the words in such an order that the construction is rendered equivocal, or made to exhibit different senses. To the former, for distinction's sake, I shall assign the name of equivocation; to the latter I shall appropriate that of ambiguity. [249]

[Unintelligibility]

I have already considered two of the principal and most common offences against perspicuity, and come now to make some remarks on the third and last offence mentioned in the enumeration formerly given. It was observed that a speaker may not only express himself obscurely, and so convey his meaning imperfectly to the mind of the hearer; that he may not only express himself ambiguously, and so, along with his own, convey a meaning entirely different; but even express himself unintelligibly, and so convey no meaning at all. One would, indeed, think it hardly possible that a man of sense, who perfectly understands the language which he useth, should ever speak or write in such a manner as to be altogether unintelligible. Yet this is what frequently happens. The cause of this fault in any writer I take to be always one or other of the three following: first, great confusion of thought, which is commonly accompanied with intricacy of expression; secondly, affectation of excellence in the diction; thirdly, a total want of meaning. I do not mention as one of the causes of this imputation a penury of language, though this, doubtless, may contribute to produce it. In fact, I never found one who had a justness of apprehension, and was free from affectation, at a loss to make himself understood in his native tongue, even though he had little command of language, and made but a bad choice of words. [266]

[Vivacity]

I come now to those qualities of style by which it (the discourse) is adapted to please the imagination, and, consequently, to awaken and fix the attention. These I have already denominated vivacity and elegance. . . . By vivacity of expression, resemblance is attained, as far as language can contribute to the attainment; by elegance, dignity of manner.

. . . . .

There are three things in a style on which its vivacity depends, the choice of words, their number, and their arrangement.

The first thing, then, that comes to be examined is the words chosen. Words are either proper terms or rhetorical tropes; and whether the one or the other, they may be regarded not only as signs, but as sounds; and, consequently, as capable, in certain cases, of bearing in some degree a natural resemblance or affinity to the things signified. These three articles, therefore, proper terms, rhetorical tropes, and the relation which the sound may be made to bear to the sense, I shall, on the first topic, the choice of words, consider severally, as far as concerns the subject of vivacity. [307]

. . . . .

I come now to consider how far vivacity may be affected by the number of words. Of this article it may be established as a maxim that admits no exception, and it is the only maxim which this article admits, that the fewer the words are, provided neither propriety nor perspicuity be violated, the expression is always the more vivid. [353]

. . . . .

I come now, lastly, to consider how it (vivacity) is affected by their (words) arrangement.

This, it must be owned, hath a very considerable influence in all languages, and yet there is not anything which it is more difficult to regulate by general laws. The placing of the words in a sentence resembles, in some degree, the disposition of the figures in a history-piece. As the principal figure ought to have that situation in the picture which will, at the first glance, fix the eye of the spectator, so the emphatical word ought to have that place in the sentence which will give it the greatest advantage for fixing the attention of the hearer. But in painting there can rarely arise a doubt concerning either the principal figure or the principal place, whereas here is it otherwise. In many sentences it may be a question, both what is the word on which the emphasis ought to rest, and what is the situation which (to use the language of painters) will give it the highest relief. In most cases, both of simple narration and of reasoning, it is not of great consequence to determine either point; it many cases it is impossible. [372-3]

SUGGESTED READINGS

Campbell, George
The Philosophy of Rhetoric. new ed. New York. Harper and Bros. 1851. xi, 435p

Sandford, William P.
English Theories of Public Address, 1530-1828. Columbus, Ohio. H. L. Hedrick. 1931. p144-52

Williams, A. M.
The Scottish School of Rhetoric. *Education.* 13:142-50 November 1892; 13:220-7 December 1892; 13:281-90 January 1893; 13:344-54 February 1893; 13:427-34 March 1893; 13:488-96 April 1893

HUGH BLAIR
(1718-1800)

Widely used in the teaching of public speaking in America during the latter part of the eighteenth and the first half of the nineteenth century, Blair's *Lectures* constitute a sort of discursive analysis of certain topics in rhetoric, criticism, poetry, philosophy, drama, and history. Without adding much that was new, Blair gave to Quintilian's doctrines a restatement which had sufficient interest value and compositional grace to win for it a wide reading public.

From the point of view of emphasis in the *Lectures,* Blair assigns to style the position of greatest prominence.

LECTURES ON RHETORIC AND BELLES LETTRES [1]

[*Definition of Style*]

The best definition I can give of it is, the peculiar manner in which a man expresses his conceptions, by means of Language. It is different from mere Language or words. The words which an author employs, may be proper and faultless; and his Style may, nevertheless, have great faults: it may be dry or stiff, or feeble, or affected. Style has always some reference to an author's manner of thinking. It is a picture of the ideas which rise in his mind, and of the manner in which they rise there; and, hence, when we are examining an author's composition, it is, in many cases, extremely difficult to separate the style from the sentiment. No wonder these two should be so intimately connected, as Style is nothing else than that sort of expression which our thoughts most readily assume. [103]

[*Qualities of Good Style*]

All the qualities of a good Style may be ranged under two heads, Perspicuity and Ornament. For all that can possibly be required of Language, is, to convey our ideas clearly to the minds of others, and, at the same time, in such a dress, as, by pleasing and interesting them, shall most effectually strengthen the impressions which we seek to make. When both these ends are answered, we certainly accomplish every purpose for which we use Writing and Discourse. [103-4]

[1] New ed., London, William Tegg, n.d.

[Use of Tropes or Figures]

First, they enrich Language, and render it more copious. By their means, words and phrases are multiplied for expressing all sorts of ideas; for describing even the minutest differences; the nicest shades and colours of thought; which no Language could possibly do by proper words alone, without assistance from Tropes.

Secondly, They bestow dignity upon Style. The familiarity of common words, to which our ears are much accustomed, tends to degrade Style. When we want to adapt our Language to the tone of an elevated subject, we should be greatly at a loss, if we could not borrow assistance from Figures; which, properly employed, have a similar effect on Language, with what is produced by the rich and splendid dress of a person of rank; to create respect, and to give an air of magnificence to him who wears it. [159]

. . . . .

In the third place, Figures give us the pleasure of enjoying two objects presented together to our view, without confusion; the principal idea, which is the subject of the discourse, along with its accessory, which gives it the figurative dress. We see one thing in another, as Aristotle expresses it; which is always agreeable to the mind. [160]

. . . . .

In the fourth place, Figures are attended with this farther advantage, of giving us frequently a much clearer and more striking view of the principal object, than we could have if it were expressed in simple terms, and divested of its accessory idea. This is, indeed, their principal advantage, in virtue of which they are very properly said to illustrate a subject, or to throw light upon it. For they exhibit the object, on which they are employed, in a picturesque form; they can render an abstract conception, in some degree, an object of sense; they surround it with such circumstances as enable the mind to lay hold of it steadily, and to contemplate it fully. [160-1]

[Definition of Eloquence]

For the best definition which, I think, can be given of Eloquence, is, the Art of Speaking in such a manner as to attain the end for which we speak. Whenever a man speaks or writes, he is supposed, as a rational being, to have some end in view; either to inform, or to amuse, or to persuade, or, in some way or other, to act upon his fellow creatures. He who speaks, or writes, in such a manner as to adapt all his words most effectually to that end, is the most eloquent man. Whatever then the subject be, there is room for Eloquence; in history, or even in philosophy, as well as in orations. The definition which I have given of Eloquence, comprehends all the different kinds of it; whether calculated to instruct, to persuade, or to please. But as the most important subject of discourse is Action, or Conduct, the power of Eloquence chiefly appears when it is employed to influence Conduct, and persuade to Action. As it is principally with reference to this end, that it becomes the object of Art, Eloquence may, under this view of it, be defined, The Art of Persuasion. [277-8]

[Distinction Between Conviction and Persuasion]

This leads me to observe, that convincing and persuading, though they are sometimes confounded, import, notwithstanding, different things, which it is necessary for us, at present, to distinguish from each other. Conviction affects the understanding only; persuasion, the will and the practice. It is the business of the philosopher to convince me of truth; it is the business of the orator to persuade me to act agreeably to it, by engaging my affections on its side. Conviction and persuasion do not always go together. They *ought*, indeed, to go together; and *would* do so, if our inclination regularly followed the dictates of our understanding. But as our nature is constituted, I may be convinced that virtue, justice, or public spirit, are laudable, while, at the same time, I am not persuaded to act according to them. The inclination may revolt, though the understanding be satisfied; the passions may prevail against the judgment. Conviction is, however, always one avenue to the inclination, or heart; and it is that which an orator must first bend his strength to gain: for no persuasion is likely to be stable which is not founded on conviction. But in order to persuade, the Orator must go farther than merely producing conviction; he must consider man as a creature moved by many different springs, and must act upon them all. He must address himself to the passions; he must paint to the fancy, and touch the heart; and hence, besides solid argument, and clear method, all the conciliating and interesting arts, both of Composition and Pronunciation, enter into the idea of Eloquence. [278-9]

[Kinds of Eloquence]

We may distinguish three kinds, or degrees, of Eloquence. The first, and lowest, is that which aims only at pleasing the hearers. Such, generally, is the Eloquence of panegyrics, inaugural orations, addresses to great men, and other harangues of this sort. This ornamental sort of Composition is not altogether to be rejected. It may innocently amuse and entertain the mind; and it may be mixed, at the same time, with very useful sentiments. But it must be confessed, that where the speaker has no farther aim than merely to shine and to please, there is great danger of Art being strained into ostentation, and of the Composition becoming tiresome and languid.

A second and higher degree of Eloquence is when the Speaker aims not merely to please, but also to inform, to instruct, to convince: when his Art is exerted in removing prejudices against himself and his cause, in choosing the most proper arguments, stating them with the greatest force, arranging them in the best order, expressing and delivering them with propriety and beauty; and thereby disposing us to pass that judgment, or embrace that side of the cause, to which he seeks to bring us. Within this compass, chiefly is employed the Eloquence of the bar.

But there is a third, and still higher degree of Eloquence, wherein a greater power is exerted over the human mind; by which we are not only convinced but are interested, agitated, and carried along with the Speaker; our passions are made to rise together with his; we enter into all his emotions; we love, we detest, we resent, according as he inspires us; and are prompted to resolve or to act, with vigour and warmth. Debate, in popular assemblies, opens the most illustrious field to this species of Eloquence; and the pulpit, also, admits it. [279-80]

[Eloquence of Popular Assemblies]

Its object is, or ought always to be, Persuasion. There must be some end proposed; some point, most commonly of public utility or good, in favour of which we seek to determine the hearers. Now, in all attempts to persuade men, we must proceed upon this principle, that it is necessary to convince their understanding. [303-4]

. . . . .

Let it be their first study, in addressing any popular assembly, to be previously masters of the business on which they are to speak; to be well provided with matter and argument, and to rest upon these the chief stress. This will always give to their discourse an air of manliness and strength, which is a powerful instrument of persuasion. Ornament, if they have genius for it, will follow of course, at any rate it demands only their secondary study. . . . [304]

. . . . .

In the next place, in order to be persuasive Speakers in a Popular Assembly, it is, in my opinion, a capital rule, that we be ourselves persuaded of whatever we recommend to others. Never, when it can be avoided, ought we to espouse any side of the argument, but what we believe to be the true and the right one. Seldom or never will a man be eloquent, but when he is in earnest, and uttering his own sentiments. [304-5]

. . . . .

Let us now consider the Style and Expression suited to the Eloquence of popular Assemblies. Beyond doubt, these give scope for the most animated manner of Public Speaking. The very aspect of a large assembly, engaged in some debate of moment, and attentive to the discourse of one man, is sufficient to inspire that man with such elevation and warmth, as both gives rise to strong impressions, and gives them propriety. [307]

. . . . .

The liberty, however, which we are now giving of the strong and passionate manner to this kind of Oratory, must be always understood with certain limitations and restraints, which it will be necessary to point out distinctly, in order to guard against dangerous mistakes on this subject.

As first, The warmth which we express must be suited to the occasion and the subject; for nothing can be more preposterous, than an attempt to introduce great vehemence into a subject, which is either of slight importance, or which, by its nature, requires to be treated of calmly. A temperate tone of Speech is that for which there is most frequent occasion; and he who is, on every subject, passionate and vehement, will be considered as a blusterer, and meet with little regard.

In the second place, We must take care never to counterfeit warmth without feeling it. [307-8]

. . . . .

In the third place, Even when the subject justifies the vehement manner, and when genius prompts it; when warmth is felt, not counterfeited; we must still set a guard on ourselves, not to allow impetuosity to transport us too far. Without emotion in the Speaker, Eloquence, as was before observed, will never produce its highest effects; but, at the same time, if the Speaker lose command of himself, he will soon lose command of his audience too. He must never kindle too soon: he must begin with moderation; and study to carry his hearers along with him, as he warms in the progress of his discourse. [308]

. . . . .

In the fourth place, In the highest and most animated strain of Popular Speaking, we must always preserve regard to what the public ear will bear. This direction I give, in order to guard against an injudicious imitation of ancient Orators, who, both in their pronunciation and gesture, and in their figures of expression, used a bolder manner than what the greater coolness of modern taste will readily suffer. [308]

. . . . .

In the fifth and last place, In all kinds of Public Speaking, but especially in Popular Assemblies, it is a capital rule to attend to all the decorums of time, place, and character. No warmth of Eloquence can atone for the neglect of these. That vehemence, which is becoming in a person of character and authority, may be unsuitable to the modesty expected from a young Speaker. That sportive and witty manner which may suit one subject and one assembly, is altogether out of place in a grave cause and a solemn meeting. [309]

[Eloquence of the Bar]

In the first place, the ends of speaking at the Bar, and in the Popular Assemblies, are commonly different. In Popular Assemblies, the great object is persuasion; the Orator aims at determining the hearers to some choice or conduct, as good, fit, or useful. For accomplishing this end, it is imcumbent on him to apply himself to all the principles of action in our nature; to the passions and to the heart, as well as to the understanding. But, at the Bar, conviction is the great object. There, it is not the Speaker's business to persuade the Judges to what is good or useful, but to show them what is just and true; and, of course, it is chiefly, or solely, to the understanding that his Eloquence is addressed. This is a characteristical difference which ought ever to be kept in view.

In the next place, Speakers at the Bar address themselves to one, or to a few Judges, and these, too, persons generally of age, gravity, and authority of character. There they have not those advantages which a mixed and numerous Assembly affords for employing all the Arts of Speech, even supposing their subject to admit them. Passion does not rise so easily; the Speaker is heard more coolly; he is watched over more severely; and would expose himself to ridicule, by attempting that high vehement tone, which is only proper in speaking to a multitude.

In the last place, the nature and management of the subjects which belong to the Bar, require a very different species of Oratory from that of Popular Assemblies. In the latter, the Speaker has a much wider range. He is seldom confined to any precise rule; he can fetch his topics from a great variety of quarters; and employ every illustration which his fancy or imagination suggests. But, at the bar, the field of speaking is limited to precise law and statute. Imagination is not allowed to take its scope. The Advocate has always lying before him the line, the square, and the compass. These, it is his principal business to be continually applying to the subjects under debate. [318-19]

[*Eloquence of the Pulpit*]

Let us begin with considering the advantages and disadvantages which belong to this field of Public Speaking. The Pulpit has plainly several advantages peculiar to itself. The dignity and importance of its subjects must be acknowledged superior to any other. They are such as ought to interest every one, and can be brought home to every man's heart; and such as admit, at the same time, both the highest embellishment in describing, and the greatest vehemence and warmth in enforcing them. The Preacher has also great advantages in treating his subjects. He speaks not to one or a few Judges, but to a large Assembly. He is secure from all interruption. He is obliged to no replies, or extemporaneous efforts. He chooses his theme at leisure; and comes to the public with all the assistance which the most accurate premeditation can give him. [333]

. . . . .

An essential requisite in order to preach well, is to have a just, and at the same time, a fixed and habitual view of the end of preaching. For in no art can any man execute well, who has not a just idea of the end and object of that art. The end of all preaching is, to persuade men to become good. Every Sermon therefore, should be a persuasive oration; not but that the Preacher is to instruct and to teach, to reason and to argue. All persuasion, as I showed formerly, is to be founded on conviction. The understanding must always be applied to in the first place, in order to make a lasting impression on the heart; and he who would work on men's passions, or influence their practice, without first giving them just principles, and enlightening their minds, is no better than a mere declaimer. [335]

. . . . .

The chief characteristics of the Eloquence suited to the Pulpit, as distinguished from the other kinds of Public Speaking, appear to me to be these two, Gravity and Warmth. The serious nature of the subjects belonging to the Pulpit requires Gravity; their importance to mankind requires Warmth. [336]

[*Parts of an Oration*]

This being the natural train of Speaking, the parts that compose a regular formal Oration, are these six; first, the Exordium or Introduction; secondly, the State, and the Division of the Subject; thirdly, Narration or Explication; fourthly, the Reasoning or Arguments; fifthly, the Pathetic Part; and lastly, the Conclusion. I do not mean, that each of these must enter into every Public Discourse, or that they must enter always in this order. There is no reason for being so formal on every occasion; nay, it would often be a fault, and would render a Discourse pedantic and stiff. [364]

[*Rules Governing the Composition of the Introduction*]

The first rule is, That the Introduction should be easy and natural. The subject must always suggest it. . . . It is too common a fault in Introductions, that they are taken from some common-place topic, which has no peculiar relation to the subject in hand; by which means they stand apart, like pieces detached from the rest of the Discourse. [367]

. . . . .

In order to render Introductions natural and easy, it is, in my opinion, a good rule that they should not be planned, till after one has meditated in his own mind the substance of his Discourse. Then, and not till then, he should begin to think of some proper and natural Introduction. [367]

. . . . .

In the second place, In an Introduction, correctness should be carefully studied in the expression. This is requisite, on account of the situation of the hearers. They are then more disposed to criticise than at any other period; they are, as yet, unoccupied with the subject or the arguments; their attention is wholly directed to the Speaker's style and manner. Something must be done, therefore, to prepossess them in his favour; though for the same reasons, too much art must be avoided; for it will be more easily detected at that time than afterwards; and will derogate from persuasion in all that follows. [367-8]

. . . . .

RHETORIC AND PUBLIC SPEAKING

In the third place, Modesty is another character which it must carry. All appearances of modesty are favourable, and prepossessing. If the Orator set out with an air of arrogance and ostentation, the self-love and pride of the hearers will be presently awakened, and will follow him with a very suspicious eye throughout all his progress. His modesty should discover itself not only in his expressions at the beginning, but in his whole manner; in his looks, in his gestures, in the tone of his voice. [368]

. . . . .

In the fourth place, An Introduction should usually be carried on in the calm manner. This is seldom the place for vehemence and passion. Emotions must rise as the Discourse advances. The minds of the Hearers must be gradually prepared, before the Speaker can venture on strong and passionate sentiments. [369]

. . . . .

In the fifth place, It is a rule in Introductions, not to anticipate any material part of the subject. When topics, or arguments, which are afterwards to be enlarged upon, are hinted at, and in part, brought forth in the Introduction, they lose the grace of novelty upon their second appearance. The impression intended to be made by any capital thought, is always made with the greatest advantage, when it is made entire, and in its proper place. [370]

. . . . .

In the last place, the Introduction ought to be proportioned, both in length, and in kind, to the Discourse that is to follow: in length, as nothing can be more absurd than to erect a very great portico before a small building; and in kind, as it is no less absurd to overcharge, with superb ornaments, the portico of a plain dwelling house, or to make the entrance to a monument as gay as that to an arbour. Common sense directs, that every part of a Discourse should be suited to the strain and spirit of the whole. [370]

[Directions Relating to the Use of the Pathetic]

The first is to consider carefully, whether the subject admit the Pathetic, and render it proper; and if it does, what part of the Discourse is the most proper for attempting it. To determine these points belongs to good sense; for it is evident, that there are many subjects which admit not the Pathetic at all, and that even in those that are susceptible of it, an attempt to excite the passions in the wrong place, may expose an Orator to ridicule. All that can be said in general is, that if we expect any emotion which we raise to have a lasting effect, we must be careful to bring over to our side, in the first place, the understanding and judgment. The hearers must be convinced that there are good and sufficient grounds for their entering with warmth into the cause. They must be able to justify to themselves the passion which they feel; and remain satisfied that they are not carried away by mere delusion. Unless their minds be brought into this state, although they may have been heated by the Orator's discourse, yet, as soon as he ceases to speak, they will resume their ordinary tone of thought; and the emotion which he has raised will die entirely away. [383]

. . . . .

In the second place, never to set apart a head of a discourse in form, for raising any passion; never give warning that you are about to be pathetic; and call upon your hearers, as is sometimes done, to follow you in the attempt. This almost never fails to prove a refrigerant to passion. It puts the hearers immediately on their guard, and disposes them for criticising, much more than for being moved. The indirect method of making an impression is likely to be more successful, when you seize the critical moment that is favourable to emotion, in whatever part of the discourse it occurs, and then, after due preparation, throw in such circumstances, and present such glowing images, as may kindle their passions before they are aware. [384]

. . . . .

In the third place, It is necessary to observe, that there is a great difference between showing the hearers that they ought to be moved, and actually moving them. [384]

. . . . .

In the fourth place, the only effectual method is, to be moved yourselves. There are a thousand interesting circumstances suggested by real passion, which no art can imitate, and no refinement can supply. There is obviously a contagion among the passions. [385]

. . . . .

In the fifth place, It is necessary to attend to the proper language of the passions. We should observe in what manner any one expresses himself who is under the power of a real and a strong passion; and we shall always find his language unaffected and simple. It may be animated, indeed, with bold and strong figures, but it will have no ornament or finery. He is not at leisure to follow out the play of Imagination. His mind being wholly seized by one object, which has heated it, he has no other aim, but to represent that in all its circumstances, as strongly as he feels it. [385-6]

* * * * *

In the sixth place, Avoid interweaving anything of a foreign nature with the Pathetic part of Discourse. Beware of all digressions, which may interrupt or turn aside the natural course of the passion, when once it begins to rise and swell. Sacrifice all beauties, however bright and showy, which would divert the mind from the principal object, and which would amuse the imagination, rather than touch the heart. Hence comparisons are always dangerous, and generally quite improper, in the midst of passion. Beware even of reasoning unseasonably; or at least, of carrying on a long and subtle train of reasoning on occasions when the principal aim is to excite warm emotions. [386]

* * * * *

In the last place, Never attempt prolonging the Pathetic too much. Warm emotions are too violent to be lasting. Study the proper time of making a retreat; of making a transition from the passionate to the calm tone; in such a manner, however, as to descend without falling, by keeping up the same Strain of Sentiment that was carried on before, though now expressing it with more moderation. Above all things, beware of straining passion too far; of attempting to raise it to unnatural heights. Preserve always a due regard to what the hearers will bear; and remember, that he who stops not at the proper point; who attempts to carry them farther in passion, than they will follow him, destroys his whole design. [386]

[*Affectation in Delivery*]

I cannot conclude without an earnest admonition to guard against all affectation, which is the certain ruin of good Delivery. Let your manner, whatever it is, be your own; neither imitated from another, nor assumed upon some imaginary model, which is unnatural to you. Whatever is native, even though accompanied with several defects, yet is likely to please; because it shows us a man; because it has the appearance of coming from the heart. Whereas a Delivery, attended with several acquired graces and beauties, if it be not easy and free, if it betray the marks of art and affectation, never fails to disgust. To attain any extremely correct and perfectly graceful Delivery, is what few can expect; so many natural talents being requisite to concur in forming it. But to attain, what as to the effect is very little inferior, a forcible and persuasive manner, is within the power of most persons; if they will only unlearn false and corrupt habits; if they will allow themselves to follow Nature, and speak in public as they do in private, when they speak in earnest and from the heart. If one has naturally any gross defects in his voice or gestures, he begins at the wrong end, if he attempts at reforming them only when he is to speak in public. He should begin with rectifying them in his private manner of Speaking; and then carry to the public the right habit he has formed. For, when a Speaker is engaged in a Public Discourse, he should not be then employing his attention about his manner, or thinking of his tones and his gestures. If he be so employed, study and affectation will appear. He ought to be then quite in earnest; wholly occupied with his subject and his sentiments; leaving Nature, and previously formed habits, to prompt and suggest his manner of Delivery. [402-3]

SUGGESTED READINGS

Blair, Hugh
    Lectures on Rhetoric and Belles Lettres. Many editions

Sandford, William P.
    English Theories of Public Address, 1530-1828. Columbus, Ohio. H. L. Hedrick. 1931. p154-9

GILBERT AUSTIN
(*fl.* 1800)

Austin's *Chironomia* deals with rhetorical delivery, embracing a large fund of material on voice and bodily action. Like Bulwer's contributions, it is detailed and comprehensive in its treatment of gesticulation.

In common with other works on elocution of the eighteenth and early nineteenth century, Austin's *Chironomia* sets up delivery as an exceedingly important part of speaking. Austin draws freely upon the classical and modern authors "for the ornament and support" of his work. Being a preacher, he comments at length on the delivery appropriate to that profession.

CHIRONOMIA [1]

[*External Parts of Oratory*]

The management of the voice, the expression of the countenance, and the gesture of the head, the body, and the limbs, constitute the external part of oratory; and relate to the personal talents and efforts of the public speaker, in like manner as the other divisions of rhetoric, invention, disposition, choice of words, and memory, relate to those of his understanding. [1]

[*Voices Subject to Improvement Through Observance of Rules*]

With certain management, few voices are so bad, as not to be rendered capable of discharging tolerably the functions of public speaking in our assemblies; and few perhaps are to be found so perfect as not to require some attention; or which may not derive benefit from the observation of some of the general rules for the proper management of that organ. These rules in the order of their importance, may be considered under the following heads:

1. Articulation. 2. Pronunciation and accent. 3. Emphasis. 4. Pauses. 5. Pitch. 6. Quantity. 7. Modulation and variety. 8. Tones. [36]

[*Pronunciation Varies with Modes of the Time*]

This knowledge is to be acquired only by conversing with correct speakers. Pronunciation (as does also the whole of language) varies

---

[1] London, printed for T. Cadell and W. Davies, 1806.

with the modes and fashions of the times: it is sometimes so fluctuating in particular words, and high authorities are often so much at variance, that the most correct mode is hard to be determined. Accent is also subject to the caprice of fashion. [46]

[*Precepts Relating to the Preservation of the Voice*]

1. The first rule for the preservation of the voice, and which is equally supported by ancient authorities, and modern experience, is, that the public speaker should, if he "strive for the mastery," be habitually "temperate in all things;"—moderate in the use of wine, and in the indulgence of the table; and not given to any personal excess. A bloated body, and an enfeebled constitution, are not only injurious to the voice, but render a man equally incapable of any other mental or bodily exertion. [70]

. . . . .

2. The voice should not be exerted after a full meal. This rule is a consequence of the first. [70]

. . . . .

3. The voice should not be urged beyond its strength; nor be strained to its utmost pitch without intermission: such mismanagement would endanger its powers altogether; and it might break. Frequent change of pitch is the best preservative. [70-1]

. . . . .

4. At that period of youth when the voice begins to break, and to assume the manly tone, no violent exertion should be made; but the voice should be spared, until it becomes confirmed and established. Neither, according to this rule, should the voice when hoarse, if it may be avoided, be exerted at any time. [71]

. . . . .

5. Certain things are found injurious to the voice, and therefore to be avoided. Butter and nuts, are accounted so among singers, and also oranges and acid liquors. The ancients considered also all cold drinks to be injurious, and dry fruits. [71-2]

. . . . .

6. Some things are found serviceable to the voice, and are used by modern singers. They may be equally advantageous to a public speaker. Warm mucilaginous and diluting drinks, in case of dryness of the fauces, or slight hoarseness, barley water and tea, preparations of sugar, sugar candy, barley sugar, and the various sorts of lozenges

which modern ingenuity prepares so elegantly: a raw egg beat up is reckoned the best substance for immediately clearing the voice, and is preferred by the Italian singers.—The ancients made use of warm baths, and the exercise of walking, and both perhaps with advantage. [72]

[*Precepts Relating to the Improvement of the Voice*]

1. The great means of the improving of the voice, as of all other improvement, is constant and daily practice. [72]

. . . . .

2. The second rule has been anticipated, which is bodily exercise. —The ancients recommend walking a certain space before breakfast; about a mile.—Riding on horseback we do not find recommended or practised as mere exercise. [73]

. . . . .

3. In order to strengthen the voice,—Mr. Sheridan advises (Lec.5) that any person who has fallen into a weak utterance, should daily practise to read, and repeat in a large room in the hearing of a friend. His friend should be placed at first, at such a distance as he may be able to reach in his usual manner; the distance is then gradually to be encreased, till he shall be so far from him, that he cannot be heard beyond him without straining. [73-4]

. . . . .

4. Mr. Walker's rules for strengthening the voice are excellent and practicable; they are his 4th, 5th, and 6th rules to which I beg to refer the reader. The general principle is this,—that in order to strengthen the higher tones of the voice, such passages should be practised as require the high tones. These are particularly a succession of questions ending with the rising inflexion. For the middle tones, passionate speeches requiring them should be practised; and for bringing down the voice, (which is apt to run wild, and not to be in our power when long continued above,) the succeeding sentence is to be begun (if the subject admit), and delivered in a lower tone. [74]

[*Precepts Relating to the Management of the Voice*]

1. The first principles of the proper management of the voice depend on due attention to articulation, pronunciation, accent, emphasis, pauses, and tones. . . . [75]

. . . . .

2. The actual practice of the various inflexions and pauses; of the pitch and the tones to be adopted, should take place previous to the public delivery of a written oration. [75]

. . . . .

3. When time or opportunity do not permit this practice, the manner in which the voice should be managed in the different parts of the oration, should be considered and determined. This practice was not unknown to the ancients, it was called the silent preparation of the voice. [75]

. . . . .

4. The difficulty of pitching the voice is very considerable, particularly in a room or situation to which the speaker is not accustomed. And as it is found easier to ascend than to lower the pitch, it is a general rule that a speaker should begin rather under the ordinary pitch of his voice than above it. [76]

. . . . .

5. As the middle pitch of the voice admits of ascending or descending freely, and is therefore favourable to ease and variety, and as the organs in this pitch are stronger from practice; every speaker should endeavour to deliver the principal part of his discourse in the middle pitch of his voice. [76]

. . . . .

6. To study variety of tone in delivery is a most important point. The opposite fault is monotony. To variety may also be referred the government of the utterance with respect to rapidity or slowness. And also the various expressions necessary to be adopted in the different passions and emotions of the mind. [79]

. . . . .

7. The lungs are to be kept always to a certain degree inflated, so that the voice shall not at any time be run out of breath. And the air which is necessarily expended, must be gradually and insensibly recovered at the proper times, and in the proper places. [79-80]

. . . . .

8. "In rooms where the quickly returning echo disturbs the speaker, he must lessen the quantity of his voice till the echo ceases to be perceptible. And when he is disturbed by the slowly returning echo, he must take care to be much slower and distinct in his utterance than usual, and to make his pauses longer. He is to attend to the

returning sound, and not to begin after a pause till the sound is ceased." (Adapted from Sheridan, *Lectures on Elocution*, 113) [81]

* * * * *

9. "In enormous buildings, as old abbeys, cathedrals, and halls, in which the speaker has no more advantage than if he were in the open air; he should regulate his voice as he ought in the open air, and make himself audible as far as he can without straining." (Adapted from Sheridan, *Lectures on Elocution*, 114) [81]

[*Estimation of the Powers of the Voice*]

1. The speaker discovers that his voice has filled the room by the return of its sound to his own ear. [81]

* * * * *

2. He will judge of the ability of his voice, by the degree of exertion necessary to enable him to fill a room of any particular size. [82]

* * * * *

3. And he may form a judgment concerning the opinion of his audience by the degree of their attention. [82]

[*Use of the Eyes in Oratory*]

To the expression of the countenance in oratory all the features contribute a share, but by far the greatest is derived from the eyes. [99]

* * * * *

As the principal object of every public speaker must be to obtain the attention of his audience; so every circumstance which can contribute to this end must be considered important. In the external demeanour nothing will be found so effectually to attract attention, and detain it, as the direction of the eyes. It is well known that the eyes can influence persons at a distance; and that they can select from a multitude a single individual, and turn their looks on him alone, though many lie in the same direction. The whole person seems to be in some measure affected by this influence of another's eyes, but the eyes themselves feel it with the most lively sensibility. [101]

* * * * *

However these circumstances may be accounted for, the public speaker will judiciously take care to avail himself of them in a proper manner. He will therefore turn his eyes upon the eyes of his audience, and in the more important and earnest passages, he will look into the very pupils of their eyes. But in the practice of this direction of the eyes, which is of such advantage towards obtaining attention, he will be most cautious not to appear to fix on any particular person as the object of invective, or as the subject and example of the vices he may condemn; unless unhappily in public debate such severity should be absolutely necessary. [103]

[*The Mouth As an Important Part of the Countenance*]

The mouth, of which we are now to treat, is next to the eyes, or even in preference to the eyes themselves, the most important part of the countenance: it is so in whatever way we consider it, whether in the variety and precision of which it is capable, or in the interest which it excites, whether by the language and tones which issue from it, or from its expression and character as it strikes the beholder. [121]

. . . . .

It is more particularly important to attend to the mouth, than even to the eyes themselves. The eyes at all times can assume the character suited to the expression of the moment. But the mouth being one of the softest features is soonest changed, and if it once lose its character of sweetness, it changes perhaps for ever. How few mouths which have been beautiful in youth (the season of happiness and smiles,) are preserved beyond that period: whilst the eyes are often found to retain their lustre, or to flash occasionally with their early brightness even in advanced life. Every bad habit defaces the soft beauty of the mouth, and leaves indelible on it the traces of their injury. The stains of intemperance discolour it, ill nature wrinkles it, envy deforms, and voluptuousness bloats it. The impressions of sorrow upon it are easily traced, the injuries which it suffers from ill-health are manifest, and accident may often deform its symmetry. It is sweetened by benevolence, confirmed by wisdom, chizzeled by taste, and composed by discretion: and these traces if habitually fixed last unaltered in its soft forms, throughout every varying stage of life. We should therefore labour in our own persons, and watch those of the youthful under our control, to form if possible this distinguished and pliant feature to decorum and grace, lest it assume an ungracious form irretrievably. [122-3]

[*Gesture Defined*]

The third division of the external part of oratory, or of delivery, is gesture. Under gesture is comprehended the action and position of all the parts of the body; of the head, the shoulders, the body or trunk; of the arms, hands, and fingers; of the lower limbs, and of the feet. [133]

[Extent to Which Gesture Should Be Used]

Though according to the system, gesture may be varied almost to infinity, it is not proposed that the speaker's gesture should be incessant; nothing could so completely defeat every expectation of the advantage arising from gesture. In many parts of an oration little gesture should be used; in many the speaker should be almost unmoved; and very few passages admit of vehement gesticulation. It is not necessary always to saw the air, far from it.—But it is necessary to consider and to judge *when* the air is to be divided by the arm of the orator; when he is to move his head, his body, and his limbs; and *how* he is to do all this with effect, with propriety, and with grace. And instead of adding much to his action, he who studies it the most carefully, will only be inclined to alter it for the better, or perhaps in many places to retrench it altogether. The art of gesture however cultivated, is not to be used for incessant flourishing; as well might the steps and bounds in dancing be adopted on all occasions, instead of the simple movement of walking: and our art may serve the same excellent purpose to the awkward gesticulator for which the father sent his clownish son to the dancing school, that he might learn to stand still. [136-7]

* * * * *

That nature without cultivation should suggest on the moment to every man all the gesture necessary to enforce his feelings, and to illustrate and grace his sentiments, cannot be maintained by any analogy from the assistance afforded by nature in the other parts of oratory, nor is it found agreeable to fact. [137]

[The Ends of Public Speaking]

The general objects of public speaking are, instruction, persuasion, or entertainment. These objects are sometimes kept distinct, sometimes they are combined in various proportions.

In their various modes of exercise, these objects will obtain their ends, that is succeed in influencing the hearer in the degree proposed, not only by the interesting matter which may be presented to him, but also by the manner in which it is presented. The manner is called the delivery. And the advantages of good delivery are such, as to conceal in *some degree* the blemishes of the composition, or the matter delivered, and to add lustre to its beauties: insomuch that a *good* composition well delivered, shall, with any popular audience, succeed better in its object (as we have already proved from high authorities), whether that be instruction, persuasion or entertainment, than a superior composition not delivered so well. [187-8]

[*Importance of Delivery in Speaking*]

First, because the majority are incapable of appreciating the matter of a discourse, separately from the manner; and secondly, because the manner has naturally considerable influence, in proportion to the degree of persuasion which it impresses on the hearer, of the sincerity of the speaker. [188]

[*The Modes in Public Speaking*]

The modes adopted in public speaking are, Reading, Recitation, Declamation, Oratory, and Acting. Of which the three first are often practised for the purpose of exercise or preparation, as well as on real occasions. [188]

[*Oratory and Reasoning*]

Oratory, which is public speaking on real and interesting occasions, is the most splendid object of all literary exertion, and the highest scope of all the study and practice of the art. To oratory belongs whatever the perfection of composition can produce, as well as all which the perfection of delivery can externally recommend and enforce.

Oratory is the power of reasoning united to the various arts of persuasion, presented by external grace, and by the whole energy of the human powers. Reasoning divested of rhetorical composition and of rhetorical delivery becomes strict demonstration. Such reasoning is found in logic, mathematics, evidences of facts, and law arguments. Reasoning in this sense is distinct from oratory: both indeed alike aim at bringing over other men to their opinions, but by different means. Reasoning appeals to the understanding alone; oratory deals with the passions also. Reasoning proceeds directly to the truth, and exhibits it in the simplest language. Oratory chooses the most favourable view of the subject, engages the attention of the hearer by the detail of circumstances, interests him by the colouring which he gives them, delights him by ornament, and, having won his favourable attention, appeals at once to his understanding and to his heart. When the subject admits of demonstration; reasoning is the most powerful, it is irresistible: but when strict demonstration cannot be had, oratory has then the advantage. And since in a very few of the most interesting enquiries which occupy the attention of men, strict demonstration can be obtained, so the demand for the talents of the orator is frequent and indispensable in the business of life. Reasoning is therefore applied principally to philosophical research, and to objects of science: oratory to the interests of men, and to objects admitting choice. It is an advantage which oratory possesses above reasoning, that oratory constantly avails itself of reasoning, where it can be applied; but strict reasoning does not condescend to call in the aid of oratory. [217-18]

[*System of Notation Needed in Study of Gesture*]

One of the reasons which may be assigned for the neglect of cultivating the art of gesture, is the want of a copious and simple language for expressing its different modifications with brevity and perspicuity. [271]

[*Parts of the Body Involved in Gesture*]

The parts of the human figure which are brought into action in gesture, cannot, in truth, be considered separate: for every muscle, every nerve, over which men can exercise voluntary action, contributes in some measure to the perfection of gesture. We may however enumerate and class in relation to them for convenience, the most distinguished parts of the body which effect the principal gestures. These are:

1. The head. 2. The shoulders. 3. The trunk or body. 4. The arms. 5. The hands and fingers. 6. The lower limbs and knees. 7. The feet. [294]

[*Notational System for Studying Gesture*]

Synoptical arrangement of the Symbolic Letters.
Letters written above the Line on which the Gesture is noted, relating to the Hands, the Fingers, and Arms.

The Hands.

First, *small letter*.

Noting the manner of presenting the Palm.

p. prone.
s. supine.
n. inwards or natural.
o. outwards.

f. forwards.
b. backwards.
v. vertical.

Noting the disposition of the Fingers.

i. index.
n. natural or inwards.
c. clinched.
l. collected.
g. grasping.

x. extended.
h. holding.
m. thumb.
w. hollow.

Elevation of the Arms.
Second, *small letter*.

d. downwards.
h. horizontal.
e. elevated.

and two Capital letters.
Z. zenith.
R. rest.

Position of the Arms in the transverse Direction.
Third, *small letter*.

c. across.
f. forward.
q. oblique.

x. extended.
b. backwards.

For motions of the Hands and Arms, and force of Gesture.
Fourth and Fifth, *small letters*.
Force of Motion or Energy.

x. extreme   *c.* contracted.   *m.* moderate

Direction of Motion.

a. ascending.
d. descending.
r. right.
l. left.

f. forwards.
b. backwards.
v. revolving.

Manner of Motion.

n. noting.
p. projecting or pushing.
w. waving.
fl. flourish.
sw. sweep.
bk. beckoning.
rp. repressing.
ad. advancing.

sp. springing.
st. striking.
pr. pressing.
rc. recoiling.
sh. shaking.
th. throwing.
cl. clinching.
ll. collecting.

Head and Eyes.

Capitals placed at the commencement of Sentences.

Head.
I. inclined.
E. erect.
As. assenting.
Dn. denying.
Sh. shaking.
Ts. tossing.
S. aside.

Looks of the Eyes and Position of the Head.
F. forwards.
A. averted.
D. downwards.
U. upwards.
R. round.
V. vacancy.

Letters below the Line for the Feet.

Positions *of the Feet.* Capitals and Numerals.

F.1. front 1st position.
F.2. front 2d position.
R.1. right 1st position.
R.2. right 2d position.

L.1. left 1st position.
L.2. left 2d position.
K. kneeling.
S. aside.

x, extended—the feet separated widely.
Steps, *small letters.*

a. advance.
r. retire.
tr. traverse.
c. cross.

st. start.
sp. stamp.
sk. shock.

Capitals substituted for the Second and Third small Letters, and relating to particular Parts on which the Hands may be Placed.

E. eyes.
N. nose.
L. lips.

F. forehead.
C. chin.
br. breast (small letters.)

A capital B. preceding and joined to a set of small Letters signifies that both Hands or both Arms perform the same Gesture.

B. both hands or both arms.

The manner of combining the fingers of both Hands is noted by two small Letters preceded by a capital B. These Letters are substituted for the whole set relating to both Hands.

B.*ap.* both applied.
cl. clasped.
cr. crossed.
fl. folded.

in. inclosing.
wr. wringing.
tc. touching.
nu. enumerating.

The Combinations of both Arms.

en. encumbered or folded.
rp. reposed.

km. a kimbo.
(either one or both B).

Significant Gestures and Expressions of Countenance which may be Noted in the Margin, after the manner of Mr. Sheridan.

Ap. appealing.
At. attention.
Vn. veneration.
Ls. listening.
Lm. lamentation.
Dp. deprecation.
Pr. pride.
Sh. shame.

Av. aversion.
Cm. commanding.
Ad. admiration
Hr. horror.
Gr. grief.
Fr. fear.
En. encouraging, and many others at pleasure.
[363-5]

RHETORIC AND PUBLIC SPEAKING

[*The Stroke of the Gesture*]

The stroke of the gesture is analogous to the impression of the voice, made on those words, which it would illustrate or enforce; it is used for the same purposes and should fall precisely on the same place, that is, on the accented syllable of the emphatical word; so that the emphatical force of the voice and the stroke of the gesture co-operate in order to present the idea in the most lively and distinguished manner, as well to the eye, as to the ear of the hearer. The stroke of the gesture is to the eye, what the emphasis and inflexions of the voice are to the ear, and it is capable of equal force and variety. [377]

[*Classification of Gestures*]

Gesture may be considered under *four* general points of view.
1. With respect to the instrument or manner by which it is performed.
2. The signification of the gesture.   3. The quality of the gesture.
4. As suited to the style or character of the matter delivered.

These general divisions are thus subdivided:

I. Gesture referred to the instrument or manner of performance is subdivided into, 1. *Principal*, performed by the advanced or more elevated hand and arm. 2. *Subordinate*, performed by the hand and arm more retired and more depressed.

II. Gesture with reference to its signification, is considered as 1. *significant*, and 2. *not significant*; these are subdivided.

Significant gestures:
1. Natural.
2. Instituted.

Gestures not significant:
1. Commencing.
2. Discriminating.
3. Auxiliary, or alternate.
4. Suspended, or Preparatory.
5. Emphatical, which are also terminating gestures.

III. Gesture is considered to be capable of the following general *Qualities:*
1. Magnificence.
2. Boldness.
3. Variety.
4. Energy.
5. Simplicity.
6. Grace.
7. Propriety.
8. Precision.

IV. Gesture, as to the proportion of those qualities requisite in the delivery, may be suited to the *Style of speaking:*
1. Epic.
2. Rhetorical.
3. Colloquial. [386-7]

[*Significant Gestures*]

The next class of gestures is derived from the established usage of certain gestures for indicating certain persons, feelings, or expressions: in arranging these there is no great difficulty, as many have been described by Quintilian and other rhetoricians and critics of good authority. Indeed this class comprehends nearly all that has hitherto been done, (as far as my information extends) on the subject of gesture: all of this class are named *significant gestures.* Thus the index finger extended towards them points out persons or things, the hand laid on the breast refers to the feelings of the speaker, the finger laid on the lips signifies an injunction of silence, and many others. [389]

[*Commencing Gestures*]

Commencing gestures begin the discourse or division, by simply raising the hand from rest; and that in general not higher than the downward or horizontal position of the arm. [390]

[*Discriminating Gestures*]

Discriminating gestures comprehend all those, which serve the purpose of indicating persons or objects; or which are used for explaining, extending, limiting, or modifying the predominant idea; or in question and answer, when made without vehemence. [390-1]

[Auxiliary Gestures]

Auxiliary or alternate gestures serve to aid or enforce the gesture of the advanced hand. They are thus performed: after the advanced hand has made its gesture on the emphatical word, instead of passing to another gesture on the next emphatical word, it remains in the attitude of the last stroke, till the retired hand is brought up in aid of it, either by a similar gesture or by a more decided one; which gives at once variety and extraordinary energy to passages admitting such gestures: they are used of course with great advantage in high passion: but are also frequent in description, where they are executed more tamely. [391]

[Suspended Gestures]

Suspended or preparatory gestures elevate the arm preparatory to the stroke which is to fall on the emphatical word; or contract or bend it for the purpose of a forcible projection unbending or stroke of the arm. Suspended gestures are so named because they hold the attention in suspense by the elevation of the arm on some less important word preceding, and because they are also expected to lead to some emphatical gesture on a more important word. [391-2]

[Emphatical Gestures]

Emphatical gestures mark with force words opposed to or compared with each other, and more particularly the word which expresses the predominant idea. Their stroke is generally arrested on the horizontal elevation, but sometimes they are directed to the highest point of the range of the gesture, and sometimes also to the lowest. Emphatical gestures when directed to the highest point serve often as suspended or previous gestures to the next emphatical gesture: and when made at the close of a sentence or division of a subject they serve as closing or terminating gestures, because when the last important idea is marked, no other gesture should be added to weaken its effect; the arm then falls to rest. [392]

[Nature of an Act of Gesticulation]

The gesture of a public speaker is essentially different from the motions of a soldier performing the manual exercise. In the latter, the object is to effect a change of position within as narrow a space and in as short a time as possible. But confined and sudden motions do not suit an orator, except when perhaps the vehemence of passion urges him to the most rapid expression. Persuasion, which is his particular office, reaches the mind slowly, and is insinuated by circumlocution not of words only, but it may almost be said, of gesture also. In the transition from gesture to gesture, his hand and arm do not therefore precipitate towards the intended position by the shortest possible line, but move in the calmer parts of the oration in a sort of waving line, or one returning upon itself, . . . [411]

[*Transition in Gesture*]

But the transition of gesture particularly relates to the change of the principal gesture from one hand to the other: which may be regulated in some measure according to the following principles. So long as there subsists a strict connection between the sentiments, uninterrupted by any considerable pause or change of persons, no transition can take place in this last sense; the same hand, which began, continues to perform the principal gesture. And the variety which it is always desirable to produce, must not be attempted by the change of the principal gesture: it must arise alone from the graceful and well regulated action of the advanced hand, supported by the combined assistance or accompaniment of the other. Neither should the positions of the feet change too freely from right to left, but they may vary in advancing, and retiring, or change from the first to the second position alternately as occasion may require. If the passage to be pronounced be of considerable length, the right hand should by all means perform the principal gesture throughout the whole of it. For the left, though, among modern speakers, allowed to take its place occasionally, according to certain rules, by no means arrives at an equality of honour. The right always continues the better hand both from long prescription and the ability arising from use. [417]

[*Variety in Gesture*]

Variety, which is a most important object to be kept in view by a public speaker, allows with advantage an interchange of the principal gesture, even when the subject may be of a more abstruse and demonstrative nature. When there is any opposition or antithesis among the ideas, or even in the structure of sentences; or where a new argument is introduced after the discussion of a former is ended, as at a new division or a new paragraph, there may be a change of the principal gesture. But it will be a point of judgment and taste in the speaker not to carry this balancing or alternation of gesture to an affected extreme, and not even in allowable cases to indulge in it over much. [419-20]

RHETORIC AND PUBLIC SPEAKING

[Function of the Subordinate Gesture]

The subordinate gesture already mentioned as performed by the retired hand will be found to bear a close analogy to accompaniment in music. It is seldom inactive, sometimes imitates exactly and with considerable spirit, but in general performs an under part supporting and adorning, but by no means moving in the same manner as the superior hand. [421]

[Change of Gesture Means Change in Circumstances]

There is no gesture or change of gesture which is not meant to enforce or to illustrate some new circumstance, which either calls into action muscles before at rest, or into a change of action those already in exertion. And this impression and influence extends not only to those muscles which are most strong and distinguished, but even to the most delicate fibres of the human frame, such as those which adjust the expression of the mouth, of the nostrils, of the brows, and of that wondrous organ the eye. [423-4]

[Gesture Must Be Used To Enforce Thought]

As gesture is used for the illustration or enforcement of language, it should be limited in its application to such words and passages only as admit, or rather require, such illustration or enforcement. That is, gesture should not be used by a public speaker on every word, where it is possible to apply it without manifest impropriety; but it should rather be reserved for such passages as require to be rendered more prominent than the others, and to be coloured higher. A judicious speaker will therefore reserve his gesture, at least the force and ornament of it, for those parts of his discourse for which he also reserves the brilliancy of language and thought. [433]

[Gestures Vary with Circumstances]

But the gesture of the public speaker must also vary considerably with the different circumstances of his situation, of his sentiments, and of his audience. [462]

SUGGESTED READINGS

Austin, Gilbert
   Chironomia; or, a treatise on rhetorical delivery: comprehending many precepts, both ancient and modern for the proper regulation of the voice, the countenance, and gesture. . . . London. Printed for T. Cadell and W. Davies. 1806. xiii,583p

JAMES RUSH
(1786-1869)

There is reason to believe that Dr. Rush's *Philosophy of the Human Voice* is the most important contribution by an American to the field of speech prior to the twentieth century. Unusually detailed, meticulously systematic, and often needlessly abstruse, this work represents what was at that time the most scientific medical approach to the problem of voice. It is the first great analytical inquiry into the physiology of vocal delivery.

Obviously, Rush's work is of greater interest to the student of elocutionary methods and of voice science, than to the student of original speech composition. Consequently, the selected passages are limited chiefly to those that discuss the pedagogical method necessary for the cultivation of a good voice.

THE PHILOSOPHY OF THE HUMAN VOICE [1]

[Constituents of the Voice]

All the constituents of the human voice, may be referred to the five following Modes:

Quality,
Force,
Time,
Abruptness,
Pitch.
[49]

. . . . .

The terms by which the *Quality* or kind of voice is distinguished, are,—rough, smooth, harsh, full, slender, thin, musical, and some others of the same metaphorical structure. [49]

. . . . .

For the specifications of *Force* we use the words,—strong, weak, feeble, loud, soft, forcible, and faint. These are indefinite in their indication, and without any fixed relationship in degree. [50]

. . . . .

Time, in the art of speaking, is subdivided into,—long, short, quick, slow, and rapid. [50]

. . . . .

[1] 4th ed., Philadelphia, Lippincott, Grambo, and Company, 1855.

I use the term *Abruptness,* to signify the sudden and full discharge of sound, as contradistinguished from its more gradual emission. Abruptness is well represented by the explosive notes which may be executed on the bassoon, and some other wind instruments. I have given this mode of the voice, the place and importance of a general head, not only as an expressive agent in speech, but because its characteristic explosion is peculiar, and quite distinct from the nature of Force; with which, from its admitting of degrees of intensity, it might seem to be identical. [50]

. . . . .

The variations of *Pitch* are denoted by the words,—rise and fall, high and low. [50]

[Definition of Elocution]

The term Elocution is applied throughout this work to signify the use of the voice, for the representation of thought and passion, under every form of correct Reading and Speech. [65]

[System for Teaching Elocution]

The art of reading consists in having all the constituents of speech, whether alphabetic, or expressive, under complete command, that they may be properly applied, for the vivid and elegant delineation of the sense and sentiment of discourse. I shall not in this section, consider the modes of the voice as expressive of feeling or thought: but shall describe the means for providing the material of speech, whenever thought or feeling may require its use.

If I were a teacher of elocution, I would frame a didactic system, of elementary exercises, similar to that which taught me, whatever the well-read critic may find to be new, in this work; and would assign to my pupil a task under the following heads:

Of Practice on the Alphabetic Elements. Notwithstanding we are all taught the alphabet, we are not taught the true elements of speech: I would therefore require the pupil, to exercise his voice on the elements, as they are sounded in a strict analysis of words. [424]

. . . . .

Let the first lesson then consist of a separate, an exact, and a repeated pronunciation of each of the thirty-five elements, in order to insure a true and easy execution of their unmixed sounds. But the pupil must be careful to pronounce, not the alphabetic syllable of the schools, but the pure and indivisible vocal element; however unusual, and uncouth, that sound may, in some cases, be to his ear. [425]

. . . . .

RHETORIC AND PUBLIC SPEAKING

Of Practice on the Time of Elements. When a true pronunciation of the elements is acquired, the pupil should not, according to the usage of the primer, pass at once to their combinations. They are employed in speech under different degrees of duration: and an exercise of the voice, through these degrees, on individual elements, creates a habit of skillful management, not so well or so easily acquired by practice on the common current of discourse. Let the pupil then consider the alphabetic elements as a kind of Time-table, on which he is to learn all their varieties of quantity. [428-9]

. . . . .

Of Practice on the Vanishing Movement. The consideration of this subject should perhaps, have been united with the last. For an attempt to prolong the elements without reference to the equable concrete of speech, is very apt to produce the note of song. The difference between these two forms of intonation, even on a single tonic, will be perceptible to an attentive ear, by keeping in mind the well known and peculiar effect of speech and of song, while trying the difference. If the effort produce an equable concrete, it will not seem to be the beginning of a song. The pupil then, without confusing his ear by other particulars, should exercise his voice in the natural radical and vanish, on all extendible elements. [429-30]

. . . . .

Of Practice on Force. It is scarcely necessary to say how loudness of voice, or the forte, is to be acquired. It is not essential to our discipline, that the elements should be uttered separately with regard to force: since after the other constituents of expressive speech are brought under command, exercise on force may be effected during the current of discourse. Still the ends of instruction would be somewhat easier attained by the elementary process in this particular. [430]

. . . . .

Of Practice on Stress. Although the elementary exercise on force, in a general sense, may not be required, I must urge its importance, in the case of particular syllabic stress. There is a nicety in this matter, that will be definitely recognized, and consequently can become familiar, only through the deliberate practice and unembarrassed observation, afforded by trials on the separate elements. [430-1]

. . . . .

Of Practice on Pitch. The several scales used in this essay, were described in the first section. The order of proximate intervals in the diatonic, and the skip of its wider transitions, must be learned from an instrument, or the voice. With a few days attention to the effect of the various rising and falling movements, on the keys of a pianoforte, or in the voice of a master, a pupil who has the least musical ear, will be able to execute the same successions in his voice, and thus to recognize the concrete pitch and change of the radical, on elemental or syllabic utterance. [431]

. . . . .

Of Practice on Melody. One difficult point regarding intonation, is the perception of the radical changes of the second, in the progression of the current melody. If the pupil has a musical ear, he may easily acquire the habit of varying the several phrases in the manner formerly mentioned. Should he not have a nice perception of sound, nor ingenuity in experiment, he must learn the diatonic progression from the voice of a master.

Melody is a continuous function; practice under this head, must therefore be made on successive syllables. The best method is to select a portion of discourse, to keep in mind, the diatonic manner in which it should be read, and at the same time, to utter only the **tonic** element of each syllable; and thus, by a sort of vocal short-hand, or instant hackings of a short cough, to go through this dotted **outline,** as it were, of the melody. [433]

. . . . .

Of Practice on the Cadence. The cadence is an important part of the melody of speech: and readers being therein liable to frequent and striking faults, the subject requires discriminative attention. Here particularly the elementary practice is to be employed; the pupil bearing in mind the different forms of intonation for terminating a sentence, and exercising his voice separately on one, two, or three elements or syllables, considered as a close.

By elementary practice on the various species of the cadence, with attention to their construction and effect, the command over intonation in this particular, will be exercised, with a propriety and precision, never yet within even the dreaming purpose of any ancient or modern system of Imitative discipline. [433-4]

. . . . .

Of Practice on the Tremor. The tremulous movement should be practiced on individual elements. With a knowledge of its nature, the pupil may correct himself in his task, and finally acquire the accuracy, so essential to this expressive species of intonation. [434]

. . . . .

Of Practice on Quality of Voice. Quality is capable of improvement; and the practice in this case may be either on the elements, or on the current of discourse. But as quality is most perceptible on the tonic sound of a syllable, perhaps the elementary lesson is the best for instruction. In whatever way the improving exercise is conducted,— by it, harshness of quality may be somewhat softened: a husky voice may be brought nearer to pure vocality; the piercing treble may be reduced in pitch, and the thin and meager voice indued with greater fulness and strength. [434-5]

* * * * *

Of Practice in Rapidity of Speech. Extreme rapidity of speech may be employed as a means for obtaining a command over the voice. The difficulty, in this case, of making transitions from one position of the organs of articulation to another, requires an exertion which tends to increase their strength and activity; and consequently enables them to perform all moderate progressions, without hesitation. I would recommend the utmost possible precipitancy of utterance; taking care not to outrun the complete articulation of every element: and this makes it advisable to set the lesson on some discourse, long fixed in the memory, that no embarrassment may arise from the distracting effort of recollection. [436]

* * * * *

We have thus enumerated both the articulative, and the expressive constituents of the whole assemblage of speech. The only question before us, on this subject, is, whether we should aim to acquire a full power over these constituents, by exercising the voice on their combination, in current discourse, or by separate and repeated practice on their individual forms.

It is needless to propose arguments in favor of the analytic and elementary system to those, who, from experience in acquiring the sciences, have formed for themselves economical and effective plans of study. Let all others be told, that one, and perhaps the only reason why elocutionists have never employed this system, is, that they have overlooked the analytic means of vocal expression; and have therefore wanted both the knowledge and nomenclature for an elementary method of instruction. There are too many proofs in science and art, of the necessity, and the success of this rudimental method to allow us to suppose, the same means would not have been adopted in elocution, if they had been known to the master. [437]

* * * * *

When an attempt is made to teach an art, without commencing with its simple elements, combinations of elements pass with the pupil for the elements themselves, and holding them to be almost infinite, he abandons his hopeless task. An education by the method we are here recommending, reverses this disheartening duty. It reduces the seeming infinity to computable numbers; and I have supposed,—one of the first comments on the foregoing history, may refer to the unexpected simplicity of means, employed by nature, to produce the unbounded permutations of speech. [440]

SUGGESTED READINGS

Robb, Mary Margaret
Oral Interpretation of Literature in American Colleges and Universities. New York. H.W. Wilson Co. 1941. p71-121

Rush, James
The Philosophy of the Human Voice: Embracing Its Physiological History; together with a System of Principles, by Which Criticism in the Art of Elocution May Be Rendered Intelligible, and Instruction, Definite and Comprehensive. To Which Is Added a Brief Analysis of Song and Recitative. 4th ed. enl. Philadelphia. Lippincott, Grambo and Co. 1855. xlviii, 49-559p

RICHARD WHATELY
(1787-1863)

In the introduction to the *Rhetoric,* Whately remarks that his object is "to adopt a middle course between these two extreme points; and to treat of 'Argumentative Composition,' *generally,* and *exclusively*; considering Rhetoric (in conformity with the very just and philosophical view of Aristotle) as an offshoot from Logic." The result is a book of real importance in the history of public speaking, a contribution in which logical proof receives a refreshing and thorough restatement. The work of Whately is thus closely related to debating practice as well as general speech composition.

The *Rhetoric* is important on still another count. In it Whately voices a sharp protest against the elocutionary methods which rely upon elaborate systems of notations to govern voice and bodily action. In turn he proposes a method for the cultivation of the natural manner in delivery.

ELEMENTS OF RHETORIC[1]

[*Nature of Conviction*]

This is, of course, what may be called, in the widest sense of the word, Conviction; but under that term are comprehended, *first,* what is strictly called *Instruction*; and, *secondly, Conviction* in the narrower sense; *i.e.* the Conviction of those who are either of a *contrary opinion* to the one maintained, or who are *in doubt* whether to admit or deny it. By instruction, on the other hand, is commonly meant the conviction of those who have neither formed an opinion on the subject, nor are deliberating whether to adopt or reject the proposition in question, but are merely desirous of ascertaining *what* is the truth in respect of the case before them. The former are supposed to have before their minds the *terms* of the proposition maintained, and are called upon to consider *whether that particular proposition* be true or false; the latter are not supposed to know the terms of the conclusion, but to be inquiring *what proposition* is to be received as true. The former may be described, in logical language, as doubting respecting the *Copula*; the latter, respecting the *Predicate*. It is evident that the speaker or writer is, relatively to these last, (though not to himself,) conducting a process of Investigation. . . . [55-6]

[1] New ed., Boston and Cambridge, James Munroe and Company, 1861.

[*Division of Forms of Argument*]

First, into Irregular, and Regular, i.e. Syllogisms; these last into Categorical and Hypothetical; and the Categorical, into Syllogisms in the first Figure, and in the other Figures, &c. &c.

Secondly, They are frequently divided into "Probable," (or "Moral,") and "Demonstrative," (or "Necessary.")

Thirdly, into the "Direct," and the "Indirect;" (or *reductio ad absurdum,*)—the Deictic, and the Elenctic, of Aristotle.

Fourthly, into Arguments from "Example," from "Testimony," from "Cause to Effect," from "Analogy," &c. &c.

It will be perceived, on attentive examination, that several of the different species just mentioned will occasionally *contain* each other; *e.g.* a Probable Argument may be at the same time a Categorical Argument, a Direct Argument, and an Argument from Testimony, &c.; this being the consequence of Arguments having been divided on *several different principles*; a circumstance so obvious the moment it is distinctly stated, that I apprehend such of my readers as have not been conversant in these studies will hardly be disposed to believe that it could have been (as is the fact) generally overlooked, and that eminent writers should in consequence have been involved in inextricable confusion. I need only remind them however of the anecdote of Columbus breaking the egg. That which is perfectly obvious to any man of common sense, as soon as it is mentioned, may nevertheless fail to occur, even to men of considerable ingenuity.

It will also be readily perceived, on examining the principles of these several divisions, that the last of them alone is properly and strictly a division of *Arguments as such.* The First is evidently a division of the *Forms of stating them*; for every one would allow that the *same* Argument may be either stated as an enthymeme, or brought into the strict syllogistic form; and that, either categorically or hypothetically, &c.; *e.g.* "Whatever has a beginning has a cause; the earth had a beginning, therefore it had a cause; or, If the earth had a beginning, it had a cause: it had a beginning," &c. every one would call the *same* Argument, differently stated. This, therefore, evidently is not a division of Arguments *as such.*

The Second is plainly a division of Arguments according to their *subject-matter,* whether Necessary or Probable, (certain or uncertain.) In Mathematics, *c.g.* every proposition that can be stated is either an immutable truth, or an absurdity and self-contradiction; while in human affairs the propositions which we assume are only true for the most part, and as general rules: and in Physics, though they must be true as long as the laws of nature remain undisturbed, the contradiction of them does not imply an absurdity; and the conclusions, of course, in each case, have the same degree and kind of certainty with the premises. This therefore is properly a division, not of *Arguments* as such, but of the *Propositions* of which they consist.

The Third is a division of Arguments according to the purpose for which they are employed; according to the *intention* of the reasoner; whether that be to establish "directly" (or "ostensively") the conclusion drawn, or ("indirectly") by means of an absurd conclusion to disprove one of the premises; (*i.e.* to prove its contradictory:) since the alternative proposed in *every* valid Argument is, *either* to admit the Conclusion, or to deny one of the Premises. Now it may so happen that in some cases, one person will choose the former, and another the latter, of these alternatives. [60-2]

. . . . .

This, therefore, is not properly a division of Arguments as such, but a division of the *purposes for which* they are on each occasion employed.

The Fourth, which alone is properly a division of Arguments *as such,* and accordingly will be principally treated of, is a division according to the "relation of the subject-matter of the premises to that of the conclusion." I say, "of the subject-matter," because the *logical* connection between the premises and conclusion is independent of the meaning of the terms employed, and may be exhibited with letters of the alphabet substituted for the terms; but the relation I am now speaking of between the premises and conclusion, (and the varieties of which form the several species of Arguments,) is in respect of their *subject-matter*: as *e.g.* an "Argument from Cause to Effect" is so called and considered, in reference to the relation existing between the premise, which is the Cause, and the conclusion, which is the Effect; and an "Argument from Example," in like manner from the relation between a *known* and an *unknown* instance, both belonging to the same class. And it is plain that the present division, though it has a reference to the subject-matter of the premises, is yet not a division of *propositions* considered by themselves, (as in the case with the division into "probable" and "demonstrative,") but of *Arguments* considered as such; for when we say, *e.g.* that the premise is a Cause, and the Conclusion the Effect, these expressions are evidently *relative,* and have no meaning, except in reference to each other; and so also when we say that the premise and the conclusion are too *parallel* cases, that very expression denotes their relation to each other. [63]

[*Presumption and Burden of Proof*]

It is a point of great importance to decide in each case, at the outset, in your own mind, and clearly to point out to the hearer, as occasion may serve, on which side the *Presumption* lies, and to which belongs the (onus probandi) *Burden of Proof*. For though it may often be expedient to bring forward more proofs than can be fairly *demanded* of you, it is always desirable, when this is the case, that it should be *known,* and that the strength of the cause should be estimated accordingly.

According to the most correct use of the term, a "Presumption" in favor of any supposition, means, not (as has been sometimes erroneously imagined) a preponderance of probability in its favor, but, such a *preoccupation* of the ground, as implies that it must stand good till some sufficient reason is adduced against it; in short, that the *Burden of proof* lies on the side of him who would dispute it. [139]

. . . . .

A moderate portion of common-sense will enable any one to perceive, and to show, on which side the Presumption lies, when once his attention is called to this question; though, for want of attention, it is often overlooked: and on the determination of this question the whole character of a discussion will often very much depend. A body of troops may be perfectly adequate to the defence of a fortress against any attack that may be made on it; and yet, if, ignorant of the advantage they possess, they sally forth into the open field to encounter the enemy, they may suffer a repulse. At any rate, even if strong enough to act on the offensive, they ought still to keep possession of their fortress. In like manner, if you have the "Presumption" on your side, and can but *refute* all the arguments brought against you, you have, for the present at least, gained a victory: but if you abandon this position, by suffering this Presumption to be forgotten, which is in fact *leaving out one of, perhaps, your strongest arguments,* you may appear to be making a feeble attack, instead of a triumphant defence. [140]

. . . . .

The following are a few of the cases in which it is important, though very easy, to point out where the Presumption lies.

There is a Presumption in favor of every *existing* institution. Many of these (we will suppose, the majority) may be susceptible of alteration for the better; but still the "Burden of proof" lies with him who proposes an alteration; simply, on the ground that *since a change* is not a good in itself, he who demands a change should show cause for it. No one is *called on* (though he may find it advisable) to defend an existing institution, till some argument is adduced against it; and that argument ought in fairness to prove, not merely an actual inconvenience, but the possibility of a change for the better.

Every book again, as well as person, ought to be presumed harmless (and consequently the copyright protected by our courts) till something is proved against it. It is hardship to require a man to prove, either of his book, or of his private life, that there is no ground for any accusation; or else to be denied the protection of his Country. The Burden of proof, in each case, lies fairly on the accuser. [141-2]

. . . . .

There is a "Presumption" against any thing *paradoxical, i.e.* contrary to the prevailing opinion: it may be true; but the Burden of proof lies with him who maintains it; since men are not to be expected to abandon the prevailing belief till some reason is shown. [142]

. . . . .

A Presumption evidently admits of various degrees of strength, from the very faintest, up to a complete and confident acquiescence.

The person, Body, or book, in favor of whose decisions there is a certain Presumption, is said to have, so far, "Authority;" in the strict sense of the word. And a recognition of this kind of Authority,—an *habitual* Presumption in favor of such a one's decisions or opinions,—is usually called "Deference." [145-6]

. . . . .

Those who are habitually wanting in Deference towards such as we think entitled to it, are usually called "arrogant;" the word being used as distinguished from self-*conceited, proud, vain,* and other kindred words. Such persons may be described as having an habitual and exclusive "self-deference." [146]

. . . . .

For it is to be observed that *admiration, esteem,* and *concurrence in opinion,* are quite distinct from "Deference," and not necessarily accompanied by it. If any one makes what appears to us to be a very just remark, or if we acquiesce in what he proposes on account of the reason he alleges, —this is not Deference. And if this has happened many times, and we thence form a high opinion of his ability, this again neither implies, nor even necessarily produces Deference; though in reason, such *ought* to be the result. [147]

. . . . .

Admiration, esteem, &c. are more the result of a judgment of the *understanding*; (though often of an erroneous one:) "Deference" is apt to depend on *feelings*;—often, on whimsical and unaccountable feelings. It is often yielded to a vigorous *claim*,—to an authoritative and overbearing demeanor. [147]

. . . . .

With some persons, again, Authority seems to act according to the law of Gravitation; inversely as the squares of the *distances*. They are inclined to be of the opinion of the person who is *nearest*. Personal *Affection*, again, in many minds, generates Deference. They form a habit of first, *wishing*, secondly, *hoping*, and thirdly, *believing* a person to be in the right, whom they would be *sorry* to think mistaken. [148]

. . . . .

It is worth observing also, that though, as has been above remarked, . . . questions of *fact* and of *opinion*, ought to be decided on very different grounds, yet, with many persons, a statement of facts is very little attended to when coming from one for whose judgment (though they do not deliberately doubt his veracity) they have little or no Deference. [150]

. . . . .

It is to be observed, that a Presumption may be *rebutted* by an opposite Presumption, so as to shift the Burden of proof to the other side. E. G. Suppose you had advised the removal of some *existing* restriction: you might be, in the first instance, called on to take the Burden of proof, and allege your reasons for the change, on the ground that there is a Presumption against every change. But you might fairly reply, "True, but there is another Presumption which rebuts the former; every *Restriction* is in itself an evil; and therefore there is a Presumption in favor of its removal, unless it can be shown necessary for prevention of some greater evil: I am not bound to allege any *specific* inconvenience; if the restriction is *unnecessary, that* is reason enough for its abolition: its defenders therefore are fairly called on to prove its necessity." [152-3]

. . . . .

Again, there is (according to the old maxim of "peritis credendum est in arte sua") a presumption, (and a fair one,) in respect of each question, in favor of the judgment of the most eminent men in the department it pertains to;—of eminent physicians, *e.g.* in respect of medical questions,—of theologians in theological, &c. And by this presumption many of the Jews in our Lord's time seem to have been influenced, when they said, "have any of the Rulers, or of the Pharisees believed on Him?"

But there is a counter-presumption, arising from the circumstance that men eminent in any department are likely to regard with jealousy any one who professes to bring to light something unknown to themselves; especially if it promise to *supersede,* if established, much of what they have been accustomed to learn, and teach, and practise. [156-7]

[*Matters of Fact and Opinion*]

Matters of opinion, (as they are called; *i.e.* where we are not said properly to *know,* but to *judge,* ...) are established chiefly by Antecedent-probability, (Arguments of the *first class, viz.* from Cause to Effect:) though the *Testimony* (*i.e.* authority) of wise men is also admissible: past Facts, chiefly by *Signs,* of various kinds; (that term, it must be remembered, including Testimony;) and future events, by Antecedent-probabilities, and *Examples.*

Example, however, is not excluded from the proof of matters of Opinion; since a man's judgment in one case, may be aided or corrected by an appeal to his judgment in another similar case. It is in this way that we are directed, by the highest authority, to guide our judgment in those questions in which we are most liable to deceive ourselves; *viz.* what, on each occasion, ought to be our conduct towards another; we are directed to frame for ourselves a similar supposed case, by imagining ourselves to change places with our neighbor, and then considering how, in that case, we should in fairness expect to be treated. [161]

[*Argument from Cause to Effect*]

When Arguments of each of the two formerly-mentioned classes are employed, those from Cause to Effect (Antecedent-probability) have usually the precedence.

Men are apt to listen with prejudice to the Arguments adduced to prove any thing which appears *abstractedly* improbable; *i.e.* according to what has been above laid down, *unnatural,* or (if such an expression might be allowed) *unplausible;* and this prejudice is to be removed by the Argument from Cause to Effect, which thus prepares the way for the reception of the other arguments. [166-7]

[Technique in Arrangement]

A Proposition that is *well-known*, (whether easy to be established or not,) and which contains nothing particularly offensive, should in general be stated at once, and the Proofs subjoined; but one not familiar to the hearers, especially if it be likely to be unacceptable, should not be stated at the outset. It is usually better in that case to state the arguments first, or at least some of them, and then introduce the Conclusion: thus assuming in some degree the character of an *investigator*. [171]

. . . . .

It may be observed, that if the Proposition to be maintained be such as the hearers are likely to regard as *insignificant,* the *question* should be at first suppressed; but if there be any thing *offensive* to their prejudices, the *question* may be stated, but the *decision* of it, for a time, kept back. [172-3]

. . . . .

And it will often be advisable to advance very gradually to the full statement of the proposition required, and to prove it, if one may so speak, by instalments; establishing separately, and in order, each part of the truth in question. [173]

. . . . .

It will often happen again that some *general principle* of no very paradoxical character may be proposed in the outset; (just as besiegers break ground at a safe distance, and advance gradually till near enough to batter;) and when that is established, an unexpected and *unwelcome application* of it may be proved irresistibly. [173-4]

. . . . .

And it may be worth observing, that we shall thus have to *reverse,* in many cases, the order in which, during the act of composition, the thoughts will have occurred to our minds. For in reflecting on any subject, we are usually disposed to *generalize;*—to proceed from the particular point immediately before us, successively, to more and more *comprehensive* views; the opposite order to which will usually be the better adapted to engage and keep up attention, and to effect conviction. [174]

. . . . .

It is often expedient, sometimes unavoidable, to *waive* for the present, some question or portion of a question, while our attention is occupied with another point. Now it cannot be too carefully kept in mind, that it is a common mistake with inaccurate reasoners (and a mistake which is studiously kept up by an artful sophist) to suppose that what is thus *waived* is altogether *given up*. [175]

[*Refutation*]

In the first place, it is to be observed that there is no distinct class of refutatory Argument; since they become such merely by the circumstances under which they are employed. There are two ways in which any Proposition may be refuted; first, by proving the contradictory of it; secondly, by overthrowing the Arguments by which it has been supported. The former of these is less strictly and properly called Refutation; being only *accidentally* such, since it might have been employed equally well had the opposite Argument never existed, and in fact it will often happen that a Proposition maintained by one author, may be in this way refuted by another, who had never heard of his Arguments. [178-9]

[*The Introduction*]

It is to be observed, however, that there is one kind of fault sometimes committed in Introductions, which does lead to this result. If a Speaker alarms his audience in the outset, by announcing a great number of topics to be handled, and perhaps also several preliminary considerations, preparatory explanations, &c., they will be likely (especially after a protracted Debate) to listen with impatience to what they expect will prove tedious, and to feel an anticipated weariness even from the very commencement. [202]

. . . . .

One of the objects most frequently proposed in an Introduction, is, to show that the subject in question is *important, curious,* or otherwise *interesting,* and worthy of attention. This may be called an "Introduction inquisitive." [203]

. . . . .

It will frequently happen also, when the point to be proved or explained is one which may be very fully established, or on which there is little or no doubt, that it may nevertheless be *strange,* and different from what might have been expected; in which case it will often have a good effect in rousing the attention, to set forth as strongly as possible this *paradoxical* character, and dwell on the seeming improbability of that which must, after all, be admitted. This may be called an "Introduction paradoxical." [203]

. . . . .

What may be called an "Introduction corrective," is also in frequent use; *viz.* to show that the subject has been *neglected, misunderstood,* or *misrepresented* by others. [204]

. . . . .

It will often happen also, that there may be need to explain some *peculiarity* in the mode of reasoning to be adopted; to guard against some possible *mistake* as to the object proposed; or to apologize for some *deficiency*; this may be called the "Introduction preparatory." [204-5]

. . . . .

5thly, and lastly, in many cases there will be occasion for what may be called a "Narrative Introduction," to put the reader or hearer in possession of the outline of some transaction, or the description of some state of things, to which references and allusions are to be made in the course of the Composition. [205]

[Persuasion]

Persuasion, properly so called, *i.e.* the art of influencing the *Will,* is the next point to be considered. [209]

. . . . .

. . . The *Conviction* of the understanding (of which I have hitherto been treating) is an essential *part* of Persuasion; and will generally need to be effected by the Arguments of the Writer or Speaker. For in order that the Will may be influenced, two things are requisite; *viz.* 1. that the proposed *Object* should appear desirable; and 2. that the *Means* suggested should be proved to be conducive to the attainment of that object; and this last, evidently must depend on a process of Reasoning. [209]

. . . . .

Persuasion, therefore, depends on, first, *Argument,* (to prove the expediency of the Means proposed,) and secondly, what is usually called *Exhortation, i.e.* the excitement of men to adopt those Means, by representing the end as sufficiently desirable. [210]

. . . . .

The Active Principles of our nature may be classed in various ways. The arrangement adopted by Mr. Dugald Stewart is, perhaps, the most correct and convenient; the heads he enumerates are *Appetites,* (which have their origin in the body,) *Desires,* and *Affections*; these last being such as imply some kind of disposition relative to another *Person*; to which must be added, *Self-love,* or the desire of Happiness, as such; and the *Moral-Faculty,* called by some writers Conscience, by others Conscientiousness, by others the Moral sense, and by Dr. A. Smith, the sense of Propriety. [222-3]

. . . . .

The first and most important point to be observed in every address to any Passion, Sentiment, Feeling, &c. is, (as has been already hinted,) that it should not be introduced as such, and plainly avowed; otherwise the effect will be, in great measure, if not entirely, lost. This circumstance forms a remarkable distinction between the head now under consideration, and that of Argumentation. When engaged in Reasoning, properly so called, our purpose not only need not be concealed, but may, (as I have said,) without prejudice to the effect, be distinctly declared: on the other hand, even when the Feelings we wish to excite are such as ought to operate, so that there is no reason to be ashamed of the endeavors thus to influence the hearer, still our purpose and drift should be, if not absolutely concealed, yet openly declared, and made prominent. [224]

[*Natural Method of Elocution*]

When however I protest against all artificial systems of Elocution, and all *direct* attention to Delivery, *at the time,* it must not be supposed that a *general* inattention to that point is recommended; or that the most perfect Elocution is to be attained by never thinking at all on the subject; though it may safely be affirmed that even this negative plan would succeed far better than a studied modulation. But it is evident that if any one wishes to *assume the Speaker* as far as possible, *i.e.,* to deliver a written composition with some degree of the manner and effect of one that is extemporaneous, he will have a considerable difficulty to surmount: since though this may be called, in a certain sense, the Natural Manner, it is far from being what he will naturally, *i.e., spontaneously,* fall into. It is by no means natural for any one to *read* as if he were *not* reading, but speaking. And again, even when any one is reading what he does not wish to deliver as his own composition, as, for instance, a portion of the Scriptures, or the Liturgy, it is evident that this may be done better or worse, in infinite degrees; and that though (according to the views here taken) a studied attention to the sounds uttered, at the time of uttering them, leads to an affected and offensive delivery, yet, on the other hand, an utterly careless reader cannot be a good one. [398]

. . . . .

To the adoption of any such artificial scheme there are three weighty objections; first, that the proposed system must necessarily be *imperfect*; secondly, that if it were perfect, it would be a *circuitous* path to the object in view; and thirdly, that even if both those objections were removed, the object would *not* be effectually obtained. [400]

. . . . .

The practical rule then to be adopted, in conformity with the principles here maintained, is, not only to pay no studied attention to the Voice, but studiously to *withdraw* the thoughts from it, and to dwell as intently as possible on the Sense, trusting to nature to suggest spontaneously the proper emphases and tones. [404]

. . . . .

He then who shall determine to aim at the Natural manner, though he will have to contend with considerable difficulties and discouragements, will not be without corresponding advantages, in the course he is pursuing.

He will be at first, indeed, repressed to a greater degree than another by emotions of bashfulness; but it will be more speedily and more completely subdued; the very system pursued, since it forbids all thoughts of *self*, striking at the root of the evil.

He will, indeed, on the outset, incur censure, not only critical but moral;—he will be blamed for using a *colloquial* delivery; and the censure will very likely be, as far as relates to his earliest efforts, not wholly undeserved; for his manner *will* probably at first too much resemble that of conversation, though of serious and earnest conversation; but by perseverance he may be sure of avoiding deserved, and of mitigating and ultimately overcoming, undeserved, censure.

He will, indeed, never be praised for a "very fine delivery;" but his *matter* will not lose the approbation it may deserve, as he will be the more sure of being heard and attended to. He will not, indeed, meet with many who can be regarded as models of the Natural manner; and those he does meet with, he will be precluded, by the nature of the system, from minutely imitating; but he will have the advantage of carrying with him an *Infallible Guide,* as long as he is careful to follow the suggestions of Nature; abstaining from all thoughts respecting his own utterance, and fixing his mind intently on the business he is engaged in.

And though he must not expect to attain perfection at once, he may be assured that, while he steadily adheres to this plan, he is in the right road to it; instead of becoming,—as on the other plan,— more and more artificial, the longer he studies. And every advance he makes will produce a proportional effect: it will give him more and more of that hold on the attention, the understanding, and the feelings of the audience, which no studied modulation can ever attain. Others indeed may be more successful in escaping censure, and insuring admiration; but he will far more surpass them, in respect of the proper object of the Orator, which is, *to carry his point.* [442-3]

SUGGESTED READINGS

Parrish, Wayland Maxfield
    Whately and His Rhetoric. *Quarterly Journal of Speech.* 15:58-79 February 1929

Whately, Richard
    Elements of Logic. Reprinted from ninth ed. London. J. W. Parker and Son. 1859. xxii,269p
    Elements of Rhetoric: comprising an analysis of the laws of moral evidence and of persuasion, with rules for argumentative composition and elocution. rev. ed. Boston and Cambridge. James Munroe and Co. 1861. 545p

THOMAS DE QUINCEY
(1785-1859)

The following short passages are taken from the review which De Quincey wrote in 1828 of Whately's *Elements of Rhetoric*.

RHETORIC [1]

[A Point of View Regarding Rhetoric]

We, for our parts, have a third, which excludes both (Dr. Whately's and Campbell's points of view): where conviction begins, the field of rhetoric ends—that is our opinion: and, as to the passions, we contend that they are not within the province of rhetoric, but of eloquence.

In this view of rhetoric and its functions we coincide with Aristotle; as indeed originally we took it up on a suggestion derived from him. . . . [218-19]

. . . . .

Whatsoever is certain, or matter of fixed science, can be no subject for the rhetorician: where it is possible for the understanding to be convinced, no field is open for rhetorical persuasion. Absolute certainty, and fixed science, transcend and exclude opinion and probability. The province of rhetoric, whether meant for an influence upon the actions, or simply upon the belief, lies amongst that vast field of cases where there is a *pro* and a *con*, with the chance of right and wrong, true and false, distributed in varying proportions between them. There is also an immense range of truths, where there are no chances at all concerned, but the affirmative and the negative are both true; as, for example, the goodness of human nature and its wickedness; the happiness of human life and its misery; the charms of knowledge, and its hollowness; the fragility of human prosperity, in the eye of religious meditation, and its security, as estimated by worldly confidence and youthful hope. In all these cases the rhetorician exhibits his art by giving an impulse to one side, and by withdrawing the mind so steadily from all thoughts or images which support the other, as to leave it practically under the possession of this partial estimate. [222-3]

[1] *Historical and Critical Essays*, vol. II, Boston, Ticknor, Reed, and Fields, 1853.

[*Definition of Rhetoric*]

Mr. Coleridge, as we have often heard, is in the habit of drawing the line with much philosophical beauty between rhetoric and eloquence. On this topic we were never so fortunate as to hear him: but if we are here called upon for a distinction, we shall satisfy our immediate purpose by a very plain and brief one. By Eloquence, we understand the overflow of powerful feelings upon occasions fitted to excite them. But Rhetoric is the art of aggrandizing and bringing out into strong relief, by means of various and striking thoughts, some aspect of truth which of itself is supported by no spontaneous feelings, and therefore rests upon artificial aids. [223-4]

SUGGESTED READINGS

De Quincey, Thomas
  Rhetoric. In *De Quincey's Literary Criticism.* Ed. with introd. by H. Darbishire. London. Henry Frowde. 1909. p37-89
  Style. In *De Quincey's Literary Criticism.* Ed. with introd. by H. Darbishire. London. Henry Frowde. 1909. p181-92

Hudson, Hoyt
  De Quincey on Rhetoric and Public Speaking. In *Studies in Rhetoric and Public Speaking in Honor of James Albert Winans.* New York. Century Co. 1925. p133-51

HERBERT SPENCER
(1820-1903)

Although Spencer's *Philosophy of Style* is more properly regarded as a contribution to literary theory, it enunciates a principle of economy of effort which is not without significance for the student of speech.

The essay appeared originally in the *Westminster Review* (October, 1852), and was prepared essentially as a commentary on Whately's *Elements of Rhetoric*, Blair's *Lectures on Rhetoric and Belles Lettres,* Campbell's *Philosophy of Rhetoric,* and Kaimes *Elements of Rhetoric.*

THE PHILOSOPHY OF STYLE [1]

[Style and Economy of Effort]

On seeking for some clue to the law underlying these current maxims, we may see shadowed forth in many of them, the importance of economizing the reader's or hearer's attention. To so present ideas that they may be apprehended with the least possible mental effort, is the desideratum towards which most of the rules above quoted point. When we condemn writing that is wordy, or confused, or intricate—when we praise this style as easy, and blame that as fatiguing, we consciously or unconsciously assume this desideratum as our standard of judgment. Regarding language as an apparatus of symbols for the conveyance of thought, we may say that, as in a mechanical apparatus, the more simple and the better arranged its parts, the greater will be the effect produced. In either case, whatever force is absorbed by the machine is deducted from the result. A reader or listener has at each moment but a limited amount of mental power available. To recognise and interpret the symbols presented to him requires part of this power; to arrange and combine the images suggested requires a further part; and only that part which remains can be used for the realization of the thought conveyed. Hence, the more time and attention it takes to receive and understand each sentence, the less time and attention can be given to the contained idea; and the less vividly will that idea be conceived. How truly language must be regarded as a hindrance to thought, though the necessary instrument of it, we shall clearly perceive on remembering the comparative force with which simple ideas

[1] *Westminster Review,* n.s., 58, 435-59, October, 1852.

are communicated by mimetic signs. To say, "Leave the room," is less expressive than to point to the door. Placing a finger on the lips is more forcible than whispering, "Do not speak." A beck of the hand is better than, "Come here." No phrase can convey the idea of surprise so vividly as opening the eyes and raising the eyebrows. A shrug of the shoulders would lose much by translation into words. Again, it may be remarked that when oral language is employed, the strongest effects are produced by interjections, which condense entire sentences into syllables. And in other cases, where custom allows us to express thoughts by single words, as in *Beware, Heigho, Fudge,* much force would be lost by expanding them into specific verbal propositions. Hence, carrying out the metaphor that language is the vehicle of thought, there seems reason to think that in all cases the friction and inertia of the vehicle deduct from its efficiency; and that in composition the chief if not the sole thing to be done, is, to reduce this friction and inertia to the smallest possible amount. Let us then inquire whether economy of the recipient's attention is not the secret of effect, alike in the right choice and collocation of words, in the best arrangement of clauses in a sentence, in the proper order of its principal and subordinate propositions, in the judicious use of simile, metaphor, and other figures of speech, and even in the rhythmical sequences of syllables. [436-7]

[*Figures of Speech and Economy of Attention*]

Turning now to consider figures of speech, we may equally discern the same general law of effect. Underlying all the rules that may be given for the choice and right use of them, we shall find the same fundamental requirement—economy of attention. It is indeed chiefly because of their great ability to subserve this requirement, that figures of speech are employed. To bring the mind more easily to the desired conception, is in many cases solely, and in all cases mainly, their object. [446]

[*Climax*]

And hence we may expect that the vividness with which images are realized will, in many cases, depend on the order of their presentation; even when one order is as convenient to the understanding as the other. We shall find sundry facts which alike illustrate this, and are explained by it. Climax is one of them. The marked effect obtained by placing last the most striking of any series of images, and the weakness—often the ludicrous weakness—produced by reversing this arrangement, depends on the general law indicated. As immediately after looking at the sun we cannot perceive the light of a fire, whilst by looking at the fire first and the sun afterwards we can perceive both; so, after receiving a brilliant, or weighty, or terrible thought, we cannot appreciate a less brilliant, less weighty, or less terrible one, whilst, by reversing the order, we can appreciate each. [456]

SUGGESTED READINGS

Spencer, Herbert
The Philosophy of Style. New York. John B. Alden. 1888. 40p

ALEXANDER BAIN
(1818-1903)

Although he was also a grammarian, logician, and rhetorician, Bain is remembered chiefly for his contributions to the field of psychology. The following short passage is of interest in that it states the principle of identity in audience analysis—a point to which many contemporary writers refer, though possibly under other heads.

THE SENSES AND THE INTELLECT [1]

[*Persuasion*]

This implies that some course of conduct shall be so described, or expressed, as to coincide, or be identified, with the active impulses of the individuals addressed, and thereby command their adoption of it by the force of their own natural dispositions. A leader of banditti has to deal with a class of persons whose ruling impulse is plunder; and it becomes his business to show them that any scheme proposed by him will lead to this end. A people with an intense overpowering patriotism, as the old Romans, can be acted on by proving that the interests of country are at stake. The fertile oratorical mind is one that can identify a case in hand with a great number of the strongest beliefs of an audience; and more especially with those that seem, at first sight, to have no connexion with the point to be carried. The discovery of identity in diversity is never more called for, than in the attempts to move men to adopt some unwonted course of proceeding. When a new reform is introduced in the state, it is usually thought necessary (at least in England) to reconcile and identify it in many ways with the ancient venerated constitution, or with prevailing maxims and modes of feeling, with which it would seem at variance. To be a persuasive speaker, it is necessary to have vividly present to the view all the leading impulses and convictions of the persons addressed, and to be ready to catch at every point of identity between these and the propositions or projects suggested for their adoption.

[1] 3rd ed., New York, D. Appleton and Company, 1888. Reprinted by permission of D. Appleton-Century Company.

The first-named qualification grows out of the experience and study of character; the other is the natural force of Similarity, which has often been exemplified in its highest range in oratorical minds. [528-9]

SUGGESTED READINGS

Bain, Alexander
> *English Composition and Rhetoric.* American ed. rev. New York. D. Appleton and Co. 1872. 343p
>
> *The Senses and the Intellect.* London. Longman, Green. Longman, Roberts and Green. 1864. xxxi,640p

EDWARD T. CHANNING
(1790-1856)

The *Lectures* from which the following passage is taken were prepared by Channing from his course in English Literature shortly after his retirement from the office of Boylston Professor of Rhetoric and Oratory at Harvard, a post which he held for thirty-two years. In addition to a small body of material on criticism, the *Lectures* contain short discussions on the nature of eloquence and on the general characteristics of demonstrative, deliberative, judicial, and pulpit oratory.

LECTURES ON RHETORIC AND ORATORY [1]

[*Argument and Persuasion*]

There is one point relative to the argumentative part of a speech which deserves consideration. Men are very apt to speak of argument and persuasion as two entirely distinct, if not hostile methods of address. As they evidently mean here, by the word argument, both the mustering and marshalling of propositions,—which is the business of rhetoric,—and reasoning from them, which belongs to logic,—we may, for the occasion, use it in the same vague way. What, then, is meant by the alleged distinction? We hear frequently that argument addresses the understanding and persuasion the passions; and that reason or the judgment is proverbially prudent and safe, while the passions are as proverbially headlong and dangerous. But how should such poor commonplaces as these, reach and explain the phenomena and the actual results of eloquence? The popular language is, that argument is characterized by coolness and deliberation. Yet, how various is its character. Sometimes it is incorporated with persuasion, so that no separate appeal to the feelings is required. Sometimes the subject-matter is such throughout, that the arguments adduced in proof are necessarily of the most popular and exciting description. They are ardent and even fierce and overwhelming. Topic follows topic, proof is heaped on proof, till we are reminded of Milton's 'piled thunder.' We seem to be in the midst of fiery shafts and grand peals, with the reason as clear as the brave eye in storms and peril, and with conviction as seated as the rock.

[1] Boston, Ticknor and Fields, 1856.

On the other hand, persuasion is said to be heated and reckless, and bent upon setting people above or beyond reason, so that they may be ruled by impulse. Yet persuasion has its proper topics and method, not less than the coolest addresses to the understanding, and is, for the most part, a brief and informal kind of reasoning. This siren or this fury is very often reason herself, kindled and inspired. Persuasion has, indeed, little appearance of proving and convincing; but this is so, probably, because feeling makes perception so rapid that steps and processes are not recognized. The heart leaps over the space required for full, formal statements, whether of proofs or reasonings, and feels all their force without stopping for them. It is not meant by these remarks to confound argument and persuasion, but to make peace between them; to show that they may and do act together with excellent effect, while in bad hands both may be equally harmful. [37-9]

SUGGESTED READINGS

Channing, Edward T.
Lectures on Rhetoric and Oratory Read to the Seniors in Harvard College. Boston. Ticknor and Fields. 1856. xx,298p

JOHN F. GENUNG
(1850-1919)

Like several other scholars in the field of rhetoric, Genung received a part of his training in theology, and was for a short time a preacher. His most distinguished contributions, however, deal with his teaching service at Amherst. He wrote chiefly on Biblical Literature and Rhetoric. In the latter field he developed a philosophy of composition which, from the point of view of the present day speech teacher, serves to bridge the gap between the older statements of rhetorical theory and contemporary practice.

THE PRACTICAL ELEMENTS OF RHETORIC [1]

[The Field of Rhetoric]

Literary discourse, properly considered, does not exist for itself alone; it is not soliloquy, but a determinate address to readers or hearers, seeking to impart to them some information or thought, with accompaniment, as occasion requires, of emotion or impulse. Hence, whatever is thus imparted must strive after such order and expression as is best fitted to have its proper power on men; consulting their capacities and susceptibilities, it must determine its work by the requirements thus necessitated. The various problems involved in such adaptation constitute the field of the art of rhetoric. [1]

[Adaptation of Discourse]

As dictated by its thought and occasion, three general adaptations of discourse are to be noted, corresponding to the three divisions of man's spiritual powers, and giving rise, as either of these is predominantly consulted, to three broad types of literature.

First and most fundamentally, discourse of whatever kind must adapt itself to the reader's understanding; that is, it addresses and compels his power of thought, whether by imparting information or by convincing of truth. Common ideas require, for the most part, merely such simple presentation as this; and the predominance of this appeal to the intellect gives rise to the great body of every-day literature—history, biography, fiction, essays, treatises, criticism—included under the general name of Didactic Prose.

[1] Boston. Ginn and Company, 1886. Reprinted by permission of Ginn and Company.

Secondly, some kinds of ideas come to the writer intensified by emotion or glowing with imagination; and hence, in their presentation, while they must still consult primarily the reader's understanding, they address themselves most directly to his sensibilities, to make him feel the thought as well as think it. Of such adaptation to the emotional nature, the purest outcome is Poetry.

A third class of ideas comprises such as, from their importance, or from the occasion of their presentation, require a definite decision in the hearer's conduct, and hence, employing persuasion as a means, culminate as an appeal to the will. This kind of discourse, as it has the highest object, must seek to enlist all the spiritual powers, imparting alike thought, emotion, and impulse; and results in the most complex literary type, Oratory. [2-3]

[*Invention*]

Invention, as applied to literary undertakings, comprehends the various procedures involved in finding, sifting, and ordering the material of discourse.

These three processes, which may be regarded as the three logical stages of the inventive act, it is important briefly to define and discriminate.

1. The first stage, the finding of material by thought or observation, is the fundamental and inclusive office of invention, the distinctive power that we designate in the popular use of the term. Herein lies obviously the heart and centre of literary production; it is what the writer finds, in his subject or in the world of thought, that gauges his distinction as an author. [217]

. . . . .

2. But a moment's thought makes it evident that the inventive act is by no means exhausted with the mere finding of material. Indeed, the material is not properly found, or at least ascertained to be what is needed, until it has been subjected to a rigorous process of testing, choosing, and rejecting. At every step it has to be held up in the light of an unspoken standard in the writer's mind: the standard mainly of his own sense of fitness and proportion, but also conditioned largely by extraneous considerations, such as the character of the audience or public, the allotted time or scope of the production, the circumstances of utterance, the exactions of the literary form adopted. [217-18]

. . . . .

3. Even yet we discern an important step involved in the work of finding; for until the material has been carefully ordered, with its parts skillfully adjusted to each other and to the whole, the question of retention or rejection, and therefore of discovering, is still open. The discourse is to be not a mere agglomeration of statements, but an organism, fitted to move as one thought, and be incorporated into the reader's mind. [218]

[*Uses of Exposition*]

Inseparably connected both with the structure of individual arguments and with the articulation of the whole course of reasoning are the various processes of exposition. They often work, when rightly employed, to make extended reasoning superfluous.

The following are the principal uses of exposition in the body of arguments that make up a discussion.

1. By exposition the question at issue is stated and explained. This is a most indispensable part of the work. Whatever in the question is obscure is to be put into accurate and lucid language; whatever is hard is to be defined; whatever is of secondary importance is to be distinguished from the main issue; and, in a word, the clearest and exactest statement possible is to be sought as the basis of discussion. [439-40]

. . . . .

2. By exposition the nature and extent of the question are determined. Whether the issue is one of fact or of principle; whether of right or of expediency; whether admitting of certain decision or only probable; whether of universal or of limited application; such questions as these must be at the outset decided, and if necessary expressed, by a careful exposition. [440]

. . . . .

3. Exposition plays a large part, often as large as argumentation itself, in the course of reasoning. A premise may depend for its clearness on the definition of a term, and the limits and relations of principles may need merely to be set forth accurately, for the question to argue itself. [441]

[*Arrangement of Arguments*]

Such, then, would seem to be the most philosophical arrangement of a body of arguments: begin with the consideration that is most near and natural, that derives its strength from its self-evident character; then make the climax in the direction of breadth and comprehensiveness, until the last argument stands as a rounder-off and finisher of the whole structure.

Arguments relatively weak are thus to occupy the intermediate place, with bulk and prominence graduated to their intrinsic value. Another fact may here aid the reasoner. An argument weak in itself may so act with other arguments as both to give and to receive more, perhaps, than its intrinsic strength. Isolated, it may be insignificant; supplementing or preparing the way for another, it may have decisive importance. This rule, then, may be applied to the minor considerations: when an argument has less relative value in itself, seek what can be done for it by skillful arrangement. [443]

SUGGESTED READINGS

Genung, John F.
Handbook of Rhetorical Analysis: Studies in Style and Invention. Boston. Ginn and Co. 1895. x,303p

Outlines of Rhetoric. Boston. Ginn and Co. 1896. viii,342p

The Practical Elements of Rhetoric. Boston. Ginn and Co. 1886. xii,488p

The Working Principles of Rhetoric. Boston. Ginn and Co. 1900. xiv,676p

SUPPLEMENTARY BIBLIOGRAPHY

Ad Herennium. In *M. Tulli Ciceronis de Oratore*. Introd. and notes by A. S. Wilkins. Oxford. Clarendon Press. 1890-93. I, p56-64

Adams, John Quincy
Lectures on Rhetoric and Oratory. Cambridge, Mass. Hilliard and Metcalf. 1810. 2v

Bacon, Francis
The Advancement of Learning. Ed. by W. A. Wright. Oxford. Clarendon Press. 1891. xlviii,376p

Baldwin, Charles Sears
Medieval Rhetoric and Poetic. New York. Macmillan Co. 1928. xvii,321p
Renaissance Literary Theory and Practice; classicism in the rhetoric and poetic of Italy, France, and England, 1400-1600. Ed. with introd. by Donald L. Clark. New York. Columbia University Press. 1939. xiv,251p

Barron, William
Lectures on Belles Lettres and Logic. London. Longman, Hurst, Rees, and Orme. 1806. 2v

Bayly, Anselm
The Alliance of Musick, Poetry, and Oratory. London. Printed for J. Stockdale. 1789. iv,384p

Blount, Thomas
The Academy of Eloquence. London. Printed by T. Johnson for P. Parker. 1670. 232p

Burgh, James
The Art of Speaking.... Baltimore. S. Butler. 1804. 292p

Clark, Donald L.
Rhetoric and Poetry in the Renaissance: a study of rhetorical terms in English renaissance literary criticism. New York. Columbia University Press. 1922. x,166p

Cockin, William
The Art of Delivering Written Language; or, an essay on reading. London. Printed by H. Hughes for J. Dodsley. 1775. xx,152p

Crane, William G.
Wit and Rhetoric in the Renaissance. New York. Columbia University Press. 1937. 285p

Demetrius
On Style. Ed. by W. Rhys Roberts. London. Cambridge University Press. 1902. xi,328p

Dionysius
On Literary Composition. Ed. by W. Rhys Roberts. London. Macmillan and Company. 1910. xiii,358p

Holmes, John
The Art of Rhetoric Made Easy. . . . London. C. Hitch and L. Hawes. 1755. 2v

Hoskins, John
Directions for Speech and Style. Ed. with introd. by Hoyt Hudson. Princeton, N.J. Princeton University Press. 1935. xl,122p

Howell, Wilbur S.
Nathaniel Carpenter's Place in the Controversy between Dialectic and Rhetoric. In *Speech Monographs*. 1:20-41 1934

Hubbell, Harry M.
The Influence of Isocrates on Cicero, Dionysius, and Aristides. New Haven. Yale University Press. 1914. xii,72p

Hudson, Hoyt H.
The Field of Rhetoric. *Quarterly Journal of Speech Education*. 9:167-80 April 1923

Jewel's Oration Against Rhetoric. *Quarterly Journal of Speech*. 14:374-92 June 1928

Jebb, Richard C.
Attic Orators. London. Macmillan and Company. 1893. 2v

McBurney, James H.
The Place of Enthymeme in Rhetorical Theory. In *Speech Monographs*. 3:49-74. 1936

Neserius, Philip G.
Isocrates' Political and Social Ideas. *International Journal of Ethics*. 43:307-28 April 1933

Philodemus
Rhetoric. Trans. by H. M. Hubbell. New Haven. Yale University Press. 1920. 139p

Priestley, Joseph
A Course of Lectures on Oratory and Criticism. Dublin. William Hallhead. 1781. xii,374p

Sandford, William P.
English Theories of Public Address, 1530-1828. Columbus, Ohio. H. L. Hedrick. 1931. 211p

Seneca, Lucius Annaeus
The Suasoriae of Seneca the Elder; introductory essay, text, translation, and explanatory notes by William A. Edward. London. Cambridge University Press. 1928. xlvi,160p

Smith, Bromley
Corax and Probability. *Quarterly Journal of Speech Education*. 7:13-42 February 1921

The Father of Debate: Protagoras of Abdera. *Quarterly Journal of Speech Education*. 4:196-215 March 1918

Gorgias: a Study of Oratorical Style. *Quarterly Journal of Speech Education.* 7:335-59 November 1921

Hippias and a Lost Canon of Rhetoric. *Quarterly Journal of Speech Education.* 12:129-45 June 1926

Some Rhetorical Figures Historically Considered. *Quarterly Journal of Speech.* 20:16-29 February 1934

Thrasymachus: a Pioneer Rhetorician. *Quarterly Journal of Speech Education.* 13:278-91 June 1927

Steele, Joshua
  Prosodia Rationalis. 2nd ed. London. J. Nichols. 1779. xvii,243p

Studies in Rhetoric and Public Speaking in Honor of James Albert Winans. New York. Century Company. 1925. 299p

Tacitus, Publius Cornelius
  A Dialogue concerning Oratory, or the causes of corrupt eloquence. In *The Works of Cornelius Tacitus.* . . . Ed. by Arthur Murphy. London. Printed by W. Green and T. Chaplin, for J. Davis. 1813. II, p397-444

Walker, John
  Elements of Elocution. 3rd ed. London. J. Johnson. 1806. xv,354p

Wallace, Karl
  Bacon's Conception of Rhetoric. In *Speech Monographs.* 3:21-48 1936

Winans, James Albert
  Public Speaking. rev. ed. New York. Century Company. 1926. xix,526p

Woolbert, Charles Henry
  Conviction and Persuasion: Some Considerations of Theory. *Quarterly Journal of Public Speaking.* 3:249-64 July 1917
  Persuasion: Principles and Method. *Quarterly Journal of Speech Education.* 5:12-25 January 1919; 5:10-19 March 1919; 5:211-38 May 1919

INDEX

Acknowledgment, as figure, 145
Action, in delivery, 154-6
Actions, causes of human, 43
Adams, John Quincy, 213
After-confirmation, 29
After-refutation, 29
Allegory, 142, 221
Ambiguity, in language, 247
Amplification, 51, 85, 182-4; distinguished from sublimity, 160; kinds of, 182-4; modes of, 159; ways of effecting, 140
Anacoenosis, 226
Analogy, as topic, 55-6
Anastrophe, 226
Anaxagoras, 31
Anticipation, as figure, 143
Antonius, 65
Antonomasia, 222
Apollodorus, 114
Apophasis, 225-6
Aporia, 225
Aposiopesis, 225
Apostrophe, 144, 228
Apparent enthymeme, 38; topics of, 57-9
Apparent syllogism, 37-8
Argument, arrangement of, 313-14; character of, 309-10; definition of, 119; forms of, 288-9; position of, 126-7; requisites for finding, 73; sources of, 73, 120-5, 165; versus fancy, 235-9
Aristotle, 35-63, 94, 110, 118, 219, 252, 287, 288, 301
Arrangement, 80-4, 136; in judicial oration, 179-82; meaning of, 133; of arguments, 126-7, 313-14; of points, 185; principle of, 237; technique in, 294-5
Art, and nature in speaking, 67-8
Arte of Rhetorike, 173-88
Arte or Crafte of Rhethoryke, 163-70
Artificial proof, 118, 119
Artistic proof, 37, 72
Asseveration, as topic, 58
Asyndeton, 228
Attendant circumstance, as topic, 55
Attention, means of getting, 236
Audience, analysis of, 73, 235-9, 307-8; analysis of as to age, 46-9; as element of speech, 39; knowledge of, 31-3

Austin, Gilbert, 263-79

Bain, Alexander, 307-8
Belief, induced by persuasion, 17
Blair, Hugh, 251-62, 303
Brutus, 65
Bulwer, John, 189-206, 263
Burden of proof, 290-3

Caesar, 65
Callicles, 11, 25
Campbell, George, 231-48, 301, 303
Catachresis, 223-4
Cato, Marcus, 156
Causal argument, 288-9, 293; as topic, 57
Cause, determination of, 83-4; kinds of, 71; modes of proceeding in, 104; nature of, 72-3, 103-5
Chaerephon, 11
Channing, Edward T., 309-10
Character, necessary in orator, 156-7
Chirologia, 189-98
Chironomia (Austin), 263-79
Chironomia (Bulwer), 189, 199-206
Cicero, 65-96, 103, 121, 133, 144, 145, 148, 151, 163, 173, 219, 225, 230
Circumstances, argument from, 122
Climax, 229, 304-5
Coleridge, S. T., 302
Common proofs, 51
Common topics, 49-51
Commonplaces, sources of, 73
Communication, as figure, 143
Compact style, 62
Comparison, 126; argument from, 124
Composition, elements of, 148
Concession, as figure, 145
Conciseness in style, 160
Conclusion, 176
Confession, as figure, 145
Confirmation, 29, 176
Confutation, 176
Conjectural cause, 115
Conjectural state, 168, 179
Connection, as condition of emotional excitation, 240
Consequence, argument from, 124
Contradiction, argument from, 123
Contrarieties, argument from, 123

Conviction, and emotional substance, 238; as related to persuasion, 309-10; distinguished from persuasion, 253; nature of, 287; versus persuasion, 210-11, 216
Copiousness of style, 93-4
Cox, Leonard, 163-70
Crassus, 65

Dactylogia, 189, 196-8
De Oratore, 65-91
De Quincey, Thomas, 301-2
Deference, in relation to presumption, 291-2
Definition, argument from, 122; as topic, 54; character of, 135; state of, 103-4
Degree, topic of, 39, 53-4
Deliberative oratory, 39-40, 41, 84, 107-9, 167-8, 176-7, 254-6
Delivery, 90-1, 149-56, 175, 187-8, 215-16, 297-9; adaptation to subjects, 154; advantages of good, 269-70; affectation in, 215-16, 261-2; bodily action, 189-206; constituents of, 60; definition of, 215; importance of, 270; need for study of, 60; vocal, 263-7, 281-6 (*See also* Gesture and Voice)
Demonstrations, as materials of enthymemes, 59; logical, 38
Demonstrative enthymemes, contrasted with refutative, 53
Demonstrative oratory, 165-7, 176
Deprecation, 136
Dialectic, and rhetoric, 35-6
Dialogue Concerning Oratorical Partitions, 96
Dialogues Concerning Eloquence, 207-8
Digression, 116
Diminution, in style, 139
Dionysius, 39, 219
Discourse, general adaptations of, 311-12
Disposition, 174-5, 184-5 (*See also* Arrangement and Organization)
Dissimilarities, argument from, 123
Dissimulation, as figure, 143
Division, 176; argument from, 123; as topic, 54; meaning of, 133
Doubt, as figure, 143

Ecphonesis, 225
Elegance, in style, 138-40
Elements of Rhetoric (Kaimes), 303

Elements of Rhetoric (Whately), 287-99, 301, 303
Elocution, definition of, 282; objections to artificial, 298
Eloquence, definition of, 252-3; distinguished from rhetoric, 302; ends of, 253-4; kinds of, 253-4; nature of, 231-5
Embellishment, 137-47
Emotion, analysis of envy, 44-6
Emotions, 76-7; analysis of, 242-3; appeals to, 232; circumstances operating on, 239-41; how calmed, 241; kinds of, 234-5; method of describing, 44
Emphasis, 140, 146
Enantiosis, 228-9
Ends of human action, 40
Ends of speaking, 40
Enthymeme, 38, 42, 51, 129, 288; material of, 38-9, 52-3, 59; species of, 53; topics of, 53-7
Envy, analysis of emotion of, 44-6
Epanaphora, 227
Epanorthosis, 225
Epideictic speech, 39-40
Epiphonema, 230
Equivocation, as topic, 58, 247
Erasmus, 177
Erotesis, 227
Ethical proof, 37, 42, 43-4, 74-5, 79-80, 180, 241-2; in deliberative oratory, 108; in exordium, 111-12; nature of, 132-3; qualities of, 213; through delivery, 270; through maxims, 52
Eulogy, 42; objects of, 176; subjects of, 105-6
Evenus, 29
Exaggeration, 42, 145
Examples, 42, 51, 293; argument from, 288-9; as materials of enthymemes, 59; in induction, 38, 39; nature of, 125-6; use of, 52
Exhortation, sources of, 177
Exordium, 29, 81, 82-3, 111-13; nature of, 63; use in deliberative oratory, 107
Expediency, as topic, 55
Explanation, as topic, 57
Exposition, uses of, 313
Extempore speaking, 149
Eye, use in delivery, 90, 155, 267-8

Feelings, of judges, 76-7
Fénelon, François de, 207-8
Figures of speech, 88-9; and economy, 304; classification of, 142-7, 225-30; definition of, 142, 224; distin-

guished from trope, 219; kinds of, 186-7; nature of, 224; nature of verbal, 147; use of, 160, 224, 252
Forensic oratory, 39-40, 42-3, 62, 256-7

Genung, John F., 311-14
Genus, argument from, 122
Gesture, 90, 154-6, 189-206, 268-79; canons on management of fingers, 203-6; canons on management of hands, 199-203; classification of, 275-7; definition of, 268-9; descriptions of fingers, 196-8; descriptions of hand, 189-96; elements of good, 187-8; extent of use, 269; function of, 279; nature of act, 277-8; parts of body used in, 271; stroke in, 275; transition in, 278; varies with circumstances, 279; variety in, 278
Gibbons, Thomas, 219-30
Good, nature of the, 41
Gorgias, 11-26
Gorgias, 27, 30, 11-23
Grand style, 93-4
Grouping, 88

Happiness, constituents of, 40-1
Harmony, in language, 87
Hermogenes, 219
Hippias, 30
Horace, 219
Humor, use of, 78, 92, 133
Hyperbaton, 142
Hyperbole, 223
Hypotyposis, 229

Identity, as topic, 56; principle of, 236-7, 307-8
Illustration, as figure, 144-5
Imagery, in oratory and poetry, 160
Imitation, 148; role of, 71; use of, 209-10
Importance, as condition of emotional excitation, 239
Inartificial proof, 118
Inartistic proof, 37, 43, 72
Indigitatio, 189, 203-6
Induction, 37-8, 51, 54
Inflections, as topics, 53
Institutes of Oratory, 99-157, 231
Intellect, appeals to, 232
Interest, as condition of emotional excitation, 240-1
Interrogation, as figure, 142-3
Introduction, kinds of, 295-6; of speech, 175; rules for composing, 258-9; technique in use of, 295-6

Invention, definition of, 174, 214, 312; meaning of, 164; stages of, 312-13 (*See also* Argument and Proof)
Irony, as figure, 145, 222-3
Isocrates, 50, 114
Issue, definition of, 178

Jointed style, 62
Judgment, as topic, 55
Judicial oratory, 109-11, 168-70, 177-82
Judicial state, 179

Kaimes, Lord, 303
Knowledge, necessary in orator, 66-7; of justice, 19-22; of politics, 41; of soul, 31-3

Language, purity of, 245; qualifications of good, 243
Latimer, Hugh, 183
Lawson, John, 35, 65, 209-12
Lectures Concerning Oratory, 35, 209-12
Lectures on Elocution, 215-16
Lectures on Rhetoric and Belles Lettres, 251-62, 303
Lectures on Rhetoric and Oratory, 309-10
Legal state, 103, 179
Licymnius, 30
Logic, and oratory, 235
Logical proof, 37, 118-30, 238-9, 287-96
Longinus, 159-60, 219
Lysias, 11, 31

Maxim, 51; definition of, 52; use of, 52
Meaning, double, 247
Memory, 84, 149-51, 175, 187
Metaphor, 60, 87, 141, 221
Metonymy, 221-2
Moderate style, 92-3
Motives, as topics, 56
Mouth, expression by, 268

Narration, 29, 83; as part of a speech, 175; rules for, 96
Natural method, in delivery, 215-16, 297-9
Nature, and art, 67-8
Necessary sign, 38
Nestor, 27
Nicomachean Ethics, 35
Notational system, in study of gesture, 271-4

RHETORIC AND PUBLIC SPEAKING

Obscurity in language, 245-6
Omission, as topic, 59
On the Sublime, 159-60
Opposites, as topics, 53
Orations, kinds of, 164; parts of, 165, 175, 258
Orator, 65, 91-5
Orator, and sophist, 26; as good man, 99; concern of, 67; defined, 67, 156; general business of, 68-70; qualifications of, 65-6; versus philosopher, 86
Oratory, and logic, 235; contrasted with poetry, 208; definition of, 100-1, 213, 270-1, 312; ends of, 102, 173-4; kinds of, 102; material of, 102; parts of, 102, 263; province of, 70-1; purpose of, 213; uses of, 101; versus reasoning, 270-1 (*See also* Rhetoric and Speaking)
Organization of materials, 29, 30, 63, 133-6
Oxymoron, 228

Palamedes, 27, 28
Panegyric oratory, 105-6
Panegyrical speeches, 84
Parabole, 230
Partition, 117-18, 133
Pathetic proof, 37, 43, 46-9, 73-5, 76-8, 81, 166, 233-4, 238-9, 242-3, 296-7; and use of syllogism, 130; in deliberative oratory, 107-8; in exordium, 111-12; in peroration, 131; in statement, 116; use in amplification, 184; use of, 77-8, 132, 211-12, 259-61
Pericles, 31, 101
Periphrasis, 228
Permission, as figure, 144
Peroration, 130-1; objects of, 63
Persons, argument from, 120-1
Perspicuity, 60, 137, 245-7
Persuasion, analysis of, 238; as artificer of belief, 17; as related to conviction, 309-10; constituents of, 72, 296-7, 307-8; definition of, 296; distinguished from conviction, 253; modes of, 37; nature of, 16-17; produced by other arts, 16; requisites for, 72; versus conviction, 210-11, 216
Phaedrus, 26-34
Phaedrus, 26-33
Phalereus, 93
Philosophers, versus orators, 86
Philosophy of Rhetoric, 231-48, 303
Philosophy of Style, 303-5

Philosophy of the Human Voice, 281-6
Pisistratus, 39
Place, argument from, 122
Plain style, 91-2
Plato, 11-34
Plausibility, as condition of emotional excitation, 239
Pleading, technique in, 79
Pleonasm, 139
Political speaking, and kind of style, 62
Polus, 11, 22-5, 26
Polysyndeton, 228
Practical Elements of Rhetoric, 311-14
Presumption, in argument, 290-3
Probability, 29, 38, 49-51, 293; as condition of emotional excitation, 239; as materials of enthymemes, 59; degrees of, 120; use in speaking, 33-4
Prodicus, 30
Prolepsis, 227
Pronunciation, definition of, 187; elements of good, 152-3; varies with times, 263-4
Proof, 29; artistic, 37; as part of speech, 117; classification of, 118; common, 51; inartistic, 37, 43; kinds of, rhetorical, 37; modes of, 37-8 (*See also* Ethical Proof, Logical Proof, and Pathetic Proof)
Properties, argument from, 123
Propositions, 176, 288-9
Propriety, conditions of, 61; in style, 89-90
Prosopopoeia, 144, 229-30
Protagoras, 30, 61
Proximity of time, as condition of emotional excitation, 240
Pulpit speaking, 257-8
Purity, elements in style, 60-1

Quality, state of, 103-4
Quantity, state of, 136
Questions, characteristics of, 102-3; fact and opinion, 292, 293; kinds of, 103
Quintilian, 99-157, 181, 219, 223, 231, 251, 276

Ratiocinatory state, 103-4
Reasoning, versus oratory, 270-1
Refutation, 29, 295; methods of, 59, 127-9
Refutative enthymemes, contrasted with demonstrative, 53
Relation, as condition of emotional excitation, 240

Relative terms, as topics, 53
Repenting, as figure, 146
Rhetoric (Aristotle), 35-63, 65
Rhetoric (De Quincey), 301-2
Rhetoric (Gibbons), 219-30
Rhetoric, and cookery, 23, 24; and dialectic, 35-6; and knowledge of just, 19-22; and knowledge of truth, 26-9; and sophistry, 26; as an art, 35-6; as art of persuasion, 15; as division of flattery, 23; as division of political art, 23; as kind of painting, 207; as science of words, 12-15; compared with medicine, 30-1; constituents of, 100-2; contrasted with other arts, 12-15; definition of, 36, 173, 302; distinguished from eloquence, 302; ends of, 207; essentials of, 164; importance of study of, 163-4; improper use of, 18-19; nature of, 11-15, 35-6; nature of skills in, 22-4; parts of, 69, 174; power of, 18-19; province of, 173, 301, 311; teaching of, 19-20; uses of, 24-6, 36; uses in politics, 25-6; view concerning, 301 (*See also* Oratory and Speaking)
Rhetorical induction, 38
Rhetorical syllogism, 38
Rhetorician, contrasted with physician, 18
Rhythm, 94-5; and style, 62; not in plain style, 91
Rules, no formal in rhetoric, 99-100; use of, 185
Rush, James, 281-6

Sallust, 228
Sarcasm, 223
Self-interruption, as figure, 145
Seneca, 219
Senses and the Intellect, 307-8
Sheridan, Thomas, 215-16, 265, 267, 274
Signs, 38, 58, 59, 293
Similarities, argument from, 123
Simonides, 84
Simulation, as figure, 144
Skill, nature of rhetorical, 22-4
Skill in speaking, essentials of, 100, 213-14; sources of, 148; studies essential to, 70
Smith, A., 297
Socrates, 11-26, 26-34
Solecism, 245
Sophists, and orators, 26

Speaking, acquiring skill in, 174; and knowledge of philosophy, 27; and knowledge of soul, 31-3; and knowledge of truth, 26-9; ends of, 216, 231-2, 269-70; inartistic art of, 27-8; methods of, 29-30; modes in, 270; sources of skill in, 148; technique in, 73 (*See also* Oratory and Rhetoric)
Speech, as social coordinator, 66; elements of, 39
Speeches, kinds of, 39-40, 176
Spencer, Herbert, 303-5
State, 136; definition of, 103, 178, 213; kinds of, 103, 168, 178-9; meaning of, 103
Statement, 83, 113-16
Statements, in deliberative oratory, 107
Stewart, Dugald, 296
Style, 60-2, 85-6, 86-90, 91-5, 136-48, 159-60, 186-7, 243-8, 251-2, 303-5; adaptation to speaking, 62-3; adapted to conditions, 214; and economy of effort, 303-4; copiousness of, 86; definition of, 251; dignity of, 61; elements of, 186; for types of speaking, 42; kinds of, 62, 147-8; meaning of, 175; ornaments of, 219-30; qualities of, 251; structure of, 62
Subjects, kinds of, 71
Sublimity of style, sources of, 159
Syllogism, 37-8, 129-30, 288
Synchoresis, 228
Synecdoche, 141, 222
System of Oratory, 213-14

Tacitus, 99
Testimony, 52
Theagenes, 39
Theme, instruments of, 165
Theodectes, 94
Theodorus, 27, 29, 57
Theophrastus, 94
Things, argument from, 121
Thrasymachus, 27, 31
Tiberius Rhetor, 219
Tillotson, Archbishop, 225
Time, argument from, 123; as topic, 54
Timidity, and speaking, 68
Tisias, 30, 33, 34
Topics, 39; common, 49-51; of apparent enthymemes, 57-9; of enthymemes, 53-7

Translation, as a state, 136
Tropes, classification of, 141-2, 221-4; definition of, 141, 219; distinguished from figures, 219; proper use of, 219-21; use of, 252

Ulysses, 27
Unintelligibility, causes of, 247
Usage, canons of language, 243-4; criteria of, 244-5

Vivacity of style, 247-8

Voice, constituents of, 281-2; estimating power of, 267; how to preserve, 264-5; improvement of, 263, 265; in delivery, 90-1, 151-4; management of, 265-7; qualities of good, 187; system for cultivating, 282-6

Walker, John, 265
Ward, John, 213-14
Whately, Richard, 287-99, 301, 303
Wilson, Thomas, 173-88
Writing, as aid to speaking, 70, 148

(2832)